School Renewal
through Staff Development

Judith Schiffer
Principal \\\
Bronxville Elementary School
Bronxville, New York

Teachers College, Columbia University
New York and London 1980

To my daughters, Lise, Beth, and Emily

© 1980 by Teachers College, Columbia University.
All rights reserved. Published by Teachers College
Press, 1234 Amsterdam Avenue, New York, N.Y.
10027.

Library of Congress Cataloging in Publication
Data

Schiffer, Judith.
 School renewal through staff development.

 Bibliography: p.
 Includes index.
 1. Teachers—United States—History.
 2. Education—United States—History. I. Title.
LA212.S35   371.1'0068'3   80-10594

Design: Romeo M. Enriquez

8 7 6 5 4 3 2 1
80 81 82 83 84 85 86 87 88
Manufactured in U.S.A.

Contents

Foreword

Shifts in sources and uses of power in making decisions about what is to go on in school are upsetting former assumptions about authority relations in education. Leaders in teaching, administering, supervising, and counseling, at all levels and in all kinds of educational agencies, struggle to understand and deal effectively with conditions created by new centers of power. In a good many communities, the public is increasingly forced to accept the reality that former notions about who makes decisions on important programs and administrative matters in schools are no longer viable.

Analyses of the exercise of power and authority in educational decision-making have been presented by several respected authors. Some of them have viewed the complex relationship between power and authority today from the vantage point of the school superintendent or other administrator; others have looked at the problem from the perspective of the organized teaching profession; and a few have represented the public in examining the situation. Still others have turned to the experience of business and industry for ideas to transfer to processes of designing and conducting educational programs. Few of the analysts have moved beyond describing and explaining the sources and nature of power and authority in educational decision-making. Most have stopped short of the critically important area of implementation of new insights in actual designing of programs.

In *School Renewal through Staff Development,* Judith Schiffer provides a unique approach to examination of power and authority as they operate in educational decision-making today. Through a brief but forceful discussion of the colonial period, this author shows that public trust was then the source of authority and power. Her concise and focused analysis of the period between the Revolutionary and Civil wars provides a backdrop for understanding the gradual development of the bureaucratic structures for managing the schools that emerged in clear design during the period after the Civil War. According to the author, the progressive era, which began in

1920, marked the emergence of the teacher as an authority.

Three major sources of power that appeared one after another—public trust, bureaucracy, the organized teaching profession—are clearly identified through the brief historical analysis in this volume. The author next proceeds to discuss continuing struggles to arrive at a reasonable and productive balance among these three. She describes contemporary conditions that impinge upon the sources and uses of power and authority in making decisions in education.

Throughout the chapters of this book, the author is centrally concerned with improvement of educational programs in schools. She examines the sources and uses of power in the past and at present to discover implications for staff and program improvement now. The implications thus identified are elucidated through the presentation of a concrete model, principles of which can be applied in all educational settings where groups of people are engaged in efforts to increase the quality of education.

To everyone interested in program improvement, this book offers unique insights into present controversies about power and authority. Strategies are outlined so that educational personnel can engage in self-development while examining goals and programs. The insights and strategies will be valuable to teachers, supervisors, and administrators at all levels of education. School board members and other citizens concerned about their schools will find the treatment of power and authority helpful as they deal with program improvement in their schools. Students preparing for educational leadership will find that this book furnishes an illuminating background for comprehending the contemporary scene.

MARGARET LINDSEY
Professor Emeritus
Teachers College
Columbia University

Preface

In the fifteen years I have worked in and with schools, I have seen many excellent plans for school improvement fail. In many situations, all the ingredients for success seemed to be there. The ideas were good, strong leadership was provided, teachers were enthusiastic, there was community support. Again and again when things did not work out as planned, my perplexity led me to consider the issues that I have now analyzed in this book.

The pivotal question for me became, "What configuration of factors ought to be present in a staff development plan if it is to lead to school renewal?" This book is the result of this concern. The motivation for writing it grew out of a conviction that school leaders need to have a realistic perspective on the nature of the school as an organization, and the factors that impinge upon school renewal in today's world.

The contemporary era has been characterized by widespread attempts to bring about change in the schools. The impetus has come from many sources, including the federal government and ordinary citizens. Large sums have been allocated for research and development and for projects aimed at diffusing innovations throughout the land. Changes have been sought in curriculum, methods and materials, program, organizational structures, and overall approaches to teaching.

In the past, when there was a high degree of teacher mobility, a school administrator could hire new teachers attuned to new goals when there was a need for change. A yearly turnover of as much as one-fifth of the staff made it possible to bring teachers into the school whose values and training fit the goals of change. Today, school staffs have become relatively stable; therefore, change must be accomplished by working with existing personnel. This need is expressed by the term *staff development*.

Studies of school change, unfortunately, point to the conclusion that despite determination, effort, and money directed to this purpose, staff development programs have not been very effective. Some have succeeded with teachers who felt the need for the training offered, but failed with those who did not. Other programs succeeded in motivating the staff to accept an innovation, but failed to get the innovation implemented or adopted in the school or school system. Still others got an innovation implemented only to have it disintegrate in response to community pressure.

Since staff development will be a priority for the foreseeable future, it is essential that educators analyze problems and issues related to staff development and develop ideas to guide research and practice.

The literature on staff development does not provide much help for the school leader who desires to make change. Although it covers a wide range of topics, it is fragmented. It deals with leadership, personal change, rational planning, and many intervention strategies; there are case studies describing programs that failed or succeeded, and models that focus on a single aspect of the change process. Lacking are frameworks that provide a basis for understanding staff development problems and for designing and evaluating programs.

The purpose of this book is to provide such a framework, and, in addition, to sketch out a model for designing staff development programs that lead to the realization of professional potential for teachers and renewal for schools.

A major theme of the book is that staff development plans often are based upon politically naive assumptions about authority prerogatives. School leaders so often are unrealistic about who are the major actors in the decision-making process.

In order to gain a clear perspective on the authority issue, we trace three principles of authority—public trust, bureaucratic, and colleague—from colonial times through the progressive era in chapters two through five. Chapter 6 is an analysis of the forces that have an impact on educational decision-making and authority relationships in the contemporary era.

Since teacher power is such a salient influence today, it is important to analyze teachers' claims for more "professional" autonomy and authority. We do this in chapter 7.

Another theme of the book is that staff development models are frequently one-sided, focusing either on making personal change or upon fulfilling organizational goals, but not on harmonizing the two thrusts. In chapter 8, we take a look at the research on school change in order to gain insights about how what is known can be incorporated into a comprehensive model of staff development.

Finally, in chapter 9, the major arguments of the book are recapitulated, and a model for staff development is presented.

Acknowledgments

It would be impossible to mention all of the friends, colleagues, professors, students, classroom teachers, and administrators who have influenced this work. During the years I have worked in the field of education, I have been a nursery school teacher and administrator, an elementary school teacher and principal, a college professor, and a "change agent." I have had my consciousness raised, my eyes opened, and my horizons widened through contacts with persons aged three through ninety-three.

Though I am grateful to so many people, I would like to give special thanks to those who provided encouragement, help, and support while I was working on the book, and to those who gave me constructive criticisms and new ideas. My professors and colleagues at Teachers College, Margaret Lindsey, Ann Lieberman, Gary Griffin, and Dale Mann provided stimulation and evaluation. Frank Peters, Ruth Licht, Corinne Lipset, and Lillian Stephens—colleagues of mine in the Department of Education at Stony Brook University—gave freely of their time and attention to discuss aspects of the book. My friend, Harold Cook, gave support and help during the time I was preparing the manuscript for publication. My mother, Fan Mechlowitz, saved the day by offering to type the manuscript. Keith Melville, a wonderful writer and very special friend, did me the great service of telling me when the book was finished.

Finally, I would like to express thanks to my family. My deceased husband, Richard, had spent hours listening to my ideas. He experienced my disappointment when the work was not proceeding well, and my elation when it was. My three lovely daughters, Emily, Lise, and Beth, were remarkable in their forbearance when their own personal crises were responded to with blank stares from mom as she sat at the typewriter. I am grateful to all of them.

Change and Educational Authority

1

$\mathbf{T}$HE NEW ENGLAND PURITANS profoundly influenced the development of American education. At an early date, they established a system of public schools and insisted that education was a fundamental responsibility of the state. But, although there were schools and schoolmasters in New England, as in the other colonies along the eastern seacoast, there was no special provision to train teachers for their classroom duties.

The colonial New England schoolmaster was considered a church functionary who was to accomplish goals deemed desirable by all citizens in the local New England community—to teach children the skills and habits necessary to read the Bible and to be good Christians. Since this was considered an easy task, one that had been performed previously by the family in conjunction with the Church, no one felt that the teacher required special occupational training, or more than an elementary school education.

As ideas about the function of the school changed and schooling became more complicated, a discrepancy developed between the aims of schooling and the teacher's ability to execute those aims. The common school, a free school open to the public, was established. In response to its lofty aspirations and mundane problems, special provision for the education of teachers before and after they began their work started in the late eighteenth century.

People training to be teachers attended institutes and normal schools established for the education of elementary teachers; practicing teachers were encouraged—and in some states required—to attend the teacher institute for the purpose of improving their knowledge of what they were teaching and to be inspired with the importance of self-sacrifice and commitment to teaching.

During the nineteenth century, provision for the education of practicing teachers improved with advances in pedagogical methodology; however, the tradition established in the beginning—that this education should be

1

focused upon improving the *individual* teacher—is one that has held until recent times.

Until the progressive era, starting in 1920, the teacher in the public schools was considered a "worker" hired to carry out the policies made by a school board or administrative staff. The notions that teachers should participate in determining school policy, or that they had needs to realize their professional potential, were unheard of until modern times. These new convictions resulted from various factors that affected one another, such as advances in research on worker motivation and administrative theory, progress in teacher education and the status of teaching as a professional career, and in the last few decades, the growth of teacher power.

These factors contributed to changing ideas about the teacher's role, and thus, to new ideas about the purpose of in-service education—that is, the education of teachers already working in the field. If the teacher is a professional person whose expertise justifies being allowed to determine as well as implement policy, then in-service education could focus upon school problems and needs; if the teacher has needs to develop professional potential, what better way to fulfill them than through school participation and involvement in making decisions and solving problems. In addition, the new viewpoint that the school is a system requiring integration of its individual parts led to the belief that organizational goals would be met best by having teachers work with others to solve common problems. Thus, the aim of in-service education changed from upgrading the individual teacher's knowledge and skills to that of promoting the professional growth of the school staff through cooperative group effort.

Another factor in the contemporary era is that teacher mobility and teacher turnover in the individual school has reduced drastically. Until recently, it did not pay for a school district to invest large amounts of money or effort to train people who could be expected to leave soon. Teachers' efforts at improvement were rewarded by credit towards salary increments, but training usually was taken outside of the local district—in colleges or conferences; when it was offered in the district, it generally was haphazard. This individualistic approach made some sense when it was possible for a school district to hire teachers whose values and background agreed with school goals. Today, more stable staffs leave districts no alternative but to develop their existing staffs in order to fulfill organizational goals.

The shift in in-service education, then, has been from an individualistic approach to that of *staff development*. This term implies that changes in teacher performance should be linked with other aspects of school renewal such as improvements in curricula, programs, administrative procedures, and school-community relations.

THREE PRINCIPLES OF AUTHORITY

The staff development literature virtually ignores the matter of educational authority, although it is becoming increasingly apparent that this issue is crucial to contemporary staff development. If staff development is aimed at some new condition in the future, then a pivotal question is, "Who decides what that future condition will be?" A second question is, "Who makes what decisions, and under what circumstances?" These questions are important today because changes have occurred that make old assumptions about authority prerogatives anachronistic.

Educational authority today takes many forms. State education departments, teacher-training institutions, teachers' associations and unions, private foundations funding educational research, federal education agencies and programs, the courts, and legislatures—all influence educational policy. On the local level, the three most influential sources of authority are the local community (presumably represented by the school board), the administrative staff, and teachers. Burton Clark has provided a framework for analyzing the relationship among the three sources of authority. He says that in the public schools there are three major principles of authority, general beliefs about who should exercise power and how. These principles are related to forms of control: "Three principles are especially important because they are now most actively in contention: the first is the principle of public trust; the second, the principle of bureaucracy; the third, the principle of colleagueship."[1]

He defines each of these principles. The principle of public trust means that public control is vested in a board of lay people. This board is legally empowered to direct the organization and is held responsible for its welfare; it is to have final authority over the work of the employed staff. This principle relates to a belief that the school should be directed by community interests rather than by professional personnel or government departments.

The principle of bureaucratic authority is that authority is delegated to or assumed by professional officials.

The principle of colleague authority is that much, if not all, authority should be in the hands of the school faculty. The school should be a self-governing community in which teachers have major control of policy and practice.

The principle of public trust was established in colonial times and held until the Civil War, when the bureaucratic principle became firmly entrenched and administrators assumed many of the prerogatives of school boards.

In the contemporary era, the principle of public trust has changed. As more decisions are made at the state and federal levels, the power of the school board has been limited even more. At the same time, at the local level, the demands of parents for a more determinative voice in school affairs have shifted the public trust concept to include participative as well as representative democracy. Perhaps the increased influence of government and professional managers on institutions, once considered the domain of the citizenry, has created a need in individuals to claim their prerogatives in decisions related to the education of their children. The call for accountability of school personnel, the demand for tax credits and school vouchers, the taxpayers' revolt, and the acceleration of parent involvement in schools reflect this need.

The Principle of Colleague Authority

Organized teachers today are struggling to increase their authority prerogatives in professional spheres and in the local school situation. The principle of colleague authority—that much, if not all, authority should be in the hands of the school faculty—is being pressed for the first time in the history of American education. As a result of increased professional status and power, teachers are now in a position to make demands they could not have made in the past.

The teachers' greater awareness of a professional role, and acceptance of the legitimacy of militant action, have encouraged them to demand the prerogatives of full-fledged professional groups such as doctors and lawyers, especially that of professional autonomy.

These demands for autonomy are predicated on teachers' claims to professional status. This claim is highly questionable, primarily because this status (and the prerogatives associated with it) has not been accorded to teachers by the public.

Sociologists have long debated the question of what constitutes a profession. Many have noted that a profession is a term applied to an ideal kind of organization—one that does not exist in reality.

An occupational group takes on more of the characteristics associated with the ideal in a process referred to as *professionalization*. This also refers to the process of an occupational group striving to achieve the right to claim professional status.[2]

Sociologists seem to be in accord that teaching is semiprofessional or quasi-professional since it is not accepted as a profession by the public and it has not yet met the few ideal criteria associated with professional status.

On the other hand, there are several trends that indicate that teachers will make strides in gaining more professional recognition. Funding of research and development by federal, private, and professional associations and the dissemination of findings will add to the codification of the technological base considered requisite to professionalism. New developments in teacher education, too, have impelled educators throughout the nation to rethink the criteria for entrance into the occupation and to take steps to ensure minimal competency. The oversupply of teachers also will make it possible to raise entry requirements. And new emphasis on staff development and continuing education for practicing teachers promises to keep them up-to-date and revitalized.

Whether or not these developments are sufficient justification for transferring school board and administrative authority into teachers' hands is a question we will consider. Certainly these advances will move the occupation closer to meeting ideal professional criteria. The principle of colleague authority, however, will still be unfeasible because the public will not relinquish its own prerogative to decide what values will be supported by the schools; the need for overall coordination and management requires administrative involvement; and teachers have neither the resources nor the right to exercise a monopoly on making decisions.

People interested in staff development must recognize that professional growth has created new needs in teachers: needs for expanding professional potential, the need to participate in making decisions, and the need to exercise autonomous judgments in the classroom. Researchers have found that there is a conflict between professional and bureaucratic orientations and modes of organization.[3] Bureaucratic orientations place highest priority upon "rationalized" activities—overall coordination, procedures, following rules—and working towards well-defined superordinate goals. Professionals value more diffuse goals, flexibility, individual autonomy, experimentation, and the expression of personal styles.

Both bureaucratic and professional modes of organization are required for the effective functioning of schools. The need to provide continuity of experience for children mandates a certain amount of standardization of rules, procedures, methods, and curricula. On the other hand, today's teachers must have considerable freedom to exercise autonomous judgments, to experiment and innovate, to express their own values, and to develop personal styles if they are to grow professionally and contribute to organizational renewal.

A problem that people working toward staff development must face is how to change existing structures, norms, rewards, and other regularities in the culture of the school to meet teachers' emergent needs in ways that enhance school renewal.

STAFF DEVELOPMENT:
CREATING A CHANGED FUTURE CONDITION

Studies indicate that the failure of many recent attempts to create school change can be attributed, in part, to faulty assumptions about the change process. One of these assumptions is that the critical variable in change is the innovation itself—if an innovation has been proven effective (through research and development) it can be successfully introduced, implemented, and incorporated into almost any setting.

Unfortunately, this assumption does not correspond with the actual process of school change. Educational innovations are not simply technical matters: improved means of fulfilling agreed-upon goals. In education, all but the most trivial innovations are controversial because they are based on values. The decision to introduce a particular innovation into a school involves choices among alternative priorities and value-orientations. In earlier times, when the aims of education were less complex, there was more general agreement about them and the means of achieving them. Today, the plurality and diversity of goals guarantees that any innovation will be incongruent with at least some people's goals and values.

In addition, authority prerogatives have shifted. The formal organizational chart that implies policy is made by the school board and handed down the line to the superintendent of schools and his staff, to the principal, and finally to the teacher—the hired functionary concerned only about implementing others' goals—is no longer realistic. Today, better-trained teachers have their own ideas about what should be done in schools. Teachers tend to consider themselves professionals. This role conception makes teachers resistant to innovations that clash with their values or require severe changes in teaching practices that have worked for them.

Teachers' professional growth has led them to demand "professional autonomy" and to press for the principle of colleague authority. Teacher power, which has drastically reduced the power of administrators, has enabled teachers to resist attempts to change their teaching behavior.

Innovation also may be resisted by parents. No longer content to let the school board represent their interests, parents are demanding direct participation in making decisions for the schools. Professional control of policy is being challenged; therefore, any innovation introduced into the school is likely to fail if it is not supported by the community.

In short, a preponderance of unsuccessful change attempts were based upon an obsolete model of authority, and on assumptions about change that did not take into account individual personality traits, needs, self-interests, habits, and expectations; these assumptions ignored conflicting goals of diverse groups in the school and its environment; furthermore, these assumptions disregarded the norms that exist in the school's culture, and failed to recognize that there is an enormous press toward systems' maintenance in a bureaucratic organization.

Strategies of change that assume it is possible to lay out long-range goals in advance and to specify in detail the sequence of steps towards the achievement of these goals are incorrect because goals and objectives written out in formal documents become modified and changed once the process of change is set into motion; it is impossible to determine in advance exactly how the process will unfold.

The most common approach to staff development is to focus upon changing individual teachers' attitudes, knowledge, and skills, or the staff's interpersonal communication. One set of approaches starts with the premise that patterns of behavior are supported by sociocultural norms, and that school change requires that old norms be replaced by new ones. These "normative-reeducative"[4] strategies focus upon making personal change; it is presumed that organizational change will occur as organizational members change their perceptions, attitudes, and values, and their behavior in line with these changes. However, studies of these strategies indicate that they are effective only if organizational patterns and procedures change to accommodate the changes occurring in people. For example, after a staff has learned techniques that make communication more productive and has gained skills in solving problems collaboratively, the people will revert to their old behavior unless time is made available for such activity; the staff development experience will be an exercise in futility.

Although it is true that school renewal is, in part, a function of personal change, this is not the only variable. Individual and group behavior are only two of the many interrelated and interdependent subsystems involved in school change.

This book takes the position that staff development attempts often fail because they have one or more of the following shortcomings: (1) they overlook the authority issue dealt with extensively in the following chapters; (2) they are overcommitted to strategies of change that focus almost exclusively on organizational goals to the neglect of personal variables; thus they fail to adequately take into account the behavioral regularities that exist in the school and its environment, and the need to make personal and normative changes; (3) they are overcommitted to making personal change and thus do not make provision for organizational accommodation to these changes.

A staff development design must provide for a process of "mutual adaptation"[5] among persons, the organization, and the desired changed future condition. This dynamic process is most likely to suceed if superordinate organizational goals are compatible with the needs, values, expectations, and goals of the people in the school and community, and if those planning for staff development are realistic about the intentions of various groups to participate in determining these goals.

In sum, a staff development model must be eclectic in its use of models and strategies of change. While it must use a variety of approaches it must focus on at least three areas: political, personal, and organizational.

In the political context, a staff development model must be based on a realistic assessment of the values, needs, expectations, and existing regularities in the school and its environment. A critical factor is that of authority: who makes what decisions and how?

At the personal level, the model must take into account the diversity and stability of values held by those who are to implement change and must provide for resocialization and education of the staff.

The model also must provide for changes in organizational subsystems—rewards, norms, technology, structures, procedures—in pari passu with changes in organizational members' perceptions and goals; conversely, it must provide changes in organizational subsystems in order to effect changes in staff members' perceptions and goals.

NOTES

1. This quote and the principles following it come from: Burton Clark, *Educating the Expert Society* (San Francisco, Calif.: Chandler, 1962), pp. 152-62.

2. Donald A. Myers, *Teacher Power: Professionalization and Collective Bargaining* (Lexington, Mass.: D. C. Heath, 1973), p. 20.

3. See Ronald Corwin, "Professional Persons in Public Organizations," *Educational Administration Quarterly* 1 (1965):1-22.

4. Robert Chin and Kenneth D. Benne, "General Strategies for Effecting Changes in Human Systems," *The Planning of Change,* 2d ed., ed. Warren G. Bennis et al. (New York: Holt, Rinehart, Winston, 1961), p. 34.

5. This is a term used by Milbrey Wallin McLaughlin, "Implementation as Mutual Adaptation: Change in Classroom Organization," *Teachers College Record* 77 (February 1976): 339-51.

Colonial Times

2

WHEN WE TRACE the three principles of educational authority—public trust, bureaucratic, and colleague—from colonial times, we have a basis for understanding how current staff development authority issues emerged.

Many current staff development problems stem from our continued acceptance of assumptions about authority prerogatives that are based upon a historical ethos incongruent with contemporary realities. Successful staff development requires alterations in traditional attitudes about authority rights, roles, and responsibilities, and the establishment of new structures for making decisions. A historical perspective will give us an understanding of how prevailing attitudes and structures evolved and will shed some light on why and how they now need to be changed.

In the following chapters, we examine five historical periods, starting with colonial times in this chapter, and emphasize aspects of education most relevant to the three principles of authority. These aspects are: important events related to the development of the school as an institution; the teacher's role, education, and professional status; and administration and supervision.

AUTHORITY AS PUBLIC TRUST

The tasks of settling the colonies and establishing the economic and political institutions of the new settlements dominated the colonial period from the seventeenth century to the middle of the eighteenth century. A continuous wave of immigrants from England, Holland, Sweden, Scotland, Ireland, Switzerland, and Germany settled colonies along the eastern coast extending from Maine to Georgia. There were three broad groups of colonies, each having different life-styles: the New England Puritan colonies characterized by religious fervor, the Middle Atlantic colonies marked by religious and cultural diversity, and the southern colonies where plantation life set the style.

9

The colonists who settled in these regions hoped to reproduce some of the cultural patterns from their European past, and to renounce other elements. Schools, like other institutions established by the colonists, reflected the persistence of European culture, as well as the peculiar aspirations of the colonists, and the needs imposed by life in the new world.[1]

In the colonial South, the class structure of society characteristic of seventeenth century England was accepted. Thus, the more affluent were privately educated, and industrial training through apprenticeship was legislated for the dependent poor.

In the middle colonies, a variety of arrangements for educating the young was made by separate religious and cultural groups. Their lack of a common inheritance of traditions, political and religious beliefs, and language did not lead to the establishment of one educational institution.

It was the New England Puritans who were in the forefront of the development of public education. Due to their great concern for preparing their young to be good Christians, they established schools, as well as the principle that providing public education was a governmental responsibility.

For the Puritan, as well as for other colonists, the family was the primary teacher. The family, however, was aided by the local community through vocational apprenticeships, and by the local church. The school was considered an extension of the church's function; ministers often were too busy attending to church matters to effectively teach young children the skills needed to learn to read Scripture, to memorize and recite their prayers, to learn by heart the precepts of Christian doctrine, and to develop in them good moral character and discipline. This task was delegated to the schoolmaster.

Bernard Bailyn, an educational historian, notes that the modern idea of public education, that is, of a line of separation between "private" and "public" was unknown before the end of the eighteenth century.[2] The transfer of responsibility for education from the home to formal institutions occurred gradually. As the colonial period progressed, the school dame who gave lessons at home, the minister, the tutor, and the schoolmaster assumed more and more of the educational responsibilities formerly held by the family.

In 1642, Massachusetts passed the first general education law. It was, in part, an apprenticeship law that provided that children neglected by their parents in "learning, labor, and other employments profitable to the commonwealth" be educated and trained.[3] This law did not require that schools be established; parents could teach their children at home or they could arrange for group instruction. The purpose of the 1642 law was to place the obligation for education upon parents and guardians of children and to provide a system of fines and punishments for neglect of this duty.

Five years later, in 1647, the General Court of Massachusetts enacted the "Old Deluder Satan" law in order to thwart Satan's intention "to keepe men from the knowledge of ye Scriptures."[4] Towns of fifty families or more were mandated to appoint a teacher of reading and writing. Towns of one hundred families or more had to employ a Latin teacher as well. Boys of all social classes (and sometimes girls) attended the town schools. Boys learned reading, writing, and ciphering, and girls learned reading and sewing. But the Latin grammar schools were attended only by the sons of the New England social, political, and religious elite; the students would go on to the colonial college.

The laws of 1642 and 1647 gave the authority for the control of schools to town officials. At first, salaries and other details pertaining to the schools were discussed and voted on at town meetings. As populations grew, selectmen, along with ministers, were often designated to manage the schools. Later, when local districts were recognized as separate entities, special school committees—the school boards—were elected by the voters. By the beginning of the nineteenth century, it was the school board that levied taxes, set the curriculum, and hired the schoolmaster for its district's schools.

The laws enacted in Massachusetts established the principles that the state could mandate education and require that towns maintain teachers, that civil authorities could supervise and control schools, and that public funds could be used to support education.[5] Education during the colonial period was a function delegated to the school by the political authority, although it generally was conducted by private or religious agencies. This pattern continued when the colonies became independent states.

The Colonial Schoolmaster

The New England lower-schoolmaster was almost always male. He was required to serve all of the community's educational needs. In a one-room schoolhouse he reigned over ten to one hundred children of varied ages and abilities. Besides developing basic skills, he instilled habits of punctuality and Christian discipline, and led his charges in rituals, singing, and prayer. The grammar-schoolmaster—also male—taught Greek, Latin, and English, as well as the principles of the Christian religion.

The schoolmaster often was also required to perform various other duties. These included serving summonses, leading the Sunday choir, ringing the church bell, digging graves, and acting as a messenger for the court.

In school, the master was expected to be a stern disciplinarian. Since, according to Calvinist theology, human beings were presumed to be basically corrupt, the master had to do whatever was necessary to control the "deep-seated wickedness of youth"[6] and put them on the path of righteousness.

As the Dorchester school rules of 1645 made clear, the view was:

The rod of correction is a rule of God necessary sometimes to be used upon children. The schoolmaster shall have full power to punish all or any of his scholars, no matter who they are. No parent or other person living in the place shall go about to hinder the master in this. But if any parent or others shall think there is just cause for complaint against the master for too much severity, they shall have liberty to tell him so in friendly and loving way.[7]

Autobiographical accounts by former pupils of the period tell of whippings administered by rods to the back and hands, hair pulling, ear pinching, boxing, and other brutalities.[8]

TEACHER STATUS, QUALIFICATIONS, AND PREPARATION. There was no interest in teacher education during this period. School teaching was not recognized as an occupation requiring special training. It was generally assumed that teaching ability was a function of knowledge and character: a person of sound character who knew his subject matter could teach it.

The most that was provided the aspiring schoolmaster was a brief apprenticeship under an experienced teacher. There were no teacher-training schools to develop pedagogical skills, to establish standards for practice, or to serve as a selective agency for the recruitment of teachers.

Standards for teaching positions were set by local lay groups and ministers according to schooling needs and available resources. Since there was a scarcity of capable people who wanted to teach, there was always a greater demand for teachers than supply; thus, willingness to teach school often was the only requirement. There were generally several other requisites, however: religious orthodoxy, loyalty to the civil government, moral acceptability, and the ability to maintain order.[9]

Only a few generalizations about the education and status of the colonial schoolmaster are possible. Teaching attracted the educated and the ignorant, the pious and the uncouth. Physicians and ministers kept school, but sometimes so did former mariners, shoemakers, weavers, and occasionally, convicts.

Some schoolmasters had only a rudimentary elementary school education; others had secondary education, college training, or even a master's degree. Generally speaking, elementary school teachers had the least education, and college teachers had the most. Grammar school teachers were often graduates of colleges such as Harvard or of English universities, who taught, often part-time, while they were waiting for an opportunity to enter a more prestigious profession, usually the ministry.

Historian Willard Elsbree describes the status of the colonial schoolmaster. He points out that the teacher's prestige varied greatly from colony to colony and within different communities in each colony, so no generalization can be made for America as a whole. In New England, however, there is some evidence that the grammar-school teacher was a respected citizen: he was frequently assigned a seat of distinction in the church meetinghouse and was often addressed by the respectful terms "Sir" or "Mr." Nevertheless, while the master may have been accorded high status in his own community, it is likely that, in general, teaching was considered a low-prestige occupation. In the catalogue of graduates of Harvard and Yale in the middle of the eighteenth century, arranged in order of the social rank of their father's occupation, schoolmasters were not even mentioned, although merchants, farmers, and mechanics were listed.[10]

SUPERVISION AND CONTROL OF TEACHERS. In New England, teachers were approved by town meetings, selectmen, school committees, and ministers. Inspectors appraised the schoolmaster's work by assessing pupils' progress in religion, reading, handwriting, and arithmetic. The schoolmaster's penmanship was examined, and the number of pupils attending was noted. In more advanced communities, inspectors evaluated the amount and character of religious instruction, the master's methods of teaching, and his ability to manage the school and use school funds appropriately. The inspections served to estimate the master's competency and knowledge, but did not function to help him improve, except that they reminded him of his duties and faults.

A report by a Boston school committee in 1710 describes the role the inspectors,

A Certain Number of Gentlemen, of Liberal Education, Together with Some of Y^e Revd Ministers of the Town: To Visit ye School from time to time . . . to Enform themselves of the methodes used in teaching of ye Schollars and to Inquire of their Proficiency, and be present at the performance of Some of their Exercises, the Master being before Notified of their Comeing, And with him to consult and Advise of further Methodes for ye Advancement of Learning and the Good Government of the Schoole.[11]

TEACHER PROFESSIONAL STATUS. Colonial schoolteachers did not consider themselves a group having common professional interests, problems, and concerns. There were no professional organizations, no uniform standards for preparation and no education for the practicing teacher. The beginnings of development as a profession did not take place until the nineteenth century.

SUMMARY

Although there were all sorts of schools in the territory eventually to become the United States, it was the New England Puritans who were most influential in shaping the future of American schooling.

The Puritans established schools for the purpose of assisting the family and Church with the job of training the young to be good Christians and to prepare them for a trade. Previously, New Englanders had relied on apprenticeship and family nurturance to socialize their children, but the exigencies of life in the new world weakened the effects of these practices. Schools were created and later mandated to promote the religious values prized by the Puritans. The principle that education would be under citizens' control (education as public trust) was thus established.

The Puritan school's function was viewed as an extension of the education process provided by the family and Church. There was little or no disagreement between the public authority and the teacher about the objectives of the school program or the means of achieving them.

The schoolmaster was essentially a church functionary who was given the task of supplementing the work of family and Church in training the young to be good Christians. Although the schoolmaster had status in the local community, he was not considered a professional person, nor was he high in the status hierarchy of occupations. The elementary school was not a bureaucratic organization. It usually was a one-room schoolhouse presided over by a lone male schoolteacher. Although he usually was not highly skilled or educated, the master had more or less complete autonomy in matters of classroom organization, curriculum, and methods of instruction as long as he was pious, civil, could keep order in the schoolhouse, and was able to teach youngsters the skills they needed.

Policy was determined and controlled by laymen. They inspected teachers to determine whether the teacher was of moral character, whether he could maintain classroom discipline, and use funds economically. If the teacher seemed to be doing his job, lay people did not interfere with him.

NOTES

1. Newton Edwards and Herman C. Richey, *The School in the American Social Order* (Boston: Houghton Mifflin, 1963), p. 3.

2. Bernard Bailyn, *Education in the Forming of American Education* (Chapel Hill: University of North Carolina Press, 1960), p. 11.

3. Nathaniel B. Shurtleff, ed., *Records of the Governor and Company of Massachusetts Bay in New England* (Boston: Press of William White, 1853), 2 (1642-1649), 8-9.

4. *Ibid.*, p. 203.

5. Gerald Lee Gutek, *An Introduction to American Education* (New York: Thomas Y. Crowell, 1970), p. 13.

6. Martin G. Brumbaugh, trans., *The Life and Works of Christopher Dock* (New York: Arno Press, 1969), p. 114.

7. Quoted in Clifton Johnson, *Old-Time Schools and School-Books* (New York: Macmillan, 1925), pp. 11-12.

8. See Walter Herbert Small, *Early New England Schools* (New York: Arno Press & the New York Times, 1969), chap. 22.

9. Freeman R. Butts and Lawrence A. Cremin, *A History of Education in American Culture* (New York: Henry Holt, 1953), pp. 131-36.

10. Willard S. Elsbree, *The American Teacher, Evolution of a Profession in a Democracy* (New York: American Book, 1939), chap. 10.

11. "Boston Town Records," *Report of the (Boston) Record Commissioners,* vol. 19, pp. 152-53.

From the Revolution to
the Close of the Civil War

3

THE DECADES FOLLOWING the founding of the Republic were characterized by expansion. The growth of frontier agricultural life, with the individualism and other traits that accompanied it, had an impact on political, economic, and social developments throughout the land.

The development of educational institutions was strongly influenced by immigration, urban settlement, the industrial revolution, the growth of the labor movement, progress in transportation, communication and technology, the growth of organized knowledge, and the rearrangement of social classes. These influences created a press for nationalism, equal opportunity for all citizens, the extension of suffrage, separation between church and state, and for a publicly supported and controlled system of education.

FOUNDATIONS OF EDUCATION: THE COMMON SCHOOL

During the Age of the Common Man—from the election of Andrew Jackson to the Civil War (1828-1860)—a crusade was launched for a new educational institution, the common school. This would be free, tax-supported, nonreligious, and state-controlled. Arguments for the common school were based, in part, upon the need for educated citizens and trained workers and businessmen, and the belief that universal education would facilitate social progress. Horace Mann, a staunch advocate of the common school, insisted that the paramount concern of a democratic society should be the education of all its citizens, not just an elite group of leaders.

But the establishment of the common school was based upon other motives as well. Nineteenth-century educators saw the common school as a vehicle for transmitting Protestant values to the masses of Irish Catholics who immigrated into northeastern cities beginning in 1830. Deep-rooted fear of Catholics and "popery" led Protestant denominations that previously favored parochial school education to support the establishment of a common school.

Another motive was to "Americanize" Irish and German immigrants. In the words of one educator:

Unless we educate our immigrants, they will be our ruin. It is no longer a mere question of benevolence, of duty, or of enlightened self-interest, but the intellectual and religious training of our foreign population has become essential to our own safety; we are prompted to it by the instinct of self-preservation. . . . The most effectual, and indeed the only effectual way, to produce this individuality and harmony of national feeling and character is to bring our children into the same schools and have them educated together.[1]

The newcomers were to become Anglo-Americans through training. They would be taught the English language, the rudiments of learning, and the virtues of patriotism and morality. It was also intended that children would be taught not to emulate their parents, but to teach their parents "American ways."[2]

The drive for the common school has been interpreted by historian Michael Katz as an attempt to preserve the social order by training the poor, and to improve city life by educating city people who worked in manufacturing. Such goals required regular attendance of all children in a prolonged, systematic, and carefully structured formal education.[3] Moral education, or the formation of right attitudes and values, was a top priority; the essential values to be instilled reflected the needs of the urban society. Educators considered punctuality, habits of precision, morality, diligence, and obedience as qualities of character that were basic goals of the school.[4]

Educational historian Ellwood Cubberley has described the general movement toward the adoption of public support for the common school. At first, education was supported by private individuals, churches, and benevolent societies; then the state began to aid schools by providing public funds. Enactment of state legislation that granted communities the authority to organize school-tax districts and levy property taxes followed. The next step usually was compulsory legislation requiring minimum taxation rates. Finally, mandatory and completely tax-supported schools were established.[5]

The Teacher: Member of an Occupation

Ideas about the teacher's role gradually changed from the Revolution to the Civil War. New thinking about human learning and development affected pedagogy. Although flogging was still a widespread practice, educators were beginning to realize that the rod was less effective than other means of inspiring learning. The graded school also altered the scope of the teacher's responsibility, and made teaching more specialized. The number of subjects in the curriculum increased, and teaching methods and materials changed. During this time, too, a new awareness of the complexity of the teaching task developed.

The search for new teaching methods grew out of changes in thinking about human nature and knowledge. New patterns of thought and action had emerged out of the colonial period. The change from religious to nonreligious or secular thinking, usually summed up as The Enlightenment, involved appeals to human reason rather than divine law, natural rather than supernatural rights, scientific method rather than established dogma, social agreements and individual freedom rather than authoritarian control, and humanitarian and democratic rights rather than aristocratic privilege.[6]

American educators brought back ideas and methods from the Swiss and German schools they visited that were based on the principles of Johann Pestalozzi, an educator from Switzerland, who lived from 1746 to 1827 and taught that the child is a natural organism with an inner life that unfolds according to natural laws. He wrote, "Sense impression of Nature is the only true foundation of human instruction, because it is the only true foundation of human knowledge."[7] Following this philosophy, educators would substitute real objects for textbooks in the classroom; teachers had to use their own ingenuity in order to create activities and materials that would facilitate the child's natural development.

One of Pestalozzi's most notable contributions was to change ideas about the qualities of the able teacher. Under his system, mere mastery of subject matter and the ability to apply the rod were insufficient. Teachers were required to understand children's behavior by observing them directly and to be responsible for their total development—social, physical, emotional, as well as intellectual. These principles were taught to teachers in 1848 in training schools like the Westfield Normal School, in Massachusetts,[8] but did not have a widespread effect on classroom practices until after the Civil War.

Historians Freeman Butts and Lawrence Cremin point out that sweeping cultural changes led to proposals for expanding the curriculum in the following ways. The task of the common school was first of all to teach "the common branches," or those studies necessary to discharge the common duties of life. In addition to the three R's, spelling, geography, history, government, constitutional law, and functional skills like writing a common business letter or bill were to be included in the school program. In order to train character and develop liberal attitudes, natural sciences, natural history, drawing, and physical training were offered. Moral education based upon Christian principles, and patriotic education—or as Mann put it, "Those precepts in the creed of republicanism, which are accepted by all, believed in by all, and which form the basis of our political faith"—were to be taught to all.[9]

The schoolmaster in the colonial period had been required only to be pious, moral, and minimally educated. Now, according to a popular teacher-training text published in 1829, the teacher had to have common sense, uniformity of temper, a capacity to understand and discriminate character, an affectionate nature, a decisive character, and a wide range of knowledge in common-school subjects.[10]

TEACHER EDUCATION. In his history of nineteenth-century American schoolmen, Paul Mattingly observes that before the 1840s and 1850s, educational processes and goals were stated in vague, poorly defined terms. The teacher's moral character and personal qualities were considered pivotal in producing knowledge, moral character, and social consciousness in students. But educators did not analyze the complexities of the learning process, nor the nature of moral character. Thus the technical aspects of pedagogy were reduced to a subordinate position.[11]

Teacher education began as it was recognized that teaching was an occupation that demanded specialized training. The influential educator Horace Mann, and others like Mann, who expressed the ideal that teaching should command the prestige and commitment to service characterized as "professional," assumed that this could only be accomplished when teacher preparation programs were placed in specialized, single-purpose institutions.[12]

According to Henry Barnard, who directed the first teachers' institute, James G. Carter did more than any other person to point out the fundamental relationship between teacher education and school improvement. Carter, a teacher and writer of educational articles for the press, wrote several pieces in 1820, pointing to teacher incompetence as the root of the problems in the elementary school, and a series of essays that suggested ways to correct this inadequacy. He proposed the establishment of normal schools—public institutions to train teachers for the common schools.

In 1823 Samuel R. Hall established a seminary for teacher preparation in Concord, Vermont, and in 1839 the first semipublic normal school was established in Lexington, Massachusetts, under the direction of Cyrus Pierce. From 1839 to 1861 twelve state normal schools were established in eight states to teach prospective teachers the subject matter to be taught and methods of teaching. These normal schools were the forerunners of the four-year teacher colleges that were established later in the century.

There was disagreement over what was a good program for teachers. Lawrence Cremin distinguishes four different positions: (1) that liberal arts instruction in secondary schools or colleges was the best preparation for teaching (a view held principally by secondary, college, and some normal school educators); (2) that a review of elementary subjects and some "helpful hints" regarding teaching were needed in addition to liberal studies; (3) that teacher education should consist of elementary subject matter combined with extensive treatment of the theoretical principles of teaching; and (4) that a normal school education that developed the "art of teaching" was needed. Advocates of this latter position placed method first; subject matter would be introduced in "professionalized" form, that is, as the substantive content that the student was learning to teach.[13]

IN-SERVICE EDUCATION: THE TEACHERS' INSTITUTE. The need for education for the practicing teacher—in-service education—arose because of the acceleration of change that characterized this period, the growing awareness of the complexity of teaching, the heterogeneity of teacher pre-service preparation, and the press towards standardization of the schools.

Before 1865, the teachers' institute was the single most important means of in-service education. These institutes were held once or twice a year for a period ranging from two to eight weeks. The institutes supplemented academic training. Their purpose was to provide brief courses in the theory and practice of teaching in the common schools. At first, attendance at these institutes was purely voluntary; teachers paid to attend. Later, private citizens contributed to defray tuition costs, and eventually, the costs were paid by public appropriations.

Samuel Bates, in a little book on the method of the teachers' institute, published in 1864, states: "There are two main purposes to be accomplished by the institute. The first consists of imparting to the teacher a knowledge of the philosophy of his profession. The second is the establishment of a common sympathy between teacher and people."[14]

To achieve the first goal, the institute would help teachers discover the "philosophical principles which underlie every department of instruction, and to properly apply these to the natural order of mental development." The institute also would help the teacher become so familiar with the fundamental principles of the branches he is to teach that he "shall be above textbooks—he himself shall be the textbook in every branch." Bates urged the teacher to go to the institute once or twice a year, at least, "to get his opinions adjusted, as the navigator comes to have his chronometer corrected before departing on his perilous voyage over restless seas."[15]

The second aim of the institute grew out of the realization that the school, if it is to produce the best results, must have the confidence of the parents. This would be accomplished by opening institute activities to the public, and publicizing the coming event in the newspapers. During the time that the institute was in session the talents of superior teachers would be made public and meritorious teachers would be brought forward and rewarded.

The methods of instruction used in the institute are described by the Massachusetts superintendent of schools, Horace Mann, in a letter to school committees in Massachusetts in 1845:

It is the design of a Teachers' Institute to bring together those who are actually engaged in teaching common schools, or who propose to become so, in order that they may be formed into classes, and that these classes, under able instructors, may be exercised, questioned, and drilled, in the same manner that the classes of a good common school are exercised, questioned, and drilled. . . . Under accomplished teachers, they are to be initiated into the best modes and processes of teaching and governing, which they are afterwards to illustrate and exemplify in their own school.[16]

Aside from stressing development of subject matter skills, a major aim of the early institute was to "awaken" aspiring teachers to the importance of self-sacrifice and commitment to teaching. As Paul Mattingly has described them, institutes were a kind of "revival agency" aimed at producing "evangelical" professionals.[17] Methods of instruction were lectures, inspirational and cultural, and elevating entertainment. For the first generation of institute participants, around 1840, professionalization was equated with the awakening of moral character rather than training in the skills and techniques of teaching. Competence and effectiveness were not measured by uniform rules or standards, but intuitively and impressionistically, and in terms suggesting that they were emanations of moral character, and of subject matter knowledge.[18]

By the 1850s professional teachers began to change the purpose of their training institutions and their criteria for effective professional preparation. Teachers came to consider themselves not as evangelical ministers but as professional persons with technical, pedagogical training.[19]

Willard Elsbree has reviewed the accomplishments of the teachers' institutes in his book on the evolution of the teaching profession. The institutes provided an impetus to inquiry about teaching, served as an agency for educating untrained teachers, supplemented normal school training, and provided additional training for practicing teachers, and infused new ideas of teaching and classroom management. They also aroused public sentiment in favor of schools and contributed to the unification of the profession through the spread of propaganda and the mobilization of teachers to take an active political role in fostering school improvement.[20]

TEACHER PROFESSIONALIZATION. A number of developments during this period facilitated the professionalization of teaching. The normal schools were established, and teacher institutes began for in-service education. County and state supervision of schools led to greater unity among members of the profession. The emergence of the graded school contributed to specialization and an increased demand for teachers. Local, state, and national teacher associations developed, with the aim of improving education and the status of teachers. Textbooks, programs of study, instructional materials, and educational literature improved and proliferated. The school year was lengthened, making teaching a full-time job. The use of examinations became widespread as a basis for certifying teachers.[21] In addition, the press towards centralization and standardization in city schools led to the need for expert knowledge, and the tasks of teaching were seen to require specialized knowledge, experience, and skills.

The professionalization of teaching was set back, however, by the increase in the number of women teachers, and a decrease in the number of male teachers. The Civil War took men out of the classroom and into the battlefield. When they returned from the war they were able to take advantage of better opportunities for employment in the expanding economy. Elementary school teaching became women's work. Since women's lives primarily were focused upon home and family, they tended to be a transient group; they were poorly educated and not committed to careers; thus, in line with accepted practices of the time, they took lower salaries than men, and submitted to greater direction from superordinates.

Horace Mann compared the wages of women and men in his *Eighth Annual Report to the Board of Education* in 1845. The average wage of male teachers was $32.46 a month, of female teachers, $13.60. He pointed out that on such wages, a female teacher would not be able "to purchase the books that belong to her profession, or command such other means as are indispensable for the general culture of her mind." He asked the board, "How can she afford to attend Teachers Institutes, or those other meetings of the learned and the experienced, where the principles belonging to the science, and the processes pertaining to the art of education are expounded and exemplified?"[22]

Nonetheless, professionalization of teaching took a great leap forward during this period. Lectures, proposals, and articles reiterated the need for professionalization. It was stressed that teachers must "organize as a profession, to be regularly recognized," and should determine standards for certification and effective teacher education.

A speaker before the Illinois State Teachers Association in 1858 declared:

The law prescribes what shall constitute a *lawyer*, but, be it observed, prescribes an examination by lawyers. But, as for teachers, the State has ordained that a teacher shall be examined, not by his own class, but by some officer who is not required to know anything of the matters he is to question of.[23]

This same speaker then posed the following question with the militancy of a contemporary union leader: "What blacksmith would not hurl his sledgehammer at the head of any lawyer who procured a law that no man should shoe horses or make a hay-knife till he had a certificate from the postmaster?"[24]

Local and state teachers' associations proliferated. The early national associations had the avowed purpose of advancing the cause of free public schools and school reform. Public school teachers were actively involved in these associations, but their economic, social, and professional welfare was not yet a focal concern.

Among the educational societies that flourished between 1826-1845 were several local associations aimed at promoting the interests of their members. State teachers' associations were established, such as the Wisconsin State Teachers Association. Article 1 of its 1853 constitution proclaimed that it was directed to the "mutual improvement of its members, and the advancement of public education throughout the state."[25] The reforms advocated included administrative reorganization, teaching methodology, and the general improvement of teacher education.

One of the important outcomes of the teachers' associations was the publication of journals that disseminated information and promoted reforms. Some of these were the *Illinois Common School Advocate,* begun in 1841; the *Massachusetts Teacher,* started in 1848; the *Ohio School Journal* (1852); and the *New York Teacher* (1853).

In 1857, teachers established the National Teachers' Association (NTA) in Philadelphia—a major event of this period of professional development. Thomas W. Valentine, president of the New York Teachers Association, speaking at the association's first meeting announced: "What we want is an association that shall embrace all the teachers of our whole country, which shall hold its meetings at such central points as shall accommodate all sections and combine all interests."[26]

This organization eventually became the National Education Association (NEA), after having subsumed, one by one, other state teachers' associations and organizations like the National Association of School Superintendents, and the American Normal School Association.

The NTA provided a forum for thrashing out controversial issues and for molding public opinion on educational and professional matters. How to prove that teaching was a profession was a problem that received continual attention during the first few decades of the association. Educational exhibits were frequent; these were aimed at informing the public and inspiring teachers. Controversial educational issues, like the use of the Bible in schools, and provision for education for Indians, were fervently discussed at meetings.

Administration and Supervision

New structures on the state, county, and local levels advanced administration and supervision during the period from colonial times to the Civil War. In 1812, New York created the first state officer to supervise schools. Before the establishment of the state superintendency, schools were administered by local school boards and their appointed delegates. These agents assumed responsibility for visiting schools, inspecting the work of teachers and pupils, and examining teacher applicants. The organization of a state system of schools led to the appointment of state superintendents who exercised educational and political leadership. The inability of a single administrator to cope with state educational problems led to the establishment of state agents and county superintendents to work in the field and study local conditions. These elected officials examined teachers for licenses, supervised instruction, and recommended ways to improve school programs.

In 1837, Buffalo became the first city to officially create the position of city superintendent. This placed public school leadership in the hands of experienced educators who promoted more systematic study of education, developed more standardized and expanded curricula, and made efforts to improve teachers' performance.

As the school population grew, the one-room schoolhouse was expanded, and young and older children were separated. "Head teachers" were released from some teaching duties to manage discipline, and to assist other teachers. The major tasks of the head teacher were planning, revising the course of study, regrading and placing students in classes, establishing time schedules, demonstrating teaching methods, and in many schools, teaching part-time. Supervision and evaluation of teachers was not a top priority.

Administration was separated from teaching around 1850, with the establishment of the position of principal in many districts around the country. The creation of this new role gradually led to a shift in emphasis from the head teacher's major task of administration per se, to inspecting teachers' work as a basis for evaluation, and supervising for the improvement of instruction.

During the period from the Revolution to the close of the Civil War, some urban educators disavowed the district or community school and argued for structured and centralized systems of education, with uniform standards of teaching performance, and standardized and systematized curricular structure and content. Schoolmen like Mann saw such centralization and standardization as the only way to counteract the "dormancy and deadness"[27] of the education provided by local communities. These developments, of course, were steps in the creation of school bureaucracy and organizational structure that became entrenched by 1880. At the same time, they were important in creating a press for professional expertise in supervision, administration, and teaching.

SUMMARY

From the Revolution to the Civil War, there were changes in the school as an institution, and in the professional status of teaching.

When this period is compared with the colonial period, we see several developments. As an institution, the school changed from providing some aspects of training for the social environment to being the dominant agency for this socialization, from the one-room schoolhouse to the graded school, from an institution that was locally controlled to one more centrally controlled, and from one in which policy was determined by lay groups to one in which professional educators increasingly determined policy and ran the schools.

The early statutes had put the maintenance and direction of the school into the hands of town officials; later, this authority was transferred to appointed (and eventually elected) committees of citizens—the school board. By the beginning of the nineteenth century, local school districts were officially recognized as separate units; their school boards chose their own schoolmaster and curriculum and raised their own funds, although they were technically responsible to the town government.[28]

Between the Revolution and the Civil War, cities and school districts began to grow in size and enrollment. The common school was established. The problems of Americanizing the new immigrants, of coping with a heterogeneous population in urban centers, and coordinating the affairs of larger schools and systems led to increased centralized control of curricula and instructional practices. The principle of local control lost ground as the state assumed authority. At the school level, full curricular and instructional discretion no longer resided with teachers; nor did such discretion reside solely with the board of education at the system level.

Schooling goals became broader and less explicit. The notion that a teacher with only an elementary school education could fulfill the grand expectations held by advocates of the common school was no longer tenable. Special arrangements were made for assisting teachers in their tasks by providing training programs in normal schools; teacher institutes were established to upgrade practicing teachers' deficiencies.

Despite their better training, teachers saw their classroom decision-making authority diminish, as administrators assumed more responsibility for the direction, coordination, and control of school practices. Teachers' autonomy continued to erode with the adoption of textbooks, workbooks, and other curricular materials throughout a school, system, and state.

On the other hand, changes toward the increased professional status of teachers were reflected in a new belief held by teachers and teacher educators that the teacher required expert knowledge and skills in pedagogy, a change from no professional training to the establishment of specialized programs and schools for teachers, and the beginning of teachers' awareness that they belonged to a common occupational group that could work together to promote their own welfare and school improvement. Finally, state, county, and local structures and positions were established that made professional supervision possible at a later date.

NOTES

1. Calvin Stowe, in *Transactions of the Fifth Annual Meeting of the Literary Institute and College of Professional Teachers* (Cincinnati: Executive Committee, 1836), pp. 65-71.

2. Frederick W. Binder, *The Age of the Common School, 1830-1865* (New York: John Wiley, 1974), pp. 10-11.

3. Michael Katz, *Class, Bureaucracy, and Schools* (New York: Praeger, 1971), p. 30.

4. Ibid., p. 31.

5. Ellwood P. Cubberley, *Changing Conceptions of Education* (Boston: Houghton Mifflin, 1909), pp. 163-212.

6. Freeman R. Butts and Lawrence A. Cremin, *A History of Education in American Culture* (New York: Henry Holt, 1953), pp. 43-44.

7. Johann H. Pestalozzi, *How Gertrude Teaches Her Children,* trans. Lucy E. Hollan and Francis Turner (London: Swan Sonnenschein, 1907), p. 199.

8. *Twelfth Annual Report of the Board of Education, Together with the Twelfth Annual Report of the Secretary of the Board* (Boston: Dutton and Wentworth, 1849), p. 89.

9. Butts and Cremin, *A History of Education,* pp. 215-17.

10. Arthur D. Wright and George E. Gardner, eds., *Hall's Lectures on School-Keeping* (Hanover: the Dartmouth Press, 1929), pp. 65-75.

11. Paul H. Mattingly, *The Classless Profession: American Schoolmen in the Nineteenth Century* (New York University Press, 1975), pp. 61-62.

12. Merle L. Borrowman, *The Liberal and Technical in Teacher Education, A Historical Survey of American Thought* (New York: Bureau of Publications, Teachers College, Columbia University, 1965), p. 21.

13. Lawrence Cremin, "The Heritage of American Teacher Education," *The Journal of Teacher Education* 4 (June 1953): 166.

14. Samuel P. Bates, *Method of Teachers' Institutes and the Theory of Education* (New York: A.S. Barnes & Burr, 1864), p. 11.

15. Ibid., pp. 12-15.

16. Samuel N. Sweet, *Teachers' Institutes or Temporary Normal Schools* (Utica, N.Y.: H.H. Hawley, 1848), p. 46.

17. Mattingly, *Classless Profession,* pp. 61-83.

18. Ibid., pp. 60-63.

19. Ibid., p. 63.

20. Willard S. Elsbree, *The American Teacher, Evolution of a Profession in a Democracy* (New York: American Book, 1939), pp. 161-62.

21. Ibid., pp. 141-42; also see Mattingly, *Classless Profession,* p. 73.

22. *Eighth Annual Report of the Board of Education, Together with the Eighth Annual Report of the Secretary of the Board* (Boston: Dutton and Wentworth, State Printers, 1845), pp. 26-28.

23. *The Illinois Teacher: Devoted to Education, Science, and Free Schools* 5 (1858): 299.

24. Ibid.

25. Elsbree, *American Teacher,* p. 254.

26. Bardeen, ed., *Proceedings of the National Teachers' Association* (1857): pp. 11-12.

27. *First Annual Report of the Massachusetts Board of Education, Together with the First Annual Report of the Secretary of the Board* (Boston, 1838), p. 46.

28. Robert Bendiner, *The Politics of Schools: A Crisis in Self-Government* (New York: Harper & Row, 1969), pp. 20-30.

From the Close of the
Civil War to the
Progressive Era

4

THE PERIOD FROM the close of the Civil War to the progressive era—1860–1920—marked the transition from old to new America. The rapid development of the big cities, the growth of industry, railroad construction, and the emergence of the corporation as the dominant form of enterprise transformed the society and revolutionized the distribution of power and prestige. Life was increasingly centralized, and power concentrated through organization: organized labor, the corporation, national coalitions of churches, the formation of political blocs of influence, and the expansion of government in national life.

Reformers turned their attention to the ills of urbanization and industrialization, and groups that experienced discrimination moved toward greater rights. Jane Addams and Ellen G. Starr founded Hull House in Chicago for the benefit of slum residents; Jacob A. Riis of the *New York Sun* wrote about deplorable housing conditions; and the Society for the Prevention of Cruelty to Children was organized in New York. Women founded two suffrage associations in 1869 and in some localities achieved the vote in specific areas, such as school elections. The nation had to grapple with the problem of "Americanizing" immigrants from southern and eastern Europe, and that of assimilating four million ex-slaves into a totally new way of life.

FOUNDATIONS OF EDUCATION:
SCHOOLING FOR SOCIAL REFORM

In the final decades of the nineteenth century, the school population became much larger. Workers' organizations began to resist the use of child labor, in self-interest as well as for humanitarian reasons. States were beginning to enact child-labor legislation. With continually increasing immigra-

28

tion, more unemployed children appeared; delinquency became a problem. There was a demand for compulsory school attendance laws in the industrial states. This legislation put recalcitrant and unruly children into the schools and created a need for new goals and strategies of teaching.

Reformers realized that the onrush of urbanization and industrialization had created innocent victims, and they took on the responsibility of seeing that children were properly fed, bathed, exercised, clothed, entertained, trained, and provided with vacations.[1]

Schooling was prescribed more and more as the cure for social ills and problems. By the turn of the century, proposals for the school included apprenticeships, instruction in hygiene, domestic science, manual arts, child care, Americanization programs, and agricultural training. The school was to take on more functions traditionally, but no longer, carried on by family, neighborhood, or shop.

Progressives such as John Dewey saw the school as the key to social reform. In *Democracy and Education,* Dewey maintained that progressive societies

endeavor to shape the experiences of the young so that instead of reproducing current habits, better habits shall be formed, and thus the future adult society be an improvement on their own . . . . We are doubtless far from realizing the potential efficacy of education as a constructive agency of improving society, from realizing that it represents not only a development of children and youth but also of the future society of which they will be the constituents.[2]

Scientific and Social Research

Intellectual life underwent a vast revolution between the Civil War and World War I. Changes occurred in fundamental notions of the universe, of man and his relation to nature, of the conceptions of knowledge and learning as they affected education. The basis for these changing ideas was the wide range of research taking place in the physical, behavioral, and biological sciences, and the theory of evolution, which had a revolutionary impact on accepted ideas about man's origin and led to revisions of thought and belief. In addition, the social conception of human nature, thinking, and learning that maintained what distinguished men from beasts was man's social relationships led social scientists to look for cultural explanations of behavior.

The Curriculum as a Field of Study

The explosion of knowledge caused by the scientific revolution led to the development of new, systematically organized disciplines in the physical and social sciences. Knowledge from these disciplines entered the school program, but it was not incorporated in a systematic way.

From 1850 to 1890, national societies had been founded in geography, history, mathematics, and eight scientific fields. The content from these disciplines was introduced into the curriculum of the elementary schools by way of textbooks written mostly by university scholars. Teachers relied upon these texts for methods of teaching as well as subject matter content. As each new text was introduced, the school program became an "assembly of parts."[3]

By 1880 educators were beginning to focus their attention on the improvement of curriculum. Given impetus by Johann Friedrich Herbart's work, educators sought systematic methods of selecting, arranging, and organizing curricula.

Herbart taught that the mind is a unity actively creating knowledge out of impressions received from the external world. He referred to the mind as an "apperceptive mass" that continually goes out to meet new ideas and to interact with them. According to Herbart, the goal of teaching should be to develop the apperceptive mass properly so that the child can be helped to assimilate new ideas in the best way. In order to do this, the teacher would have to present material in the systematic way described in detail by Herbart and the Herbartian educators.

Scientific method was to be applied to curriculum-making. This was based upon the assumption that both the subject matter to be taught and the basic laws of learning that would indicate *how* these subjects would be taught could be empirically determined. The essentialist position, which had been adhered to previously, had held that the content of the curriculum should be made up of bodies of knowledge; this position was modified to take into account the "needs of children" or the "needs of society," or both. What these needs might be were presumed to be "scientifically" determinable.

Curriculum builders like Franklin Bobbitt, Charles H. Judd, and W. W. Charters attempted to select curriculum content and method in relation to the empirical realities of society. They suggested that educators could determine curriculum content by looking at societal and institutional regularities to find out what skills were needed to cope with life, and make them available. In Bobbitt's words, curriculum should reflect "that series of things which children and youth must do and experience by way of developing abilities to do the things well that make up the affairs of adult life."[4]

Educators looked to the findings of psychologists such as Edward Thorndike, G. Stanley Hall, Arnold Gesell, and Lewis M. Terman for insights about child development and learning that would make it possible to introduce and present subject matter most efficiently in terms of the child's ability to assimilate it. Curriculum-building involved a process of discovering the facts, principles, and laws that existed out in the world, organizing them according to the laws of learning, and then applying them.

The Rise of Progressivism and the Progressive Impulse in Education

The growth of scientific knowledge and methodology led progressive thinkers to believe that science had the power to enable people to understand and control their world and achieve their purposes.

Michael Katz states that the term progressivism encompasses a wide variety of activities directed toward changing American political and institutional behavior between 1890 and 1920. The dominant effort of the era was to obtain improved conditions through the use of science. He points out that as applied to education, the goals were: to alter the political control of schooling, to reformulate educational thought, to promote pedagogical change, to introduce educational innovations, and to inject scientific management into administration.[5]

In the area of political control, the focus was on municipal reform. Centralization of power in small school boards of elected members was proposed to bypass the tendency toward graft and corruption inherent in the existing ward system that granted educational jobs as a form of patronage.

There were three strands of progressive educational thought: child-centered, social-reformist, and scientific. Some historians like Michael Katz, Clarence Karier, Paul Violas, and Joel Spring believe that these strands of thought, aside from being humane and democratic, also grew out of an impulse for social control and order.

Many changes in pedagogy grew out of new conceptions of childhood development and learning, the teaching-learning process, and the nature and role of subject matter. The focus changed from an emphasis on logically ordered subject matter to be learned to meaningful expression and purposeful activity. Friedrich Froebel, a disciple of Pestalozzi, introduced activity methods and the idea that social participation should be a prominent phase of school life. Francis W. Parker, in the Quincy and Cook County schools, developed Pestalozzian child-centered methods and attempted to develop the mutual relationships of curriculum subjects in such a way as to enhance their meaning for a child. Dewey's laboratory school sought to train youngsters in "cooperative and mutually useful living"; experimentation, play, and self-expression had high priority in the school.

Educational innovations introduced in this period included industrial education, kindergarten, the junior high school, guidance programs, ability grouping, and the use of tests and measurements to evaluate and track students. Some of the innovations of this period represented extensions of bureaucratic structure, introducing more specialized elements into a hierarchical form of organization that was being subdivided more and more.[6] The impetus for many of these changes grew out of the industrial scientific-management movement that correlated efficiency with progress and reform. Efficiency procedures were widely applied to classroom learning, to teachers, programs of study, the organization of schools, administrative procedures, and the operation of the entire school system.

"Objective" achievement tests in language arts and arithmetic were developed and used, as were scales for rating teachers' efficiency. School system surveys conducted by outside efficiency experts were common during the early part of the twentieth century. The purpose of these surveys, in the words of Calvin N. Kendall, commissioner of education in New Jersey, was to determine "What return is the community getting from its investment in the schools?" and "How can the investment be made to yield greater returns?"[7]

In many places uniform texts were adopted, and much attention was paid to making the maximum use of the school plant. In Gary, Indiana, for example, a "platoon system" was developed that had widespread publicity and use in the rest of the country. This platoon system involved having only half of the student population in regular classrooms at one time; the other half would be utilizing the shop, laboratories, playground, and auditorium.

Scientific management affected the administration of schools. The rise of business and industry to a position of prestige and influence, the reform movement in politics and education, and the vulnerability of school administrators to public criticism led to an infusion of industrial values and practices into the school. Raymond Callahan's review of the educational literature indicates the pervasiveness of business terminology and the concern of many administrators to demonstrate that they were using the most efficient and "scientific" means of school management.[8] Influential works by educational leaders Ellwood P. Cubberley, Franklin Bobbitt, and Frank Spaulding, and the National Society for the Study of Education reiterated the need to operate the school like a well-run business organization.

Franklin Bobbitt, who taught educational administration at the University of Chicago, analyzed the tasks of management in organizations and published his conclusions in 1913. He stated that education was "rather backward" in applying proven principles of good management, so educators should borrow from business.[9] Bobbitt stated two basic principles that should be applied:

Principle I.—Definite qualitative and quantitative standards must be determined for the product.

Principle II.—Where the material that is acted upon by the labor processes passes through a number of progressive stages on its way from the raw material to the ultimate product, definite qualitative and quantitative standards must be determined for the product at each of these stages.[10]

Bobbitt insisted that these principles were applicable to education, since "education is a shaping process as much as the manufacture of steel rails."[11]

Frank Spaulding, an influential educator and Superintendent of Schools in several cities at one time or another, spelled out the way schools could be made more efficient by using industrial methods. He emphasized "the analysis and comparison of conditions under which results are secured," and "the consistent adoption and use of the means that justify themselves most fully by their results, abandoning those that fail so to justify themselves."[12] Some of the "products" that could be measured, according to Spaulding, included "the average length of time required for each child to do a given definite unit of work, and the quality of education that the school affords."[13] He also advocated analyses of the budget in order to secure "a maximum of service at a minimum of cost in every school and every subject."[14]

It should be noted, however, that there also was great criticism of this trend by administrators, professors, and teachers. One teacher complained in an issue of the American Federation of Teachers' journal, the *American Teacher:*

We have yielded to the arrogance of "big business men" and have accepted their criteria of efficiency at their own valuation, without question. We have consented to measure the results of educational efforts in terms of price and product—the terms that prevail in the factory and the department store. But education, since it deals in the first place with organisms, and in the second place with individualities, is not analagous to a standardizable manufacturing process. Education must measure its efficiency not in terms of so many promotions per dollars of expenditure, nor even in terms of so many student-hours per dollar of salary; it must measure its efficiency in terms of increased humanism, increased power to do, increased capacity to appreciate.[15]

Influential educators like William C. Bagley and John Dewey also argued eloquently that some of the so-called "scientific" methods being lauded as panaceas, such as the achievement tests, were being applied inappropriately to classify and standardize students instead of being used for diagnostic purposes. These educators also questioned whether business and industrial values and procedures ought to be applied to schools, which, after all, had very different goals from the factory.[16]

Bagley considered especially unfortunate the "tendency toward the 'factory system' in school organization—toward a 'hierarchy' of authority and responsibility which makes the school board a 'board of directors,' the superintendent a 'general manager,' the assistant superintendents so many 'foremen,' and the principals equivalent to 'bosses,' while the teachers, to complete the picture, have the status of 'hands' or 'routine workers.' "[17]

The Teacher: Industrial Worker

Despite new perceptions about the importance of schooling in creating a better society, elementary school teachers' standing remained that of low-status employees who were to be monitored by administrators in the school, and by the public in their private lives. The restrictions on teachers' personal freedom stemmed from the requirement that they be exemplars of good behavior within and without the classroom. The extent to which these freedoms were curtailed, however, and the harsh sanctions that were applied for minor infractions also indicate that teachers did not have the power of high-status employees.

Teachers' dancing, cardplaying, gambling, smoking, drinking, staying out late at night, and failing to attend church were frowned upon by the public in many parts of the country. Even until World War II, in some communities in the South and Midwest, teachers were forbidden to go to the theater or to a dance. In Kansas in 1929, eleven high school teachers were dismissed by the board of education for attending a local country club dance.[18]

Political activity, "subversive" beliefs, and community activities also were scrutinized carefully by school boards. For example, in 1920 the board of education in St. Louis demanded the dismissal of any teacher who joined a union. In many places, teachers were not permitted to actively campaign for a political cause.[19]

School boards also regulated teachers' opportunities for marriage and divorce. Divorced teachers were considered unsavory characters, and were rarely appointed or retained. But married female teachers were also considered less desirable, since a married woman was providing a second income in her family and was taking the place of someone more "needy" of the income. In 1903, the New York City Board of Education enacted a by-law forbidding a woman teacher to marry, and hundreds of other school boards acted similarly, calling for a married woman to resign immediately after the wedding or at the end of the school year.[20]

Before the turn of the century, elementary school teachers usually had only a high school education, which made them much less educated and "professionally expert" than those in the newly emerged administrative profession. Even after the normal school was instituted, certification requirements upgraded, and in-service education made available, teachers still retained a docile relationship to superordinates in the school and school district. They frequently were referred to as industrial workers and were expected to execute, under minute prescription and careful supervision, the plans developed by management.

TEACHER EDUCATION. After the Civil War, the conceptions of education changed; the primary goals of teaching—the inculcation of character and the training of will—were modified. Teacher education began to emphasize the development of personal teaching style, pedagogical skills, and uniform standards for the measurement of effective teaching.

As educators began to consider criteria for effective teaching, the institutes took on greater responsibility for establishing teaching standards. A review of elementary subjects was less important than considering these subjects from "the teacher's point of view." Activities at the teachers' institutes increasingly included lectures and discussions regarding pedagogical methods and principles, and school management, in addition to instruction in the common branches.[21]

The period from the close of the Civil War to the progressive era is marked by tremendous exploration, experimentation, and change in teacher education programs. Institutes changed eventually; the reading circle flourished for a while and then faded; the normal school became the teachers college; and departments of education in colleges and universities proliferated.

The normal schools, which Nicholas Murray Butler once referred to as "academies or high schools with a slight infusion of pedagogical instruction,"[22] underwent a transformation between 1911 and 1920. Gradually, these normal schools became teachers colleges by going through an evolution that usually included raising entrance requirements to include high school graduation, adding liberal arts subjects to the courses in professional education and methodology, lengthening the program of studies from two to four years, incorporating studies in the theory of education, securing the right to grant degrees through state legislative action, and improving facilities.[23] The first normal school to become a modern teachers college was Michigan State Normal College. The Michigan legislature designated it a Normal College in 1897, recognizing that the school was actually giving college-level instruction. In 1903, the legislature mandated the board of education to organize courses there leading to the Bachelor of Arts degree, and the first degree was granted in 1905.[24]

By 1920, nineteen state normal schools became teachers colleges; by 1930, sixty-nine had made the transition.

Primarily because of the growing interest in improving the preparation of secondary school teachers, education became increasingly common as a subject of study in liberal arts colleges and universities. By 1890 there were over 100 colleges out of a total of 400 that offered teachers courses, and this trend accelerated after the turn of the century.[25]

The number of departments of education and faculty positions also increased after 1910, as well as the functions of departments of education. Programs began with the training of secondary teachers, but later specialized training was given to elementary teachers, administrators, supervisors, researchers, and normal school and college teachers. Graduate programs were established.

Conflict continued between those who believed that a liberal arts education was the best preparation for teaching, and those who emphasized the importance of professional preparation. The most commonly held position of teacher educators was that both liberal and professional studies should be included in teacher preparation programs. As Dewey reminded an audience at Columbia University in 1923:

> The more theoretical studies do not attain their highest development until they find some application in human life, contributing indirectly at least to human freedom and well-being, while the more practical studies cannot reach their highest practicality save as they are animated by a disinterested spirit of inquiry.[26]

In the schools of education in the early twentieth century, the liberal and technical functions achieved balance in the curriculum.[27] Three strands of professional development were stressed: the principles of pedagogy based upon the development of educational sciences; foundations of education, which, by reference to other disciplines, threw light on the practice of education; and laboratory experiences that would link theory and practice.[28]

SUPERVISION AND CONTROL OF TEACHER EDUCATION. Two important agencies led to greater standardization of teacher education: state departments of education, and voluntary professional associations.

The state departments exerted their influence primarily through certifying teachers; state authorities assumed functions in evaluating teacher education programs previously performed by local superintendents and school boards. The certification power of local authorities was taken over by state authorities. Standards were made more objective when the state education departments acted to establish standards for certification, supervise certifying examinations, and grant statewide certificates.[29]

Early professional groups like the American Institute of Instruction and the National Education Association gave extensive attention to teacher education. In addition, there were regional associations of colleges and secondary schools. These groups exerted their influences by providing the opportunity for leaders to exchange ideas on the theory and practice of education and on teacher education, appointing committees that studied specific problems and made recommendations, and beginning to establish standards for colleges and secondary schools, and to accredit secondary institutions.[30]

IN-SERVICE EDUCATION. From 1890 to 1930 the demand for skilled and cultured teachers increased. This need was reflected in in-service education programs, as was the improved level of education of teachers. The teachers institute was attacked by teachers and teacher educators at the turn of the century as being inadequate to fulfill the needs of well-trained teachers. Nonetheless, in 1910, institute attendance was still compulsory in twenty-eight states and sanctioned by inducements or penalties in other states.

Reading circles, which exposed teachers to outstanding books to upgrade teachers' academic and professional skills, became common as a means of in-service education. Generally, they were organized on a statewide basis and controlled by state authorities. By 1910 reading circle participation could be applied toward meeting certification requirements in twenty-seven states.

Other means of education for practicing teachers were summer schools, extension courses, after-hour classes, and correspondence study. Colleges and other teacher-training institutions reorganized their extension programs, and granted college credits for work done. More courses were offered in summer schools and after hours, and correspondence courses from the high school to the graduate levels were available.

These innovations began in the nineteenth century, but were not in widespread use until the first decades of the twentieth century. Their importance was that they enabled practicing teachers to extend their professional training while holding full-time jobs.

TEACHER PROFESSIONALIZATION. Because Horace Mann believed, "As the teacher goes, so goes the school," he campaigned for conditions that would facilitate the creation of a teaching profession, such as careful selection of personnel, well-designed advanced training, and increased status and authority for teachers.[31]

These goals were shared by many progressive educators who wanted reform through an improved teaching cadre. They pressed for the establishment of strong teacher associations to promote educational reform, and for research that would develop the "science of education."

Teachers' organizations grew gradually between 1865 and 1900. Newly created associations had different objectives than did those of the previous period. In the early associations, greater emphasis was placed upon broad educational questions than upon the improvement of the teachers' economic lot. Later, this situation was reversed. (Even during the earlier period, however, there had been concern for teachers' welfare benefits.)

Professional associations worked to countervail the restrictions placed upon teachers and to improve their position. Teachers' associations began to fight for better teacher education, certification requirements, and in-service education to improve teachers' status. As early as 1887, a National Education Association committee report supported tenure to protect academic and personal freedom. (But the NEA did not publicly commit itself to advocating protective tenure until 1915. As late as 1938, tenure for teachers was not a widespread practice.) Because of the efforts of these associations, salary schedules in some cities were set up as early as 1898, city union pension funds began in 1885, and state pensions in 1896.

The NEA established divisions and departments that provided an opportunity for all types of educators to promote their own interests and still be associated with the larger association. The association turned its attention to problems and issues of immediate concern to members; after 1890, research efforts and special committee investigations conducted by NEA had a considerable impact upon educational decision-making.

During this period, new kinds of teachers' groups began and traditional associations expanded. The American Federation of Teachers (AFT), an affiliate of the American Federation of Labor, was organized in 1916, when 2,800 teachers in eight locals united. The AFT had 12,000 members four years later. (The slow growth of the AFT can be attributed to the reluctance of teachers who aspired to "professional status" to join a trade union movement.) Despite its small membership during the early part of the century, the influence of AFT was still felt. Focusing on matters related to teachers' welfare, working conditions, and academic freedom, and on activity in shaping public opinion and lobbying for pro-education legislation, the AFT was a strong catalyst for teacher professionalization.

Another influential organization formed in the second decade of the century was the Progressive Education Association (PEA). Rooted in the philosophy of John Dewey and inspired by the work of Francis Parker in the Quincy, Cook County, schools, the PEA "aimed at nothing short of reforming the entire school system of America."[32] According to the original platform of the association, "The aim of Progressive Education is the freest and fullest development of the individual, based upon the scientific study of his mental, physical, spiritual, and social characteristics and needs."[33]

In 1924, the PEA began to issue a journal entitled *Progressive Education.* In its articles designed for professionals and lay persons, it publicized progressive programs and encouraged schools, especially elementary schools, to break with traditional practices.

In addition to these two organizations, state teachers associations grew in number and membership, as did local teachers associations, during this period. The state organizations had a powerful influence upon state educational policies and administrative practices, and they played an active part in improving teachers' salaries and working conditions. The local associations were primarily interested in the economic and professional welfare of their own members, but they played a part in teacher professionalization by raising teachers' awareness of educational issues and by creating a sense of mutual identity.

Administration and Supervision

Michael Katz suggests that the bureaucratic organization of schools became entrenched by 1880, not because there were no alternative models, but because bureaucracy best met the demands of industrialization and urbanization, and best reflected the social values and priorities of the time. He maintains that bureaucracy fit with dominant social and industrial practices. Children were treated as raw material to be processed and sorted into existing social patterns and inequalities.[34] Whether or not this interpretation is correct, the victory of bureaucracy over alternative models of organization went hand in hand with centralization, standardization, rational procedures, and the growth of administrative professionalization.

Education became "big business" following the Civil War, and school budgets became enormous. With this tremendous growth came a great increase in the techniques and agencies of school administration. By the end of World War I, 27,000 administrative and supervisory officers were reported; coordinating state and local educational authorities became a problem. Educational administration emerged as a profession that was separate and distinct from teaching by the second decade of the twentieth century.

During the first quarter of this century, too, the municipal reform movement succeeded in depoliticizing schooling, and further shifted educational authority from lay to professional hands. Laurence Iannocone points out that the reform movement rested on three doctrinal tenets: that public service should be separated from politics, that city communities were unitary in their values and educational needs, and that schools were best run by competent professionals.[35] In order to remove power from strong urban, ethnic machines, and to transfer it to upper-middle-class reformers and professional educators, school boards were reduced in size, school districts were redrawn so that they did not coincide with other local governments, and local school district elections were separated from other local elections. In many cities, like Boston, reformers hoped that by replacing the large school boards elected from the wards run by political machines, with a small centralized board with members elected at large, they would be able to introduce regulations and procedures that would substitute efficiency and equity for nepotism and graft.[36]

These changes resulted not only in diminished power for the ethnic machines, but also in reduced influence and control by neighborhood communities in school decisions.

In the cities, administrators had to manage huge enterprises involving large staffs and appropriations. The dominance of business values, especially the concern for efficiency and economy and the demand for school reform, put pressure on school administrators to demonstrate that they were operating the schools like a well-run industrial organization. These needs led to specialized graduate work in school administration to train the "professional executive." It was argued that special technical preparation was needed to handle these problems and to demonstrate to the public that administrators could provide efficient, educationally sound service.

THE NATURE OF SCHOOL SUPERVISION. During this period characterized by the establishment of bureaucratic schools, the growth of a professional administrative staff, and the application of "scientific" approaches to school management, curriculum design, and instructional methodology, efficiency and standardization were top priorities. The supervisory staff had the authority to determine the curriculum, textbooks, and methods of instruction to be used. This staff evaluated teachers on the basis of whether they succeeded in teaching prescribed materials by prescribed methods.[37]

The improvement of teachers became a major function of administrators and supervisors. The superintendent of schools, who was the executive officer of the lay board, delegated more and more of the supervisory function to head teachers, principals, teaching specialists, and special supervisors. The development of supervision as a function of administration, the organization of supervisory staffs, the empirical nature of professional knowledge, and the advanced training of administrators and supervisors helped shape the concept of teacher improvement as "bringing teachers up to a standard of performance contrived out of the superior knowledge of specialists."[38] Administrators and supervisors would be planners; teachers, specialists in practice.

Bobbitt, in his influential work for educators "Some General Principles of Management," stated: "The worker must be kept supplied with detailed instructions as to the work to be done, the standards to be reached, the methods to be employed, and the appliances to be used."[39] Bobbitt declared, "Teachers cannot be permitted to follow caprice in method." He insisted that the "workman" should be trained prior to and during service, so that he would be familiar with the "controlling science." Still, the work of the "planning department" had to be "transmitted to the teachers so that there can never be any misunderstanding as to what is expected of a teacher in the way of results or in the matter of method. This means that instruction must be given as to everything that is to be done."[40]

Teacher freedom no longer was justifiable at a time when supervisors were trained experts. Bobbitt taught that management must discover and supply the most effective tools, arrange the division of labor, provide teacher incentives to stimulate productivity, and see that the "raw material or partially finished product is actually passed on from process to process, from worker to worker, in the manner that is most effective and most economical."[41]

Although the previously held assumption that teachers could not analyze their own weaknesses or improve their own performance without direction from administrators was becoming untenable, careful control by supervisors was the norm.

At the same time, teachers were getting better training before they began teaching, and were beginning to define themselves as a professional group.

SUMMARY

In this era, four trends have implications for contemporary staff development: bureaucracy was established as the major organizational structure of schools, administration became a career distinct from teaching, control of schools became more centralized, and teachers worked to improve their professional status.

The centralization of urban schools and the establishment of a bureaucratic school structure conducted by a cadre of administrators trained specifically for the job took control out of local school boards' hands, despite the persisting myth of local control. The principalship and the city superintendency were institutionalized, and bureaucracy became the predominant structure of school organization. Thus, the principle of bureaucratic authority was firmly established after the Civil War.

The school board's power began to decline with the advent of the city superintendency. Despite the maxim that the school board makes policy and the superintendent carries it out, boards gradually delegated more and more of their policy-making authority to their hired professional official, the superintendent, as the tasks of schooling became more complex.

Administration emerged as a career different from teaching. The administrator claimed an expertise not shared with his subordinate, the teacher. And, since efficiency and standardization were priorities, curricula, textbooks, and instructional materials were determined by administrators, and not the individual teacher.

Although teachers were considered and treated as hired employees who had to produce a "product" according to administrative specifications, they were making advances in professional development. Teacher education improved, and certification standards were upgraded. Moreover, teachers were beginning to define themselves as a professional group. They established voluntary organizations; through these associations, teachers initiated research and investigations of school practices. Better teacher education and the strengthening of teachers' professional associations provided a foundation for the emergence of teachers as an authority source, and for the principle of colleague authority in the contemporary period.

NOTES

1. David Nasaw, *Schooled to Order: A Social History of Public Schooling in the United States* (New York: Oxford University Press, 1979), p. 97.

2. John Dewey, *Democracy and Education* (New York: Macmillan, 1916), p. 92.

3. Mary L. Sequel, *The Curriculum Field: Its Formative Years* (New York: Teachers College Press, Teachers College, Columbia University, 1966), p. 12.

4. Franklin Bobbitt, *The Curriculum* (Boston: Houghton-Mifflin, 1918), p. 43.

5. Michael Katz, *Class, Bureaucracy, and Schools* (New York: Praeger, 1971), pp. 113-46.

6. Ibid.

7. *Proceedings of the National Education Association* (1915), pp. 376-80.

8. Raymond E. Callahan, *Education and the Cult of Efficiency* (Chicago: University of Chicago Press, 1962), chap. 1, pp. 1-18.

9. Franklin Bobbitt, *The Supervision of City Schools: Some General Principles of Management Applied to the Problems of City-School Systems,* Twelfth Yearbook of the National Society for the Study of Education, pt. 1 (Bloomington, Ill., 1913), pp. 8-9.

10. Ibid., p. 11.

11. Ibid.

12. Callahan, *Education and the Cult of Efficiency,* p. 68.

13. Ibid., p. 69.

14. Ibid., p. 73.

15. Benjamin C. Gruenberg, "Some Economic Obstacles to Educational Progress," *American Teacher* 1 (September 1912): 90.

16. John Dewey, "Education as Engineering," *New Republic* 32., No. 407, 20 September 1922, p. 91.

17. William C. Bagley and John A.H. Keith, *An Introduction to Teaching* (New York: Macmillan, 1942), p. 379.

18. Howard K. Beale, *Are American Teachers Free?* (New York: Charles Scribner's Sons, 1936), pp. 374-75.

19. Ibid., p. 396.

20. Ibid., p. 384.

21. Herman G. Richey, "Growth of the Modern Conception of In-Service Education," in *In-Service Education*, Fifty-sixth Yearbook of the National Society for the Study of Education (Chicago: University of Chicago Press, 1957), pp. 39-40.

22. Willard S. Elsbree, *The American Teacher, Evolution of a Profession in a Democracy* (New York: American Book, 1939), p. 321.

23. Jessie Pangburn, *The Evolution of the American Teachers College* (New York: Bureau of Publications, Teachers College, Columbia University, 1932), pp. 2-12.

24. Lawrence Cremin, "The Heritage of American Teacher Education," *The Journal of Teacher Education* 4 (June 1953): 167.

25. Ibid., p. 163.

26. Merle L. Borrowman, *The Liberal and Technical in Teacher Education, A Historical Survey of American Thought.* (New York: Bureau of Publications, Teachers College, Columbia University, 1965), p. 21.

27. Ibid., pp. 156-62.

28. Ibid.

29. Cremin, "The Heritage of American Teacher Education," pp. 169-70.

30. Ibid.

31. Lawrence A. Cremin, *The Genius of American Education* (New York: Random House, 1965) pp. 187-88.

32. Stanwood Cobb, "The Romance of Beginnings," *Progressive Education* 6 (1929), p. 68.

33. Ibid.

34. Katz, *Class, Bureaucracy, and Schools,* pp. xxi-xxii.

35. Laurence Iannaccone, "Three Views of Change in Educational Politics," in *The Politics of Education,* ed. Jay D. Scribner, Seventy-sixth Yearbook of the National Society for the Study of Education (Chicago: University of Chicago Press, 1977), pp. 277-83.

36. Katz, *Class, Bureaucracy, and Schools,* p. 115.

37. Richey, "Growth of the Modern Conception of In-Service Education," p. 52.

38. Ibid., p. 51.

39. Bobbitt, "General Principles of Management," pp. 74-96.

40. Ibid., pp. 92-94.

41. Ibid., pp. 95-96.

The Progressive Era

5

DURING THE PERIOD of the progressive era, from 1920 to the launching of the Russian satellite Sputnik, the United States went through a great depression and two world wars. These events, among others, led to reassessments of the American way of life, and to conflicts and clashes among competing ideologies and power groups. After World War I, the question arose whether western democracy could adjust to industrial life and the problems created by the technological explosion while still retaining its traditional freedoms. The depression of the thirties resulted in questioning of the free enterprise system and modifications of the system through social legislation, the policies of the New Deal, and the expansion of the labor movement. The growth of fascism, communism, and the outbreak of World War II led to new thinking about the aims of education and the role of the school in society.

During the decade of 1950 to 1960, new conditions emerged: booming technology, industrialization and urbanization, the development of urban slum ghettos, the problems of poverty and racial inequality, the cold war, and fear of world communism. These brought on a new storm about the educational system.

THE FOUNDATIONS OF EDUCATION: PROGRESSIVE EDUCATION

Lawrence Cremin cites the following factors that contributed to the receptiveness to experimentation in the schools in accord with suggestions for action by progressive educators: a steady rise in school enrollments, with expansion of an increasingly diverse clientele receptive to reform; centralization of school districts that could then afford richer programs and were able to try many of the recommendations of progressive educators; newly developed and professional state departments of education that supported and aided progressive experimentation and disseminated information through publications, instructional materials, curricula, conferences, institutes, and seminars; the involvement of the United States Office of Education, which became the main source of the spread of progressivism through persuasion and administration of legislation; the centralization in professional educational matters accomplished by the National Education Association, which increased its membership greatly in the era after World War I, and published research bulletins, an influential journal for classroom teachers, and technical publications for administrators; a growing perception that a rapidly changing society demanded a responsive effort on the part of education; and the acceptance of progressive education as respectable.[1]

The twenties and thirties were an age of reform in American education. Educators tested methods of making a curriculum in which various important elements were considered, ranging from the nature of the child to the needs of society.

Some educators like William Heard Kilpatrick, A.S. Neill, and L. Thomas Hopkins focused upon the needs and interests of the child. Approaches appropriate to the child-centered school were developed: with the "project method," the curriculum was organized around topics, problems, or themes; the "activity methods" involved children in activities that required thinking as well as doing; the "emergent curriculum" was a curriculum that unfolded as the class pursued interests and problems of concern to them.

Other approaches focused upon the school's responsibility to help build a better social order. Reconstructionists like John L. Childs and George S. Counts saw the schools as cultural instruments for humanizing industrial society. Still others like John Dewey, William Boyd, and Hollis L. Caswell sought to harmonize children's interests and needs, social functioning, and organized knowledge in curriculum designs.

In addition to these approaches, many new plans were devised to apply theoretical principles to childhood education, starting in the 1920s. These included contract plans to individualize instruction, like the Dalton and Winnetka plans; ability grouping; life-adjustment education for youth, which emphasized vocational and practical experience and training; and the play school, a child-centered community in which children, through play, learned to master their environment and express their creative potential. Thousands of local districts experimented with progressive innovations.

Several new approaches to curriculum reform were formulated; for example, Alice Miel and Hollis L. Caswell maintained that the central problem for curriculum design was neither the reordering nor reconstituting of subject matter, but instead the revitalizing and redirecting of the individual school and teachers.

By the end of World War II, progressive education and "good education" were, for the most part, considered synonymous by educators and the public alike. Educational rhetoric included phrases like "recognizing individual differences," "the whole child," "social and emotional growth," "creative self-expression," "intrinsic motivation," "persistent life situations," "real-life experiences," and "teacher-pupil relationships."

Cremin summarizes the imprints made by the progressive movement on American schools. Among those he lists are: educational opportunity was expanded steadily upward and downward, expansion and reorganization of curriculum continued to develop at all levels, extracurricular activities were added to the formal curriculum, more variation and flexibility were used in the grouping of students, guidance programs were established, the character of the classroom changed from passive to more active and informal, materials of instruction had principles of learning and child development incorporated into their designs, audiovisual and other supplementary materials were created, school architecture changed, teachers were better educated, administrative relationships changed, and there was increased parent and teacher participation in making policy.[2]

Progressive education also came under attack. Criticism from educators might be summarized by Arthur Bestor's comment in 1953 that the ultimate purpose of education is "the deliberate cultivation of the ability to think." Intelligent training through study in the basic academic disciplines should be the *raison d'etre* of the schools. Progressive education had subverted American education by divorcing the schools from scholarship and teacher training from the arts and sciences.

Along with the growing dissatisfaction among the intelligentsia with progressive education, there were other negative factors—tremendous pressures placed upon the schools due to the problems of rampant inflation, a teacher shortage, the flood of war babies enrolled in the schools, the need for new school buildings, concern about communist expansion, the demands of an expanding industrial economy, and the need for intelligent manpower. These combined forces led to the demise of progressive education in the fifties.

Schooling in the Fifties

In the 1950s, the education profession was called upon to deal with new concerns.

There were four major sets of controversial issues. One set of issues revolved around the problem of providing equal educational opportunity for all Americans. Most of the controversy centered on the conflict between the ideal of equal opportunity and the practice of racial class segregation and discrimination. A second set of issues concerned support and control of education: the conflict between public and private control of schools, between church and state, and the conflict over federal aid to education. The third group of issues related to the nature of the educational program: the relative merits of traditional subject matter versus the needs and interests of the child, the advisability of teaching about controversial issues, the debate over whether schools should take leadership in social change or should follow accepted societal customs, and the merits of religious instruction. Finally, there were issues related to the social role of teachers and the teaching profession: the nature of academic freedom, loyalty oaths, and the proper role of teachers in political action.[3]

By 1953, the organized educational enterprise in the United States had come to have several general characteristics. For one thing, centralized authority and decentralized administration had developed. Overall authority for the control of education increasingly had been vested in the state, but direct administration of schools had been directed largely to local units.

In addition, public support came from larger and larger units—public funds from local, state, and federal units—rather than private sources of endowment, gift, or tuition. The proportion of funds raised by taxes by local districts, towns, and counties has declined, and the proportion by the states and the federal government has risen.

Other general characteristics included: the expansion and complexity of knowledge, strengthened conception of the teaching profession, and improved professional preparation. Additionally, the attitude held three hundred years previously by the Puritans, that the child was born in sin and had to be severely disciplined to be kept in the path of righteousness, gradually gave way to the humanistic concept that the child is basically good, and that this goodness could and should be nurtured by humane methods of child rearing and education.[4]

The Teacher: Artist

Cremin observes that progressivism cast the teacher in an impossible role: "He was to be an artist of consummate skill, knowledgeable in his field, meticulously trained in the science of pedagogy, and thoroughly imbued with a burning zeal for social improvement."[5]

In a book written in 1955, Harold Rugg and William Withers paint a picture of the "ideal" teacher that is a far cry from the "pious and civil" colonial schoolmaster or the "worker" teacher of the first part of the twentieth century. They proclaim: The true teacher loves to teach—would rather teach than do anything else. "He likes people, is a deep believer in humanity, has great faith in the potentialities of human beings; is a friend, comrade, and guide—not a policeman and taskmaster—respects his students and is respected by them. He is a student of our civilization, of the psychology of learning and the development of personality, and of human expression and appreciation. He is sensitive to others, keeps the channels of communication open; plans his teaching carefully, is a master of the art of developing thinking ability. Above all, he is a dynamic, creative person of integrity and scholarship—an artist-teacher with great capacity for feeling."[6]

TEACHER EDUCATION. In *The Scientific Movement in Education,* the Thirty-Seventh Yearbook of the National Study of the Science of Education, E.S. Evenden outlines changes that affected or occurred in teacher education from 1900 to 1938. At the level of education for teachers before they began service, there was an increase in the number of faculty with higher qualifications, and in the number and importance of professional elements in teacher education. There was development of education as a field of study, of principles and techniques of curriculum construction, of methods of measuring educational procedures, and of graduate departments for professional preparation of teachers. Emphasis on the study of the technology of teaching increased, as did attention to guidance and selection of prospective teachers, and the use of in-service education.[7]

The most rapid growth of teachers' colleges came after World War I. A major factor was a rapid increase in high school enrollment during the twenties and thirties; by the forties, this increase created a severe teacher shortage. Additionally, the research in related fields such as educational psychology and tests and measurements, and the work of educational thinkers like John Dewey, gave impetus to the development of professional content in teacher education.

By the end of the fifties, almost all teachers' colleges had converted to liberal arts colleges or universities. This was due to the need for general and professional education for teachers that was broader and deeper.

A pattern had been set earlier that prevailed as a model for teacher preparation in all institutions, whether they were teachers' colleges, four-year liberal arts colleges, universities, or graduate schools of education. General education courses were required of all students. To obtain depth in a major subject area for secondary teachers, or in the elementary education area of specialization, students followed a sequence of courses. The sequence of professional courses included foundations in educational history, philosophy, sociology, and psychology, and methods courses. A series of laboratory and clinical experiences culminated in a supervised student-teaching experience.

PROFESSIONAL STATUS OF TEACHERS. The standardization of teacher certification and accreditation of teacher-education programs, as well as the growth of teachers' organizations affected the development of teaching as a profession during this period.

The major criterion in teacher certification is the successful completion of a course in an accredited institution of teacher education. Therefore, control of the accreditation of programs is the crucial element in the process of teacher certification.

Prior to 1927, there were no standards for the accreditation of teacher education programs, nor even a list of institutions with accredited programs. Accreditation began in 1927 by the American Association of Teachers' Colleges (AATC), which merged with two other organizations to become the American Association of Colleges for Teacher Education (AACTE) in 1948.

In the period beginning in the mid-forties and extending to the present time, there has been a struggle for the control over accreditation of teacher education.

In 1946, the NEA established the National Commission on Teacher Education and Professional Standards (NCTEPS), in part to give teachers a voice in accreditation. The commission advocated the bachelor's degree as the minimum level of preparation for any teaching position. NCTEPS also wanted to assume responsibility for the profession in matters of selection and recruitment, certification, in-service growth, and the advancement of professional standards.

By the 1950s the selection, preparation, licensure, assignment, retention, and authority for the approval of teacher education programs were consolidated and centralized in state agencies.

In 1952, the National Council for Accreditation of Teacher Education (NCATE) was established. The initial council shifted control out of the hands of the colleges and universities by giving only six of its twenty-one representatives to higher education, and fifteen to school people (teachers, state education department representatives, school board representatives, and chief school officers).

In 1956, after some struggle, the colleges again gained control of teacher education through increased representation in NCATE.

Teachers' organizations also grew tremendously in membership and influence during this period.

The two large rivals, the AFT and the NEA, changed and expanded. In the beginning of this era—before the depression—the AFT was widely thought to be communistic and nonprofessional; the NEA began an anti-union campaign that contributed to the decline of the AFT until after the depression. But the AFT began to increase its membership after World War II, as a result of the protests of teachers over the lessening of their buying power due to inflation and cutbacks. With the resurgence of the AFT, the NEA began to modify its anti-union stance. Although it still fought to preserve and develop the teacher's image as "professional," it began to take a more militant position.

Before the 1960s, the major means used by both groups to improve teacher benefits were lobbying, personal diplomacy, and other nonmilitant tactics.

IN-SERVICE EDUCATION. In earlier times, in-service education was thought of as some kind of out-of-school activity planned for the working teacher. It was hoped that participation in any professional growth activity would inspire better performance and give the teacher some additional "tricks of the trade."

From 1920 to 1960 in-service activities came to be viewed as those that would lead to the growth of the entire school staff, not just to the improvement of the individual teacher. Although teachers continued to take college courses for in-service credit toward salary increments, or professional enlightenment, there was a new focus on developing individual skills that were relevant to the local situation. This new approach was predicated on the belief that the school program as well as teacher performance would improve as teachers worked together on problems significant to them. This new approach was possible because teachers were receiving better training before they became teachers, and because there was less turnover in teaching staffs.

Several trends are apparent in the in-service literature of this period. The literature stressed change in school goals and methods, a supportive school climate and good supervisor-teacher relationships, cooperative group effort by the entire staff, the identification of needs felt by individuals and groups, opportunities for working teachers based upon these needs, and the use of research to identify problems, needs, and concerns, and to solve problems.

In the area of change, the literature emphasized that programs of in-service education should exist for the dual purpose of helping the members of the staff become more competent to deal with their professional roles as teachers and administrators and of improving the quality of the school system's educational program. This would require change in people as individuals and professionals as well as changes in the nature and quality of the instructional program. In order to facilitate this change, administrators, consultants and other people working toward change would need to understand what happens when individual change confronts institutional elements.

The line between in-service education and supervision became hard to draw as educators came to realize that the improvement of staff performance was related to school climate, administrative support, and interpersonal dynamics, as well as the acquisition of new knowledge and skills. Writers emphasized the importance of morale, administrative support of teacher experimentation and personal style, and the need to develop an atmosphere that is conducive to building mutual respect, support, and creativeness.

In professional growth, the emphasis shifted from upgrading the teacher's performance to promoting the growth of the entire staff. Roles and responsibilities were less tied to position, and more a function of personal interests or talents. The supervisor was part of the team, a person who might assist, consult, advise, or instruct. Some writers advocated the change of title "supervisor" to that of "educational consultant," "technical assistant," "helping teacher," or "instructional advisor." Leadership was seen as a function of the person, not of the role. In-service programs involved group activity; leadership was alternated among people as it emerged from the staff. Activities included curriculum-planning committees, policy-making boards, workshops, and action research—in-depth investigations of school problems identified and conducted by teachers and administrators.

The literature of the progressive era also emphasized participation in planning the in-service program and the involvement of the entire school staff in group activities and solving problems. This was based on the assumptions that "all who are affected by or take part in an action should participate in making the decision leading to that action."[8] A leading educator, J. Cecil Parker, wrote that in-service education should provide many opportunities for people to relate to one another, continuous attention to individual and group problem-solving processes, and continuous attention to the interrelationship of different groups.[9]

In contrast to the scientific-management era, when it was assumed that improvement would result from administrative directives to teachers, educators of the progressive era believed that a desire for improvement on the part of the participants in the in-service program was an essential requisite for success.

Parker's first guideline was expressed in the title of one chapter, "People Work as Individuals and as Members of Groups on Problems That Are Significant to Them." He explained that a problem is significant to an individual "when he can become involved in it emotionally as well as intellectually; when it can be seen as a basis for actions; and when a solution is demanded by the exigencies of the situation as he perceives them."[10]

In line with the concern for developing in-service programs responsive to individual needs, was a new emphasis on self-appraisal. In contrast to the earlier assumption that administrators and supervisors were in a better position to identify the teacher's needs than was the teacher, there was a shift to the modified position that self-evaluation supplemented by supervisors' observations and appraisals would help individuals identify their own in-service needs.

Procedures were developed to identify the needs felt by teachers—"felt-needs," as it was called in the literature. These included checksheets, attitude-rating scales, inventories of instructional practices, opinion surveys, and questionnaires. The assessment of teacher needs usually was limited to asking teachers what were their needs.

These assessments often were used as the basis for in-service plans, however. Surveys also were used to evaluate existing in-service programs, to discover how extensively in-service education was being provided by school systems, and to identify the kinds of programs in existence.

Other kinds of research in the progressive era were used to solve or investigate school problems. Such research included community studies aimed at identifying community resources and needs, and action research. For example, teachers investigated and developed new procedures for grouping children, for improving reading or mathematics instruction, and compared programs and materials for their effectiveness in meeting stated goals.

The in-service literature of this period emphasized various other considerations. Educators wanted: time during the school day for in-service activities, and diversity and variation in these activities; in-service programs to be evaluated, and then modified on the basis of these evaluations; programs individualized to take into account varying needs, levels of seniority, and problems; schools and universities to cooperate in developing local in-service programs; programs focused upon the problems of the local school and district, and held at local sites; and the active participation of the principal, as school leader, in the planning and other phases of the in-service program.

MODELS OF IN-SERVICE ACTIVITIES IN THE 1950s. Two major types of activities emerged during this period: the workshop and, as has been indicated, action research.

In the middle 1950s, the workshop was the most widespread in-service technique used. This generally involved a number of teachers working together, with resource persons and a director, on problems of concern to the participants. Theoretically, there was no preplanned schedule of activities; the participants worked on problems of their choice; and leadership was a function of the workshop members.[11]

Stephen Corey saw action research "as research undertaken by practitioners in order that they may improve their practices."[12] Staff members collaborated in designing, planning, and evaluating solutions to problems that they had identified. The problems attacked by action research involved many uncontrollable variables. Because of its practical relevance, however, many educators supported action research, despite its methodological shortcomings. Furthermore, it was hoped that the process of searching for improved practices would, in itself, produce growth.

Administration and Supervision

The scientific-management approach to supervision and administration followed before 1920—that the administrator's function was planning, organizing, directing, and controlling—underwent a transformation during the progressive period. Before this time, supervision had emerged as an important function of administration; in this period, the methods of supervision changed from that of authoritative direction to that of guidance. In Courtis's words supervision should be "creative," having as its goal "the facilitation of the natural process of growth" in teachers.[13]

The major goal of supervision also shifted from that of teacher improvement to that of improving the school program through cooperative group effort by the entire professional staff.

Numerous authorities realized that scientific-management minimized the psychological and sociological aspects of personnel management. The administrator-as-manager viewpoint was challenged by the growth of a better understanding of the importance of morale, and why and how behavior is changed. Goodwin Watson told educators, in a 1942 article in *Progressive Education,* that knowledge related to the motivation of behavior suggested that the belief should be modified that direction by an expert was the most effective means of improving a worker's performance.[14]

Several landmark publications by such writers as Mary Parker Follett, Elton Mayo, and J. L. Moreno emphasized the human relations viewpoint. The famous studies done at the Western Electric plant in the 1920s, pointed to the importance of worker morale, and the influence of the informal system of group norms, interaction patterns, and leadership upon worker productivity. A study by Kurt Lewin, Ronald Lippitt, and Ralph K. White at the University of Iowa on the psychological dynamics of democratic, authoritarian, and laissez-faire leadership styles found that democratic leadership was most effective in eliciting high motivation, contentment, individuality, group-mindedness and friendliness compared to the other two kinds of leadership.[15]

These influential research studies and advances in the fields of psychoanalysis, social psychology, and field psychologies led to an outpouring of literature with a human relations and group dynamics point of view. These had a great impact upon concepts of administration and supervision.

Another trend was the social science approach formulated by Chester Barnard in 1938. He called for a general theory of administrative relationships placed in the context of the social science of behavior.[16]

In 1945, Herbert Simon pointed out that a theory of administration had to be based on concepts derived from empirically observed phenomena of organizational relationships and events.[17]

New practices in school administration were informed by the work of organizational theorists such as Talcott Parsons, Chris Argyris, E. W. Bakke, Neal Gross, and Robert K. Merton, and social psychologists researching the process of individual change in organizational settings.

By the 1950s the school as a social system came to be considered the basic unit for administrative analysis.[18] The assumption was that a social system involves two related classes of phenomena, the normative dimension of behavior and the personal dimension.

Strategies for bringing about change in professional behavior changed as it became clear that individual change can be facilitated or hindered by the norms and expectations of groups within the institution. Attention was focused upon how individual needs, expectations and personality dispositions related to organizational components.

The growing knowledge of the psychology of human relations led to a revision of the goals of school supervision. Correcting teacher deficiencies took second place to promoting professional growth. This new goal required a new relationship between the supervisor and teacher, that is, from that of authoritative direction by the supervisor, to guidance and motivation.

Another influence upon more democratic supervisory-teacher relationships was the increased professional preparation of the teaching staff. Although in 1952, half of the nation's 600,000 public elementary school teachers did not hold college degrees, according to the National Education Association's estimate, the financial and social status of teachers, and the quality of their professional preparation had improved to the point that they could be considered specialists in the practice of teaching. Rating of teachers by checklists, inspections, and the results of student achievement tests became less common; cooperative problem-solving on the part of the staff and clinical models of supervision and evaluation in which teachers participated actively in setting goals and judging results became more commonly used.

Although the concept of supervision changed from that of direction from above to guidance, it should be noted that the goal of supervision remained

that of advancing administrator's objectives. Teachers were asked to participate in identifying and solving problems, but they rarely were involved in
determining policy. One writer, a schoolteacher, bluntly stated that "in their
eagerness to be known as democratic administrators, some school principals
deny that there is such a thing as a school hierarchy. But the denial does not
alter the fact."[19] She expressed skepticism about whether participatory
decision-making could actually work, given the constraints of time and the
bureaucratic hierarchy, as well as the power of administrators to sanction
experimentation. She suggested that instead of denying the fact of a hierarchy, administrators should set out clear limits within which teachers could
make decisions, take action, and experiment in the classroom.

SUMMARY

The progressive era marked the emergence of the teacher as an authority.
This was a result of better teacher education and improvements in professional standards and requirements for entry into teaching.

The development of teaching as a profession created new needs in teachers for autonomy in exercising professional judgments in the classroom, and
for participation in making decisions about school practices and problems.
The principle of bureaucratic authority remained entrenched; increasingly,
though, challenges to this authority from the teachers were made. (In the
contemporary period, these challenges solidified in the form of teacher
power manifested by militant action and collective bargaining.)

During the progressive era, managerial ideologies shifted from "scientific
management" to "democratic administration," and the major goal of supervision became the improvement of pupil learning through the cooperative
group effort of the entire school staff. The hierarchical structure of the
school organization persisted, but teachers shared in day-by-day decision-
making about school affairs and had relatively high amounts of autonomy
in the classroom.

Although "participation" in school affairs was considered important to
inspire motivation to do effective work, and for commitment to school
goals, teachers were not considered legitimate sources of policy-making authority. They were consulted on matters such as textbook selection, student
placement, and report card construction; they did not have an important
role in establishing overall goals or policies, however.

By the 1950s, the board of education's major responsibility was the hiring
of a superintendent of schools, who would see to it that their broad goals
were carried out, and communicating and gaining community support for

the superintendent's policies and programs.[20]

Principals had the authority to run their schools as they wished as long as the principals remained within the limits defined by the central administration. Though principals exercised leadership and supervised staffs, by and large it was left to teachers, now considered "experts in practice," to implement school goals through daily activities in the classrooms.

Better teacher education and teacher professionalization led to changes in the teachers' ideas of their roles, and in their career commitments. The foundation was laid for developments in the contemporary period.

As we shall see in the next chapter, teachers would begin to claim authority prerogatives in local policy determination and in professional matters such as certification, accreditation, and teacher education before and after they began service. For the first time, the principle of colleague authority will emerge to challenge the other two principles of authority.

NOTES

1. Lawrence Cremin, *The Transformation of the School: Progressivism in American Education 1876-1957* (New York: Vintage, 1964), pp. 274-76.

2. Ibid., pp. 306-08.

3. Freeman R. Butts and Lawrence A. Cremin, *A History of Education in American Culture* (New York: Henry Holt, 1953), p. 516.

4. Ibid., pp. 563-68.

5. Ibid., p. 168.

6. Harold Rugg and William Withers, *Social Foundations of Education* (New York: Prentice-Hall, 1955), pp. 689-90.

7. E.S. Evenden, "Contributions of Research to the Education of Teachers," *The Scientific Movement in Education,* Thirty-seventh Yearbook of the National Society for the Study of Education, pt. 2 (Chicago: Public School Publishing Company, 1938), pp. 33-52.

8. J.W. Carrington, "Developing and Sharing the Power of Group Dynamics," in *The Teaching Profession Grows In Service* (Washington, D.C.: National Commission on Teacher Education, pt. 1 (Chicago: University of Chicago Press, 1957), p. 104.

9. Cecil J. Parker, "Guidelines for In-Service Education," in *In-Service Education,* Fifty-sixth Yearbook of the National Society for the Study of Education, pt. 1 (Chicago: University of Chicago Press, 1957), p. 104.

10. Ibid.

11. James R. Mitchell, "The Workshop as an In-Service Education Procedure" (Study conducted and reported by the Subcommittee on In-Service Education of Teachers), *North Central Association Quarterly* 28 (April 1954): 421-57.

12. Stephen M. Corey, *Action Research to Improve School Practices* (New York: Bureau of Publications, Teachers College, Columbia University, 1953), p. 10.

13. S.A. Courtis, "A Philosophy of Supervision," *Educational Supervision,* First Yearbook of the National Conference on Educational Method (New York: Bureau of Publications, Teachers College, Columbia University, for the National Conference in Educational Method, 1928), p. 251.

14. Goodwin Watson, "The Surprising Discovery of Morale," *Progressive Education* 19 (1942): 33-42.

15. See Ralph K. White and Ronald Lippitt, *Autocracy and Democracy: An Experimental Inquiry* (New York: Harper & Row, 1960).

16. Jacob W. Getzels, James M. Lipham, and Roald F. Campbell. *Educational Administration As a Social Process: Theory, Research, Practice* (New York: Harper & Row, 1968), p. 40.

17. Herbert A. Simon, *Administrative Behavior* (New York: Macmillan, 1945), cited by Jacob W. Getzels, *Educational Administration*, p. 43.

18. Getzels, *Educational Administration*, p. 40.

19. Jo Kinnick, "The Teachers and the In-Service Education Program," *In-Service Education*, Fifty-sixth yearbook of the National Society for the Study of Education, pt. 1, p. 133.

20. Norman D. Kerr, "The School Board as an Agency of Legitimation," in *Governing Education*, ed. Alan Rosenthal (New York: Anchor Books, 1969), pp. 137-72.

The Contemporary Era

6

IN THE PREVIOUS chapters, as we traced the three principles of authority from colonial to contemporary times, we saw that the historical ethos that policy-making should be in the hands of the local board of education gradually altered in actual practice. Administrative influence over school policy became a reality that has endured for at least a century.

The nationalizing trend in educational policy-making, during the contemporary period, has had the effect of increasing administrative power vis-à-vis the school board and has created new community-professional tensions.

Challenges to the bureaucratic principle of authority, however, have come from two major sources: parents and teachers.

In this chapter, we explore three contemporary developments that have altered the relationships among the three principles of authority: schooling and the national interest, community power, and perhaps most important, teacher power.

FOUNDATIONS OF EDUCATION: THE NATIONAL INTEREST

The launching of Sputnik in 1957 dramatically demonstrated the demise of the superior technological position of the United States and confirmed the suspicions of critics of progressive education that the schools were not adequately preparing students to be literate, mathematical, and scientific. A wave of criticism was directed towards schools, teachers, and teacher education.

Schools were called upon to provide the business and scientific communities with technologically sophisticated workers. Thus, the focus changed from the prewar curriculum emphasis on social adjustment to that of organizing subject matter for instruction.

The resources of the federal government, of universities, and of industry and the private foundations were mobilized to study and improve the curriculum and teacher performance.

The Curriculum Reform Movement

The concern led to special national meetings of educators. In 1958, teacher educators and school teachers from all over the land met with liberal arts professors at Bowling Green, Ohio, to consider teachers' educational needs. In 1959, thirty-five prestigious scientists, scholars, and educators gathered at Woods Hole, Massachusetts, to discuss how teaching, especially science teaching, could be improved.

The National Science Foundation, which had been created in 1950, became the vehicle for dealing with the national concern for curricular reform. The Foundation and the National Defense Education Act (NDEA) of 1958 poured funds into improvements in the teaching and course content of the physical and natural sciences.

The curriculum reform movement initiated in the 1950s had a central goal of giving students the intellectual power to cope with a technological society in which knowledge rapidly becomes obsolete. Future Americans would have to be problem-solvers in order to survive. They would have to be equipped to effectively identify problems; gather, weigh, and interpret pertinent data; and find creative solutions based on such inquiry. Since each academic discipline has a unique structure, key concepts, and modes of inquiry, and requires a different problem-solving process, the reform projects focused upon the context and methods of teaching discrete subjects.

These changes required a parallel change in teachers' attitudes, knowledge, and skills. Although some academic curriculum developers sought to "teacher proof" materials by preparing curriculum packages containing everything they considered necessary to ensure student learning, it soon became apparent that a teacher could distort even the most rigidly structured curriculum package if the teacher did not have a deep understanding of its objectives and underlying concepts and principles. Teachers had to be trained to use the materials in the way they were intended, and to understand the principles of learning on which they were based.

In-service training became an integral part of the curriculum reform movement. Teachers who would be testing or using the new materials spent summers with people who designed curriculum projects and trained teachers to use the projects; others took graduate courses on university campuses, or special workshops given in local settings.

A new interest in teacher education developed within university academic departments. Colleges and departments of education began a dialogue about priorities in teacher education, and a movement began to redesign programs and course offerings—both substantively and pedagogically. Three conferences were called by the National Commission on Teacher Education and Professional Standards (TEPS), in 1958, 1959, and 1960, to discuss the possibilities of collaborative efforts between academic and education departments to improve teacher education.

During the 1950s and 1960s, numerous efforts were made to find better ways of preparing teachers. Included in teacher-training programs were courses focusing upon the use of new programs and equipment. In other courses, teachers were encouraged and trained to use innovative teaching approaches, such as "open classroom," an orientation towards teaching based upon the British Primary School; individualized instruction; and inquiry and discovery methods for social studies and science, which emphasized involving children in solving problems and in experimenting. Teachers were taught to use collaborative teaching approaches, such as team-teaching, where two or more teachers share responsibility for a large group of children; and differentiated staffing, where a senior teacher and several junior teachers work together but have different levels of responsibility and authority.

Many of the innovative programs received support from philanthropic foundations such as the Fund for the Advancement of Education, established by the Ford Foundation.

Nationalizing Trends in the 1960s

The 1960s saw an acceleration of the 1950s trend toward the expectation that the schools should fullfill national goals and needs, and an increase in extralocal involvement in the educational enterprise.

The expanded federal force in education during the 1960s was rooted in public policy objectives related to the war on poverty, economic growth, civil rights, national defense, and other national goals.

The federal government initiated programs in the war on poverty that included the Office of Education's Job Corps; community action programs; Head Start; Follow Through; and Upward Bound; the Elementary and Secondary Education Act's Title I programs, which provided federal funds to equalize the educational opportunities of "disadvantaged" children; the "war on prejudice" programs, to provide the technology, education, and training to further school integration; and vocational education and training programs for better job opportunities.

In addition to programs directed towards alleviating poverty and racism, the federal government supported vocational rehabilitation programs for juvenile delinquents and for prison inmates, adult education programs, student aid programs, higher education programs, and teacher-training and in-service programs of great variety.

Creative Federalism

In 1964, President Johnson used the term "creative federalism" to describe a concept of federal-local program design that would bypass the states and bring to bear a wide range of resources, including those of business, labor, and private institutions in dealing with local problems.

As it applied to schools, creative federalism emphasized: new administrative planning methods, research and development, and innovation.

At the administrative planning level, agencies were encouraged to establish more effective planning capabilities and more systematic evaluation of educational and organizational performance. Systems such as PPPS (Planning-Programming-Budgeting Systems), PERT (Program Evaluation and Review Techniques), and a National Assessment were to be used to increase efficiency, improve decision-making, and pinpoint objectives.

In the 1960s the federal government became the chief source for educational research and development. From 1958 to 1971, spending for this purpose more than quintupled. The major aim of these efforts was to create local school change.

The United States Office of Education, through its National Center for Educational Research and Development, supported four kinds of research and development institutions: research and development centers, regional laboratories, educational policy research centers, and the National Laboratory for Early Childhood Education. By 1973, the National Institute of Education had been created to provide national leadership and support to educational research and development.

The Office of Education also established cooperative research grants or contracts with state or local agencies, private nonprofit organizations, and individuals for a wide variety of research projects, surveys, and demonstrations. These included educational laboratories, new curriculum development, and information dissemination. Contracts were made with private corporations for research and development in the field of educational technology, such as for the manufacture and programming of teacher computers. Research into the study of teaching, teacher education, and the development of training materials for teacher education were supported. The National Institute of Education provided funds for ERIC, the Educational Resources Information Center, to set up a linkage system for information dissemination.

Educational decision-making moved from the grassroots to Washington as a result of the great number and variety of federal categorical aid programs. Some of the categories that have been funded are manpower training; counseling and testing; science, mathematics, and foreign language instruction; work-training programs; community action programs; programs for the culturally deprived; National Teacher Corps; vocational education; and learning disabilities detection. Although application for funds is voluntary, and although many receiving institutions and individuals do not use the funds exactly as intended,[1] it is clear that the availability of federal money has changed the federal-state-local balance of power.

Education for the Seventies: Renewal and Reform

The decade of the sixties was a time of educational innovation. Federal grants for educational purposes grew from $1.7 billion in 1960 to $8 billion in 1969. In the 1970s federal programs and support remained strong; the 1977 budget for educational grants amounted to about $17 billion. In retrospect, most of the innovations of the sixties had only a limited impact on school renewal. This fact (confirmed by major nationwide studies conducted by the Rand Corporation and the Ford Foundation, and sensed by the public), combined with a growing conservative trend in the nation, in the 1970s resulted in the "back to basics" movement, with its emphasis on accountability.

In March of 1970, President Richard Nixon set the tone for the new decade of accountability in his message to Congress: "Education for the 1970s: Renewal and Reform." Nixon emphasized that schools should be held accountable for their performance. One result of this message was that during the early 1970s the federal government sponsored accountability innovations. Another result was that the states began to enact accountability legislation that imposed upon the local education authorities (LEA's) minimal competency requirements measured by standardized student tests.

Among the federally sponsored accountability projects were performance contracting, where business firms guaranteed the school that they would produce tangible results and would not ask for payment if they did not; educational vouchers for parents so that they could pay for educational services at schools of their choice; and a range of business-management systems.

In the early 1970s, one state after another enacted educational accountability acts to require schools and teachers to be accountable for the quality of their educational programs. Michigan was one of the first states to mandate an accountability system. The Michigan State Department of Education used test scores as the major criterion to evaluate teachers, and withheld funds from schools because of low test scores.

In 1972 the United States Office of Education established the Cooperative

Accountability Project (CAP) to encourage accountability efforts. This agency established the State Education Accountability Repository (SEAR) to disseminate accountability information to state education agencies.

CAP and SEAR were phased out in 1976, but the effects of their activities continued. States have legislated requirements for "minimum competency," the term that has replaced "accountability."

Private Large-Scale Agencies

Private foundations such as Ford, Rockefeller, Kellogg, Kettering, Carnegie, and Mott have given large grants for educational purposes. When they operate individually or in concert with government and universities to research an innovation or support a policy, they have tremendous power to influence national policy. Team teaching, teacher aids, preschool programs, and educational television all originated as foundation-supported and publicized projects. Foundations have supported research into teacher education, created teacher-education programs, developed curricula, conducted investigations of the public schools, and sponsored a program of national assessment. The results of the work supported by foundation funds—curriculum materials, reports, surveys, books, programs, recommendations, and pilot programs—have great impact on the policies of the public schools.

Another influence on curriculum and teaching has been the widespread use of standardized tests. Since entrance into college is, in part, predicated upon a student's college entrance test scores, pressure is exerted on schools and teachers to prepare their children to succeed on these tests. Further, since test results are considered a measure of school effectiveness, teachers and administrators often feel constrained to "teach to the test" in order to produce scores that demonstrate the effectiveness of their teaching programs and methods.

The tests produced by the Educational Testing Service, and the American College Testing Program, which are nationally standardized, also have the effect of discouraging local school innovation that may not produce results measurable by the tests.

Many change agents have experienced the disappointment of seeing their successfully implemented innovations discontinued because they did not appear to lead to higher test scores. This writer once spent two years developing open classrooms in an elementary school. Although the teachers and administrators saw demonstrable evidence of increased student learning and motivation to learn, and felt strongly that the new approach was superior to methods they had used in the past, the open classroom innovation was disbanded and replaced by drill methods after the middle-school children in the district made a bad showing on standardized tests.

Business firms, too, have affected education in the contemporary era. Roald Campbell points out that today's educational business firms differ from those of the past in that they seek to develop markets for materials and services that are largely of their own making, whereas traditional firms designed their products to support the practices of educational institutions.[2] In the late sixties, publishing houses joined with industrial companies; these large firms, such as GE-TIME-LIFE, IBM-SRA, and Xerox-University Microfilms, have developed instructional programs and total educational systems, such as computer-assisted instructional plans, and reading and language arts programs used from kindergarten through twelfth grade. These industries are linked formally and informally with foundations, universities, state departments of education, and with federally sponsored research and development efforts.

Federal Courts

In the last two decades the federal courts have made over fifty decisions directly related to education. Since 1950 the federal courts have made far-reaching decisions about integration, eligibility to receive federal funds, and church-state relations in education. The courts have ruled on the flag salute; school prayers; releasing children for religious instruction; Bible reading; the use of tax funds to support post-elementary school education; the students' right to wear long hair and buttons, to dissent and to see their "confidential" file, to organize, strike, and bargain collectively.

After the 1954 desegregation decision, the courts played an increasingly important role in creating a national policy for education. This has had the effect of further limiting the local school board's discretionary authority.

The courts also have influenced school board-administrative-teacher relationships by supporting teachers' rights to organize and negotiate, by clarifying the legal restrictions on teacher behavior both in and out of the classroom, by beginning to spell out teachers' rights. Moreover, the courts have influenced school-student relationships by defining children's rights.

Other Nationalizing Trends

There are a number of other major nationalizing trends. A likely result of the movement to develop national standards for accreditation of teacher education programs and teacher certification is that the values embodied by departments of education in universities and colleges of education will become more homogeneous. In addition, colleges of education affect schools through in-service programs, research dissemination, and services to school boards.

National organizations such as the Daughters of the American Revolution, or anti-pornography groups press their concerns through local political parties, publicity, and efforts to sway local boards.

Special interest groups such as the National Parent Teachers Association (PTA) and local advocacy groups supported by nationwide networks that provide funding and information are dramatically increasing in number. These groups use television advertising, telephone networks, information dissemination, and lobbying in state and federal legislatures. The National PTA, for example, played an important role in defeating tuition tax credit legislation, and in 1979 supported the establishment of a separate, cabinet-level Department of Education.

Professional associations that operate on a national level also influence policy. Teachers, librarians, administrators, subject matter specialists, and school boards have organizations that influence their members aims and values, and work to shape educational decisions.[3]

Implications

Contemporary nationalizing influences, individually and in interaction with each other, have had a great impact on local school authority. These influences have resulted in a decrease in the policy-making power of the local school board, an increase in the power of the superintendent and his staff, an increase in the local citizens' challenge to the school board and its professional staff, and a greater likelihood that teachers will resist local directives if they are incongruous with national priorities.

The local school board has seen its power decline because local communities cannot set policies that are contrary to national policies established by federal legislation or court decisions—establishing segregated schools or requiring children to pray. Furthermore, curriculum is influenced by nationwide projects, testing programs, and available instructional products. Finally, the availability of federal funds for innovation that promotes national goals is in itself a powerful influence on policy decision-making at the local level. School boards may sanction an innovation more in line with national than community interests in order to bring extra money and resources into the district.

More and more, the citizens of the local community challenge the school board, as well as the professional staff. When a policy is introduced into the school district that is in line with national mandates or goals, but not supported by the local community, there is ferment. Or, citizens' groups can bypass the local board to redress grievances; they may turn to extralocal agencies, lobby for legislation, or sue in the courts.

Teachers, too, may refuse to go along with local rulings that conflict with national priorities. With the nationalizing trend, teachers have become more cosmopolitan.

Community Power

The "depoliticizing" of the educational bureaucracy that took place early in the century as a reaction against the machine-dominated urban political structure caused schools to move away from parent-community collaboration. Educators, freed from political constraints, were better able to apply professional judgments in running the schools. One of the unfortunate effects of this removal of the school from the political arena is that it became possible for professionals to isolate the school from community concerns and interests. The insularity of the educational bureaucracy became a focus for the recent dissatisfaction with urban school systems; in addition, it contributed to the demand for professional accountability and for community control.

Middle-class parents in nonurban districts also have been demanding a voice in school decision-making, in part because they no longer believe that the school board represents the needs and aims of all community groups. The principle of public trust has shifted to include a demand for participative instead of representative democracy.

In the contemporary era, much criticism was directed at the institution of schooling, which, once again, was viewed as the public agency best equipped to produce social change.

In the fifties, sixties, and early seventies, changes were proposed in curriculum, teaching methods, organizational structure, and traditional authority relationships.

A myriad of experiments were aimed at overcoming the shortcomings of schools accused of being irrelevant, obsolete, and inhumane. These experiments included the Philadelphia Parkway School Program—the school without walls—which aimed to merge school and community in the use of the city as an extended classroom; and New York's Open Corridor schools, where activities and programs were geared to the individual child's developmental needs, abilities, and interests, and where the corridors as well as the classrooms were used for activities.

The national goal of equalizing educational opportunity led to a host of innovations, including compensatory education, vocational education, desegregation, and busing.

Another set of innovations was directed at altering the power and authority structure within the public schools. Decentralization—administrative or political or both—and community control were advocated by those who felt that existing professional bureaucracies were not responsive to the needs and concerns of local constituencies.

Paralleling the concern for equity and humaneness was a demand for "accountability," backed by federal and states efforts, as has been discussed. This demand has come from diverse groups. Advocates have included those who desire radical changes in educational goals, those who want traditional goals met with greater efficiency, and those who desire to put previously excluded groups into the mainstream of American life. Leon Lessinger, Myron Lieberman, and Kenneth B. Clark stressed that schools should be accountable to those who use them to fulfill the promise they have made to teach all children basic reading, writing, communication, and computational skills. Such fulfillment should be tangible and demonstrable. Others, such as Robert J. Nash and Russell M. Agne, called for educators to analyze, criticize, and reconstruct the profession to make it more directly responsible to the cries of those who suffer from the defects of the social order.[4]

Both of these demands converged in the community control issue represented by the Ocean Hill-Brownsville confrontation. Minority group parents and others thought that the New York schools and their teachers were racist. They were concerned that their children would continue to be kept out of the mainstream, unless the community had a deciding voice in policy-making in the local schools. Community control was presumed to be the factor that would make the schools more responsive to the needs of minority-group children.

Community groups that felt powerless and unrepresented by urban boards of education led the drive for community participation and control. They wanted to gain power over the hiring of school staffs and to have a voice in setting curriculum policy at the district and individual school levels.

The demand for total community control has declined in the seventies, but its radical potential has caused administrators in cities and elsewhere to attempt to develop a more workable equilibrium between the public and professional bureaucracy. In large school systems, decentralization is a common means of accomplishing this balance.

As of 1979, decentralization was under consideration or was a reality in most large and medium-sized school systems. The usual pattern of decentralization is to break up the existing school district of 50,000 to 100,000 students into smaller districts averaging between 15,000 and 25,000. The assumption is that declining educational quality is related to large, impersonal school administrations, and the hope is that smaller units will provide a mechanism for local control. Decentralization gives community advisory groups a say in curriculum, hiring and firing, and matters of finance.

Urban minority group parents were not the only ones to demand participation. As the costs of education skyrocketed, as confidence in public institutions declined, and as parents became more concerned about their children's futures in a competitive job market, middle-class parents also clamored for a say in school policy-making.

Parents are resuming their role as sources of authority in the public schools. An NEA report lists three factors that have led to this development: the importance of education in a changing employment market, parents' resentment of poor schooling for their children, and federal programs that emphasized evaluation and the importance of producing tangible results.[5]

Parents have indicated their intention to participate more powerfully in decisions about what schools their children attend. A Gallup poll conducted in the early seventies indicated that citizens gave fairly strong support to the voucher plan, proposed by the Nixon administration in 1969. This plan gave parents vouchers equivalent to the sum of money that would normally be invested by a city school system for their child's education. If parents were dissatisfied with their neighborhood school, they could "shop around" among private and public schools. Clearly, this plan would have given parents leverage in their neighborhood schools: if decision-makers did not attend to parental wishes and grievances, their children could be withdrawn.

In a 1978 article, Professor Tyll Van Geel pointed out that in recent years parents have appealed to the courts in their attempts to have their preferences count in the operation of the schools. Although parents have met with mixed results in the courts, they have been surprisingly successful in getting the courts to hold that parental preferences are to count as long as the request is reasonable and not disruptive of the schools. Parents have tried, sometimes successfully, and sometimes not, to be allowed to have a greater voice in decisions affecting their children. Some parents have sued to control the courses offered and not offered, to have their children given access to or to be exempted from a course. Other parents have sought reforms of the procedures by which children are assigned to a course of study. Parents of handicapped children have claimed that before the school may make basic changes in a child's status, such as assigning the child to a slow-learner group, special-education programs, special schools for students with disciplinary problems, or excluding the child from public school altogether, certain procedures must be followed—procedures that involve the parent in the decision-making process.

In another body of cases, parents complained about the discriminatory exclusion of their children from schools, courses, and programs. In one case, the courts agreed with the parents' demand that their child be assigned to a program they perceived to be of higher quality than the one to which the child had been assigned by the school.

Parents and their children also have gone to court in attempts to assure that their preferences with regard to the books used in the classroom and made available in school libraries be followed. In a 1976 Ohio case, the courts said that although the parents could not compel the school board to buy certain books, they did have the right to block the board from removing certain other books from the library shelves. As Van Geel notes, it is possible that in the future, students and parents may successfully claim the right to demand that certain materials, ideas, beliefs, and opinions be made available within the school on an equal basis with those that school officials would like to be made available.[6]

During the 1970s there has been a growing trend in federal legislation towards requiring that parents be officially involved in decision-making. This was evident in Public Law 94-142 (the Education for All Handicapped Children Act), which mandated that educational plans for a child had to be approved by the child's parents. According to an article in *American Education,* a journal of the Department of Health, Education, and Welfare, the 1978 education amendments to the Elementary and Secondary Education Act continue a trend also evident in the amendments of 1976: an emphasis on involving parents and teachers in planning and carrying out programs. Parental involvement is basic to Title I (Financial Assistance to meet Special Educational Needs of Children), and the amendments to the Indian education programs. The mechanism for this involvement is advisory councils; in several instances these councils have become policy determiners more than advisory bodies. The legislation specifies the establishment of district-wide parental advisory councils, and, in addition, project school advisory councils for large programs, with members "elected by the parents in each project area or project school."

Congress also recognized the need to train parents participating in advisory councils. Each local agency is required to provide a training program and training materials for advisory council members and pay the expenses of attending training sessions.

At the federal level, the Commissioner of Education must conduct a series of regional workshops each year to train parental advisory councils and to facilitate parental involvement in Title I programs. The National Institute of Education (NIE) is also involved: it will assess the effectiveness of the advisory councils and the training methods used.

Increased parental involvement in the education of their children is also reflected in the Basic Skills Improvement Program in the new Title II of ESEA. It authorizes the development and dissemination of materials to be used at home by parents to improve their child's basic skills.[7]

The need for increased community participation in school affairs is re-flected in several other trends. Community education is offered by many universities and teachers colleges; associations promoting such goals have been formed. Courses for teachers before they begin service increasingly emphasize home-school cooperation; parent-teacher education centers also have become more common.

In some school districts, alternatives to the overall school mission are being made available to meet the goals of those parents who do not agree with the goals or methods underlying the mission. These alternatives, such as an "open classroom wing," may be set up within each school, or each school in a district may be established as an alternative to the others, giving parents a choice about which school their children will attend.

In addition, there is a growing trend towards involving parents in the daily life of the school. Parent-teacher organizations and programs that en-courage parents and senior citizens to share their talents and resources with students by offering minicourses, or to work as teacher-aides, are a few of the mechanisms for parent involvement.

Community-Professional Tensions

One of the arguments for community involvement is that it will elicit increased community support. The Institute for Responsible Education studied trends in community involvement. Don Davies, director of the in-stitute, pointed out that the term "citizen participation" takes many forms and serves a wide variety of functions, from "window-dressing" to true collaboration.[8] In some cases, the impetus behind citizen participation is a belief, or perhaps a wish, on the part of school people that citizens will be supportive of school goals if they are given an opportunity to participate in school affairs. As Dale Mann's study of urban advisory councils indicates, this is often a naive point of view. Mann found that increased support of the school is the result of participation only when there is congruency between the needs and interests of the community and those of school officials. When this is not the case, increased community involvement can be accom-panied by increased skepticism and tension.[9]

Ronald Corwin sheds some light on possible reasons for incongruency between the community's and educators' interests. He distinguishes between two kinds of goal orientations, the "cosmopolitan" and "local." He defines a cosmopolitan orientation as one that is up-to-date with reference to re-gional and national standards, with little credence given to policies and pro-grams based simply upon community tradition. A local orientation repre-sents a desire to maintain traditional policies and programs; it is a status quo, not a change, orientation.[10]

These orientations may not be shared in common by professionals and the community. Corwin describes four typologies of community-school relationships: (type 1) both the professional and community groups have a local orientation; (type 2) the community is more cosmopolitan than the school staff; (type 3) the staff is more cosmopolitan than the community; and (type 4) both the staff and the community have a cosmopolitan orientation.

The demand for citizen participation is a demand that schools be responsive to community needs and concerns. In some cases, community needs reflect "cosmopolitan" concerns that require changing traditional structures and programs. This was the case in cities where citizens demanded a restructuring of zoning or busing in order to desegregate schools in accordance with Supreme Court mandates.

Corwin predicts that the type 4 relationship will become more typical as local pockets of folkways disappear under the bombardment of national standards, as social mobility due to population growth forces schools to hire teachers from all parts of the nation, and as professionalization increases the national orientation of teachers.

If teacher professionalization increases at a faster rate than changes in community attitudes and goals, type 3 may be the more typical relationship. Teachers would then be more resistant to local directives that conflict with the broader orientation developed and supported by their pre-service and continuing education, and by their professional organizations and training institutions.

In any case, the relationship between the teaching cadre and the communities in which they work will be affected increasingly by events in the larger society, and this relationship will be in dynamic flux.

Implications

The contemporary movement toward community participation has implications at various levels in education. For one thing, the members of the community that support the school, or send their children to it, are demanding participative rather than representative democracy. This alters the concept of *authority as public trust* to include parents, other citizens, and students, not just the school board.

Secondly, the assumption of a hierarchical chain of command, with policy originating in the school board, directed by administrators, and implemented by classroom teachers, is no longer tenable. Shared decision-making by a more inclusive group of participants is the trend, as evidenced by the rapid increase in urban decentralization and community control, as well as the popularity of parent-administrator-school board-teacher councils that make a wide variety of decisions, from textbook selections to the hiring of teachers and administrators.

In addition, the behavior of school boards, administrators, and teachers is apt to become more political and defensive as their decisions and actions are held up to public scrutiny and challenged by citizens.

Teacher militancy, too, may increase in response to increased citizen involvement.

Finally, staff development plans must take citizen involvement into account, and provide for it. The kind and amount of participation will depend upon situational variables, such as the local-cosmopolitan orientations of professionals and community members.

The shift from a demand for participative instead of representative democracy represents a challenge to the principle of bureaucratic authority; it also conflicts with the demands now being made by teachers for more authority.

Teacher Power

The contemporary development that has most altered the relationship among the three principles of authority is teacher power, and its most salient feature on the local level—collective bargaining.

We sometimes forget that teacher power is a new development. As recently as 1969, Dan Lortie wrote:

The current situation reflects the centuries during which teachers were defined solely as employees. It is interesting that teachers have not challenged their formal subordination; unlike most who claim professional status, teachers have not contested the right of persons outside the occupation to govern their technical affairs.[11]

What a difference a few years have made! In the seventies, teachers have negotiated for control, or representation, in groups that set curricular policy, select textbooks, and recommend educational programs; they are demanding a say in setting promotion and evaluation policies and determining student placements and grading practices; they are negotiating for control of in-service programs. Not only have they challenged public prerogatives to make local decisions, they also have challenged higher education's control of teacher certification and accreditation of teacher education programs, and are insisting upon having a role in the design, implementation, and evaluation of teacher education programs.

A consequence of teacher professionalization and power is conflict with other sources of authority: with higher education over the control of teacher education, with administrators over curricular, personnel, and other school issues, and with school boards over policy determination. As these other authorities attempt to maintain their own positions of control, teachers press their claims through the use of political action, collective bargaining, and strikes—the manifestations of teacher militancy.

Teacher Militancy: Its Causes and Its Growth

Militancy has revolved around the issues of salaries, working conditions, and policy. Jack Culbertson defines teacher militancy as: "The collective articulation by teachers of demands for political participation in organizational decision-making and/or for desired extractions, regulations of behavior, allocations of resources, or statements of policies or intents."[12] Robert Bendiner notes that the trend towards militancy has been so "fast and feverish" since the mid-sixties, that is "hard to appreciate how fresh a phenomenon it really is."[13]

As late as 1961, the NEA was officially opposed to the use of the strike by teachers. Since 1960, NEA affiliates have initiated a huge percentage of the total work stoppages, strikes, and interruptions of services, including a statewide strike in Florida in the spring of 1968.

According to the Bureau of Labor Statistics, there were only 91 strikes by teachers during the period from 1940 to 1962, in contrast to 131 in the single year 1968-69. Tallies by NEA show that there were 94 strikes in 1976, 81 in 1977, and 132 in the fall of 1978, by teachers and a very few university professors.

In 1979, the NEA claimed 1.8 million members; the AFT more than 500,000. The AFT maintains a $5 million militancy fund to assist locals on strike and the NEA provides millions of dollars for legal defense of members and leaders and for the support of collective bargaining at the state and local levels.

The number of school systems reporting teacher-school board contracts increased 70 percent between 1966 and 1968. By 1970, more than half of the nation's elementary and secondary school teachers were working under some form of negotiated agreement, and twenty-one states had enacted legislation mandating local negotiations between school boards and teachers as a unit.

Welfare issues such as salaries and working conditions had top priority in the early struggles. In recent years, policy issues are coming to the forefront.

Contracts increasingly specify that teachers be represented on committees that set curricular policy, recommend educational programs, and select textbooks and other materials. Frequently, contracts have provisions related to standards for teacher and administrator selection, evaluation, promotion and tenure; in-service education; pupil discipline; and testing practices. In some districts, teachers have negotiated the right to challenge administrative decisions about teaching and grading methods, and the placement and transfer of teachers.

Legally, what is negotiable is far from settled; it varies from state to state, and new rulings alter precedents. In some states, like Michigan, there have been judicial rulings giving teachers the right to negotiate "curriculum and class schedules, size of classes, selection of textbooks, materials, supplies, planning of facilities and special education; establishment of in-service training of teachers; procedures for the rating of effectiveness of teachers."[14]

Recently, teachers' organizations have turned more and more to political action to accomplish major legislative changes, and to put candidates of their choice into office. In 1978, NEA endorsed 271 candidates for Congress. In 1978, on a national level, the AFT lobbied against the establishment of a separate federal Department of Education, and in 1978-79, for an expansion of the Elementary and Secondary Education Act and the Middle Income Student Assistance Act, among other things. Affiliates of AFT have lobbied for and against a variety of city, state, and local legislation and have supported political candidates. For example, in 1978, the New York State United Federation of Teachers (NYSUT), supported candidates who were elected governor, lieutenant governor, and attorney general. As the UFT president, Thomas Y. Hobart wrote in the *New York Teacher*, the union's official publication:

The real significance in NYSUT's support goes beyond the considerable impact that our 200,000 members have when they go to the voting booth. In many respects the value of NYSUT's endorsement can be measured in terms of the thousands of hours of work that are put forth on behalf of a candidate once an endorsement has been made. As I wrote in this column in late September, "Ours is not a paper endorsement or an empty gesture." In every region of our state our members proved this as they manned telephone banks, distributed leaflets, or coordinated mailings on behalf of our endorsed candidates.[15]

CAUSES OF TEACHER MILITANCY. The reasons for the acceleration of militancy fall into two overlapping categories: psychological readiness and practical necessity.

As "aspiring professionals," teachers traditionally eschewed tactics that might be associated with organized labor and blue-collar workers. Recently, teachers have become more accepting of the union model. Some of the forces that have altered attitudes and behavior are: civil disobedience; the American Labor movement; changes in the characteristics of the teaching cadre; status incongruity; teachers' response to bureaucratization, urbanization, and standardization; the professionalization of teaching; and the resultant need of teachers to have a stronger voice in school decision-making.

In recent years, militancy has gained acceptance in American society as a means of achieving social change. The labor movement moved from successfully organizing workers in the private sector to success among public workers, and militant tactics, such as the strike, became more acceptable in the nation at large. As a result, unionization and union tactics gained approval by teachers.

The teaching cadre also has changed in the contemporary era. There has been an increase of upwardly mobile male teachers, and career-oriented female teachers, as well as an increase in the number of teachers from labor-oriented families. Teachers are more committed to teaching as a career, as evidenced by lower turnover rates. Since there are few career ladders within teaching, teachers who expect to spend their lifetimes in the occupation want to improve their benefits and working conditions, and their opportunities for professional development.

Status incongruity provides another push toward militancy. When various dimensions of status, such as salary, authority, and level of education, are not commensurate with one another, a state of dissatisfaction, referred to as status incongruity, can occur. Teacher authority has not kept pace with advances in salary and education in recent years; this discrepancy probably is an important incentive behind recent efforts of teachers to achieve new levels of authority.[16]

The professionalization of teaching also added to the impetus for militancy. Higher educational qualifications, specialization of teaching skills and roles, and stronger professional role conceptions have led teachers to improve their salaries, status, and decision-making authority. For example, teachers claimed that their expertise required that their salaries be increased commensurately with administrators' salaries, which had increased disproportionately. In 1949, the average salary of high school teachers in urban school districts over 500,000 was $4,689, considerably lower than that of high school principals, which was $7,321.[17]

Urbanization and centralization play a role in encouraging militancy. Teacher-administrator relationships in small districts tend to be paternalistic and personalistic. In large districts, there is a greater need for universalistic, contractual relationships; teachers in large districts are therefore more willing to support a professional organization. In fact, organizing activities have been largely directed at large districts.[18]

The bureaucratic characteristics of schools also can feed militancy. This happens to the extent that bureaucratic characteristics block professionally oriented teachers from carrying out their professional roles. Ronald Corwin, in a study of militant professionalism, found that a desire for more influence over school policy and disagreement with central-level decision-making and district goals account for a good part of teacher dissatisfaction and militancy. In professional matters, authority issues were of greater concern to the militants than to the rank and file teachers, and the positive correlation between professionalism and conflict was stronger in the most bureaucratic schools than in the less bureaucratic ones.[19]

Teacher militancy is also, in part, an attempt by teachers to countervail the power held by school boards and administrators. Through collective bargaining, strikes, and other strategies, teachers have been able to receive a greater share of the available rewards. These rewards include the opportunity to have a greater voice in determining school policies. There is evidence that teachers gave strong support to the union movement in the late 1960s and 1970s because they felt powerless to fulfill "their desire to do more, and better, for students, the classrooms, and the school system."[20]

According to a 1978 study of 454 New York City school teachers, most union activists perceived affiliation with the union as a vehicle through which teachers hoped to strengthen their position in the power structure controlling the school system. They perceived the existing structure as relatively unresponsive to internal staff pressures."[21]

THE GROWTH OF TEACHER MILITANCY. These and other reasons prepared teachers around the nation for a positive response to union victories in the early sixties. In New York, one of the first successes occurred in the struggle over the principle of collective bargaining and the right to choose a bargaining unit. When the board of education did not succumb to the union's demands, the United Federation of Teachers called for a one-day work stoppage in the autumn of 1960; still, the board did not give in. In the following election, the UFT's dues-paying membership quadrupled. When bargaining negotiations broke down in the spring of 1962, 20,000 teachers went on strike. The salary agreement framed after the strike made a tremendous impression on the nation's teachers—in the NEA as well as the AFT. As a result, the NEA changed its stance on strikes, and on militant tactics in general.

Myron Lieberman and Michael M. Moskow consider the organizational rivalry between the NEA and the AFT (both under increasing pressure to demonstrate that one can do more for its members than the other) perhaps the most important single factor underlying the rapid spread of collective negotiations.[22]

In addition, they cite other reasons for this proliferation. Teachers needed more effective representation at the local level. Previously, they had been fairly ineffectual in dealing with local boards and administrators. There is a snowball effect in teacher negotiations. Every time a teacher organization and school board negotiate collectively, it is more difficult for other teacher organizations and school boards to refuse. Developments outside of education also have an effect. These include legislation favoring collective bargaining for state and local public employees, and the willingness of federal employees to engage in negotiations.

Teacher Power and the Profession

Some writers have implied that educationists—teachers, administrators, education professors, and public officials concerned with schooling—constitute a monolithic establishment, sharing not only a community of interest, but goals and values as well.

While it is true that educationists share many mutual interests and values, it is also true that disagreement, conflict, and competition is rife among groups in this so-called "establishment."

The conflict over educational authority has not been simply a matter of the community versus the educationists; professional groups have been striving to establish their own roles in deciding educational questions.

Within the profession there has been a power struggle over accreditation, certification, teacher education, and in-service education. For teachers, gaining control in these areas represents advances in professionalization and collective strength.

ACCREDITATION. From 1927 to 1952, the control and responsibility for accreditation was in the hands of the colleges. In the 1950s, a struggle began between the American Association of Teachers Colleges and the NEA for control over accreditation.

In the aftermath of Sputnik, the NEA's National Commission on Teacher Education and Professional Standards established a project in 1959 to develop statements in areas of responsibility that would serve as guidelines for professional organizations and individuals for action on the local, state, and national levels leading to the complete professionalization of teaching.

The project task force maintained that the responsibility for accreditation of preparatory programs and certification should be in the hands of the organized teaching profession. It urged that every state establish a Commission on Teacher Education and Professional Standards, composed of representatives of the teaching profession, mainly classroom teachers. The commission would serve as the advisory board on accreditation, program approval, certification, and licensure.

In the 1960s, the teaching profession continued to make strides in its efforts to gain control of governance. The NEA in 1961 adopted as minimum requirements for membership a bachelor's degree and eligibility for certification, where required.

In 1971, NCTEPS developed a "Model Teacher Standards and Licensure Act" to be used as a guideline for the creation of a Teacher Standards and Licensure Commission to control accreditation and certification.[23] This original model act called for a thirteen-member commission, consisting of eleven licensed teachers or administrators, and two from higher education. Since then, the NEA has asked only for a majority.

As a result of the 1967 demand by the National Commission Accreditation (NCA) to revise the representation of the Council and Governing Board of NCATE, control went to institutions of higher education. Because the NEA had been reduced to a minor role in NCATE, the NEA announced in 1972 its plan to withdraw its financial support from the Council.

There was a restructuring of the NCATE Council and Coordinating Board in 1974; AACTE and teachers now have an equal number of votes. As a result, more classroom teachers are working on visitation teams and evaluation boards.

The swing of the control pendulum towards the teacher's side has aroused AACTE to action. In a 1975 *Journal of Teacher Education* article, AACTE's executive director, Edward C. Pomeroy, bluntly stated that "we're in the midst of a power struggle" and called for higher education to retain its place in teacher education by strengthening its power base through action on state and federal levels.[24]

Certification

Teachers have asserted themselves in the area of teacher certification as well. The 1971 Teachers Standards and Licensure Act called for both certification and accreditation to be in the hands of the organized teaching profession. Bush and Enemark have reported on the national picture. Autonomous commissions, having a majority of classroom teachers sitting on them, have been established in California and Oregon. Advisory commissions to the state boards of education have been established by legislation in seven other states, and advisory commissions on professional practices exist in fourteen states. In ten other states, legislation pertaining to such commissions was either a possibility or was actually pending in 1975. Although these commissions are weak, the tide is running strongly in the direction of giving teachers a larger voice in setting certification standards, as well as a greater voice in other aspects of the governance of the profession.[25]

Teacher Education

The trend toward states mandating competency-based teacher education has intensified the conflict between the organized teaching profession and higher education, but it also has led to a collaborative dialogue between the research and development community, state officials, college professors, and administrators and teachers, in attempts to establish a sounder base for certification.

The 1974 report of the Higher Education Task Force on Improvement and Reform in American Education (HETFIRE) defined power as shared responsibility and expressed a strong commitment to collaboration in teacher education.[26]

Shared decision-making or parity is a concept underlying the governance of teacher centers or consortia. Parity suggests that students, teachers, principals, parents, and professors come together on a par to design, conduct, and evaluate a teacher education program.

IN-SERVICE EDUCATION. Recent publications and directives to union leaders promulgated by NEA and AFT are unequivocal about these organizations' intention that in-service education should be governed by teachers and based upon needs identified by teachers. NEA advocates that opportunities for in-service education should be related to day-by-day job needs and made part of teachers' job assignments; in-service offerings should be based on assessment by teachers of their own job needs, and teachers should have a preeminent voice in determining both the content of their in-service education programs and the ways and means that are most meaningful to them in aquiring new skills and relevant knowledge, and in gaining new insights.[27]

NEA literature on in-service education indicates that, at the local level, contracts—or agreements having the force of contract language—that give teachers a greater voice in determining their in-service education have been negotiated.

Organized teachers want to get rid of the faculty meeting that has traditionally passed for in-service education. They also want to diminish the influence of professors and administrators in planning and carrying out in-service activities.

Maurice Leiter and Myrna Cooper, of the United Federation of Teachers, have spelled out three basic goals for in-service: first, that it should be a top priority for the union; second, that organized teachers should be the major partners in the partnership among colleges, administrators, and the union; and finally, that the teachers' organization is the best agency for generating in-service education activities, since "teachers are more ready to trust those who represent them than those who rate them."[28]

Governance and control of in-service education is an issue in the federally supported "teacher centers." In 1978, the government provided grants for the establishment of fifty-five centers. Allen A. Schmieder of the United States Office of Education, and Sam J. Yarger of the Syracuse Teacher Center Project defined the teacher center as:

A place, in situ, or in changing locations, which develops programs for the training and improvement of educational personnel (in-service teachers, preservice teachers, administrators, para-professionals, college teachers, etc.) in which the participating personnel have an opportunity to share successes, to utilize a wide range of education resources, and to receive training specifically related to their most pressing teaching problems.[29]

NEA and AFT recognize that there can be collaboration between boards of education, colleges, community agencies, and teachers' organizations in the running of teacher centers. Organized teachers are determined that they keep control of their own professional development, however. Federal legislation supports this aim by placing the teacher center facilities under policy boards composed of teachers.

An NEA document declares:

If ever the accepted spelling for teacher center becomes "teachers' center," it will mean that the NEA concept of a teacher center has prevailed. . . . It implies a planning program, and administrative process in which teachers have more than simply the right to participate in a continuing education program, once a program has been established. A teachers' center implies proprietary planning rights.[30]

The teachers' center "should be the teachers' own turf and be run and operated by teachers themselves," the NEA has said.[31] The center would be run by a full-time manager-expediter supported by clerical and technical staff. This manager would not be a professional educator of teachers. Resources, mostly materials, would be provided, based upon needs and problems that teachers have identified. The center also would provide an opportunity for cultural enrichment, for meeting state certification requirements, or for preparing for a new field of work.

The belief in the necessity for teacher control of in-service education is not shared by those in higher education who have responded to this demand with a counter-proposal for collaboration. The AACTE Commission on

Education for the Profession of Teaching warns that colleges of education must not surrender their role in the teacher center; pre-service, in-service, and continuing education are interrelated components of one professional delivery system and require the active involvement of the teaching profession and teacher-training institutions.

IMPLICATIONS. The organized teaching profession is making demands for the control of accreditation, certification, and in-service education, and for a powerful voice in teacher education. These demands are part of a larger trend towards teacher power. Justification for these demands is based upon the rhetoric that teachers will be motivated to improve their work, and to improve the instructional programs they implement, if they have control over the profession. If they are to be accountable, they must have authority. Others, expressing a different point of view, say that since both higher education and teachers are responsible for teacher education and its outcomes, control should be jointly held and equally shared.

The differences in these two viewpoints are not merely philosophical or pragmatic. The issues are political, centering on questions of power and authority.

Teachers undoubtedly will continue to make militant demands for control. But because they do not have the resources of time or expertise to control all phases of the profession, the collaborative model will probably prevail, at least for a time.

If the struggle over control does lead to productive dialogue and collaborative efforts to improve the profession, the end result of the conflict is bound to be a strengthening of professional education and standards, and of professional role ideas. This, in turn, will provide a more solid basis for teacher demands for authority over curricula and other policy matters at the local level.

Teacher Power, Collective Bargaining, and the Three Principles of Authority

Collective bargaining between teachers and the board of education is the major vehicle through which organized teachers have increased their local authority prerogatives. Collective bargaining has altered the roles and responsibilities of administrators, relationships between administrators and the board of education, between administrators and teachers, and between teachers and their organizations.

Wages, salary, hours, and other conditions of employment are the categories that are negotiable under teacher-school board collective bargaining. These categories include: trade union welfare objectives; service objectives:

those that assist students, such as remedial and guidance programs; and professional objectives: those that further professionalize teachers as an occupational group, such as school time and resources for the development of an in-service program.

Since everything that happens in schools affects teachers' working conditions, AFT and NEA have interpreted the term "conditions of employment" to include "anything two parties can agree on." NEA's *Guidelines for Professional Negotiations* state:

Teachers and other members of the professional staff have an interest in the conditions which . . . go far beyond those which would be included in a narrow definition of working conditions. *Negotiations should include all matters which affect the quality of the educational system.*[32]

AFT president Albert Shanker told a group of university professors in 1978 that he did not know of a better method of achieving true collegiality than through collective bargaining. He explained that collective bargaining is not merely a method of determining wages and hours of employees; it is a system of decision-making, joint planning and problem solving. He added that the alternative to collective bargaining is a "system where decisions are handed down from high by a bureaucratic authority and received passively, if not resentfully by the faculty."[33]

Now that teachers have made gains in welfare benefits and have consolidated their power base, they are increasingly placing policy issues related to curriculum, instruction, and other matters on the bargaining table. A 1979 Rand Corporation report financed by the National Institute of Education in the Department of Health, Education, and Welfare, involved analysis of more than 150 teachers' contracts from a national sample of school districts. The researchers, Lorraine McDonnel and Anthony Pascal, report, "Regulation of class size may be one of the most dramatic gains, but negotiated provisions covering assignment and transfer policy are another important achievement. At the same time, organized teachers now play a major role in decisions about the length and composition of the school day, how teachers are evaluated, and how supplementary personnel are used in the schools."[34]

Often, placing policy issues on the bargaining table is only a tactic used to get concessions on other issues or to achieve other objectives. Conversely, school boards often will make concessions on policy matters in order to avoid having to negotiate a welfare issue. In any case, the further teachers advance into the areas of policy and decision-making, the less control the school board has over these matters.

Curriculum revision has been the subject of bargaining in Newark, New

Jersey; Toledo, Ohio; and Salem, Massachusetts, among other places. As a result of these negotiations, teachers have been able to take an active role in changing the content and sequence of course offerings; make specific recommendations on what shall be taught and how; and review the final curriculum packages and designs.

Detroit teachers have worked to eliminate culturally biased tests; Kansas City teachers have won the right to serve on committees to formulate plans for discipline in school buildings; and in Chicago, Washington, D.C., and Cleveland, Ohio, AFT locals have bargained for courses, textbooks, and counseling that will help "all children in our multiracial, multireligious, and multiethnic school systems."[35]

Collective bargaining also has altered the roles of administrators. It has put the principalship into a state of flux by altering the role from one of "educational leader" to that of "implementor of the agreement," even though the principal may have had little or no part in framing the agreement.

Collective bargaining also has changed the role of the superintendent, and has introduced other power elements into the schools' authority structure, namely that of professional negotiators for both management and the teacher-unit, and the teachers' organization itself (and its leadership) as distinguished from the individual practitioner.

TEACHER POWER, COLLECTIVE BARGAINING, AND THE AUTHORITY PRINCIPLE OF PUBLIC TRUST. As we have seen, the authority for school policy-making was originally vested in town officials, and eventually in the school board, which was presumed to represent the needs and interests of the community. As school districts became urbanized and centralized, and as administration became a distinct profession, policy decision-making increasingly became the prerogative of the superintendent of schools. The school board's major function became the hiring of the superintendent and legitimating his or her policies to the community.

Collective bargaining has increased the demands made upon the school board and at the same time has further eroded its power. Boards are once again involved with the details of school administration, since teachers' work conditions are specified in the contract. Although the superintendent plays a major role in collective bargaining, the contract and the negotiations that lead up to it are the board's responsibility. The school board thus is more directly involved in decision-making than it was before the advent of collective bargaining, when details of school life were decided by administrators. Because school boards must now negotiate several hundred items with teacher representatives, however, boards have much less autonomy than they had several decades ago. Furthermore, organized teachers are challenging school board authority directly. A past president of AFT, Charles Cogen, stated this challenge: "The sooner our boards of education realize the obsolescence of the 'right to manage' concept . . . the sooner will there be more peaceful and constructive approaches in the rapidly spreading process of teacher collective bargaining."[36]

Articles in the *American Board Journal* have affirmed that school board members fear their authority prerogatives will be increasingly eroded. Many articles decry developments in teacher unionization, give advice to school board members on negotiating, urge school board members to try to redress the imbalance between the resources of the weak National School Board Association and the combined resources of the AFT and NEA. Other articles point out the threat to school boards should the NEA and the AFT ever merge, and remind readers that these two organizations have been lobbying for a federal collective bargaining law that would force boards to negotiate policy with their employees and would establish the federal government as the final arbiter in labor disputes between teachers and boards. (A 1977 ruling stated that such a law would be unconstitutional. This ruling, however, is bound to increase lobbying for similar laws at the state level.)

TEACHER POWER, COLLECTIVE BARGAINING AND THE PRINCIPLE OF BUREAUCRATIC AUTHORITY. The principle of bureaucratic authority that has been preeminent for the last century is being seriously challenged by a new principle—that of colleague authority. Although administrators encouraged teachers to participate in school decision-making during the progressive era, administrators were the acknowledged leaders. They selected the school's overall aims, decided upon the means to be used to achieve these aims, and evaluated teacher performance and program outcomes. Innovations were initiated by administrators, and teachers were expected to implement them.

Teacher professionalization and its effect on teachers' professional role ideas has made this approach unacceptable to many teachers who consider their own expertise equal or superior to that of administrators on pedagogical matters. Teacher power, and especially collective bargaining, has done much to alter the de facto authority relationships between teachers and administrators.

SUPERINTENDENT OF SCHOOLS. In the recent past, it was the superintendent who was expected to make the major decisions about the school's mission and the means of achieving it. The superintendent's expertise and position gave him or her the authority to lead the line administrators in decision-making about policies, programs, curriculum, and teaching methods, as well as the responsibility of implementation.

Today, superintendents are besieged by challenges to their previously overwhelming authority. National and state policies and mandates are circumscribing their decision-making autonomy, and the availability of federal funds creates pressures to bring in federally sanctioned innovations. Black power, white power, student power, parent power, and teacher power have placed the superintendent in the center of the political arena.

One of the great impediments to superintendents' leadership is collective bargaining, which places limitations on their decision-making authority, and makes it more difficult to side with both teachers and the school board at the same time.

A 1968 study by the NEA Research Division, *Patterns in Negotiations,* found that the modal situation in the nation was that school boards were the negotiating agents, with superintendents serving as advisors to negotiators as well as the board. In some states, however, superintendents have operated as negotiators for the board, and this is the likely trend. Superintendents will encounter increasing difficulty maintaining the traditional role of teacher advocate or even the neutral middle-person serving both teachers and the board; more and more, the superintendent will act as agent for the board.

The finalized contract further constrains the superintendent's decision-making powers. Since minute details about curriculum, textbook selection, testing, school building and district organization, class size, personnel assignments and transfers, discipline, and the number of faculty meetings to be scheduled during a semester often find their way into the contract, superintendents lose the flexibility they previously had to meet new conditions with decisive action.

THE PRINCIPAL. Before 1920, the principal had nearly total autonomy in the school. Rarely did the superintendent interfere with individual schools. The principal was given free rein to make decisions about teacher selection, placement, promotion, and salaries.

Although it is generally conceded that the principal is the key person for improvement of curriculum and instruction in the individual school, the principal's authority and flexibility has recently begun spiraling downward. This is the result, in part, of teacher-school board collective bargaining. Recent evidence indicates that principals feel that their power has been greatly eroded and both their administrative and educational roles are markedly diminished.

A 1970 University of Oregon study of 291 school principals in all fifty states found that one of the most critical problems for principals was defining and establishing an appropriate role for themselves. They expressed feelings of low status and of being left out of school district decision-making and had an uneasy feeling about their relationships with their teaching staffs as a result of collective bargaining. They were also troubled by a conflict between their managerial and educational leadership roles.[37]

A survey conducted by the *American School Board Journal* in 1975 found that a basic complaint of principals was that they have no part in devising policies and procedures that they are ordered to implement, and they are given little or no authority to enforce these policies and procedures.[38]

The teacher's contract is negotiated between the school board and the teachers' representatives. While the superintendent usually serves in an advisory capacity to the board, the principal generally is not consulted. Since teachers have insisted upon the right to negotiate matters that affect the daily operation of the school, the principal is in the position of having to enforce policies that may be incongruous with his or her own goals.

Furthermore, although the principal sits neither on the teacher's side of the bargaining table, nor the school board's, she or he is seen more and more by teachers as part of management, and thus suffers a degree of alienation from her or his staff. And since the principal is expected to enforce management's prerogatives, she or he frequently is in an adversary relationship with the teaching staff.

Another problem is that an aim of both NEA and AFT and their affiliates is to shift many of the principal's traditional prerogatives into teachers' hands, or to make them contractual, to resolve conflicts between labor and management that occur frequently.

As a result of such threats to the principalship, and the feeling of principals that their rights are being bargained away, principals are mobilizing to maintain their power. Articles from 1975-1979 in the *American School Board Journal,* the *National Elementary Principal,* the *National Association of Secondary School's Journal,* and other publications indicate that principals intend to strengthen their professional organizations; to lobby for laws that will guarantee their rights to due process, and one that will enable them to negotiate directly with the board; to take political action; and to learn conflict-management skills.

Although professors conceptualize the principal's role as curriculum leader, the reality is that collective bargaining on curricula matters limits the principal's leadership and flexibility. The list of concerns of administrators subjected to mandatory collective negotiations for several years indicates how keenly principals feel this limitation.

The concerns of 1,800 members of the Michigan Association of Elementary School Principals in 1968 were: How can the principal function as an instructional leader in a district that engages in negotiation? If teacher militancy continues, will the principal be stripped of his responsibility for educational leadership in his building? What happens to curriculum planning when the staff bypasses administration leadership and negotiates directly with the board of education in the area? If authority and responsibility for instruction are granted to the teachers' group through negotiation, then who is responsible for the districtwide implementation of curriculum and instruction? It would appear that the teachers want the authority but not the responsibility. How can teachers grow into new responsibilities for curriculum planning, school organization, and the like, without working at cross-purposes with present personnel who have always performed these roles? Will negotiation dampen the principal's authority to establish textbook and curriculum committees? Will he be allowed to remind the committees that there has been no action from them?[39]

Many of today's principals, caught between the demands of their superordinates and the expectations of their teacher-subordinates, find it increasingly difficult to exercise either the administrative or leadership roles.

In a study of 165 New York State administrators, Mann found that about one-third of them felt unhappy about their lack of autonomy. Only a few of this group felt constrained by those above them in the hierarchy. More than half complained that they lacked autonomy in their jobs because of their subordinates, especially teachers' unions, and also because of community members.[40] Other research indicates even more discontent on the part of principals about their autonomy.[41]

Collective bargaining has been a major factor in diminishing the principal's authority, but it is not the only one. Teachers' professional role ideas, grievance procedures that permit teachers to bypass the principal and deal directly with a grievance committee, the principals' lack of sanctioning power, court decisions that have upheld teachers' and students' rights, and citizens' demands have contributed to the principals' sense of eroding power.

But principals are not powerless. The norms regulating their behavior have changed; in order to be effective, principals must accommodate to these new norms, modify old assumptions about their role, and carve out new roles and role relationships. In any case, while it is still true that the principal is the key figure for change in the individual school, it is not true to the extent, or in the same way, it was true before the 1970s.

TEACHER POWER, COLLECTIVE BARGAINING, AND THE PRINCIPLE OF COLLEAGUE AUTHORITY. The principle of colleague authority states that much, if not all, authority should be in the hands of the school faculty.

Although teachers today increasingly are demanding that this principle prevail, recent events indicate that they are ambivalent about whether they are willing to accept the responsibility that goes along with authority. In addition, the question of whether colleague authority will give the individual teacher more or less professional autonomy has not been faced.

Ambivalence about professional authority and responsibility was reflected in teachers' negotiated contracts analyzed by Herbert C. Rudman.[42] One contract called for teacher involvement in curriculum updating, but also limited the amount of time that a teacher might spend in faculty meetings to five per semester. Another contract stipulated a given day of the week for curriculum meetings, which made it impossible for university professors to attend, or for other resources unavailable on that day to be utilized.

The fact that curriculum mandates, specification of textbooks, and stipulations of the names and exact dates of pupil testing find their way into contracts indicates that some teachers are willing to restrict their own professional choice and freedom in order to curtail administrative authority. The truly professional approach would be to restrict negotiated agreements to the process of solving curriculum problems.

Norman Boyan states that teachers have confronted the authority structure of the school in order to achieve two aspirations: to establish a pattern of school government in which teachers participate as equal partners with administrators and school boards on the basis of their technical expertness, and to change the traditional prerogative of administrators to assess teaching performance. Teachers have not proposed self-regulation as an alternative to administrative assessment, though; they continue to insist upon the seniority principle, tied to years of teaching experience and level of preparation as the criteria for promotion and tenure.

As Boyan points out, the discrepancy between teachers' professional aspirations for enlarged participation in decision-making and their reluctance to assume greater responsibility for self-regulation as professionals generates tension in teacher-administrator relationships.[43]

Organized teachers also have exercised teacher power in order to protect themselves from community criticism, demands for accountability, and the threat of job loss. Their willingness to make decisions for political rather than for educational reasons is another symptom of a conflict between their professional and employee role ideas. For example, teachers resorted to collective action defensively in New York City in the late sixties when they joined management for the first time against the community that urged decentralization and community control. Robert Braun points out that this stance was taken for political reasons although it was justified on educational grounds—namely, that it would establish racially segregated and provincial schools. He suggests that one reason the union opposed decentralization is that the union's own power is greater when it can deal with a central board than when it must become involved with many different boards.[44]

Teacher Power Reviewed

By the 1960s organized teachers were beginning to suspect that it was time to shift from a professional to a union model in their efforts to exert influence and to gain benefits. Many interacting forces—including the willingness of public employees to bargain collectively, and a general climate of protest in the nation—set the stage for a new approach. In addition, since the sixties was a period of economic prosperity, teachers had career alternatives and were thus willing to risk job loss if they went on strike. Victories by the AFT and UFT (United Federation of Teachers) demonstrated to teachers the efficacy of militant action; the result was that the more professional NEA markedly altered its stance on militant action and collective bargaining. In fact, the organizational rivalry between the two major teachers' organizations, the NEA and AFT, became a major force in the acceleration of militancy. Collective bargaining is now an accepted practice buttressed by legislation and court decisions, and work stoppages and strike threats have become widespread.

During the more conservative seventies, teachers' jobs are less secure and taxpayers are less willing to support increased school expenditures, either for programs or teachers' benefits. In part because teachers have made considerable gains, they are modifying their demands for increased benefits; they are directing their teacher power toward gaining more authority over professional matters and school policy.

In professional spheres, there are two power struggles: one over control of teacher education, and the other over the control of the profession (accreditation and certification). In the individual school and district, teachers continue to strive for less administrative control and greater collegial authority. Teacher associations have used two major strategies to achieve their ends—political activity and collective bargaining.

Negotiations between teachers and school boards have had far-reaching effects on the balance of power; school boards have relinquished many of their traditional prerogatives and administrators have lost a good deal of authority. Sometimes shifts in roles and responsibilities of teachers and administrators are mandated by the contract, as when faculty committees are constituted to handle problems previously under the control of a department chairman or principal. Often administrators are put into an adversary relationship with teachers—a shift from the tradition of democratic supervision, long considered the sine qua non of effective leadership. School boards now are negotiating what were once considered nonnegotiable items, such as the number of faculty meetings that can be scheduled per year, thus limiting the principal's flexibility and eroding his or her prerogatives.

Ironically, collective bargaining has in many ways diminished the autonomy of the rank and file teacher who is constrained to consult the "union rep" or the written agreement before participating in school improvement activities, lest he or she be in violation of the contract. Teacher power has implications for staff development. Most importantly, teacher power has changed teacher-administrator relationships and weakened administrative control and flexibility. Moreover, the struggle of teachers to increase their control over professional matters such as teacher education, certification, and in-service education is significant because increased professionalization is likely to lead to increased demand for colleague authority. The effects that teacher power and collective bargaining have on local authority relationships and decision-making prerogatives also will influence staff development.

SUMMARY AND IMPLICATIONS

During the contemporary period the definition and balance of power among the three principles of authority—public trust, bureaucratic, and colleague—have shifted.

Three factors have led to an alteration in the authority structure in the present era: the nationalizing trend, community involvement, and teacher power.

Pressing national needs and priorities caused reformers to focus upon the school as a major means of solving societal problems. Federal courts, programs, agencies, grants-in-aid, and legislation, as well as research and development units and projects conducted by foundations have all influenced policy at the local level. National testing programs and educational business firms with a national market are additional influences that have limited local control of educational policy. This trend also has altered authority relationships between the school board and the central administration, the teacher and the administrator, and the community and the professional staff.

Public trust now includes citizens' groups that demand participatory involvement and no longer are willing to leave policy decision-making up to governing boards, which they feel do not adequately represent them. It also includes extralocal influences on local policy, such as state education departments, courts and legislatures, big business, foundations, and professional associations.

Bureaucratic authority, once overwhelmingly strong, is now being constrained by citizen power and teacher power. Administrators are bombarded by demands from parents; the administrators' decision-making authority is challenged by teachers backed up by strong unions and associations; the management prerogatives of administrators have been curtailed by collective bargaining, legislation, and judicial decisions.

The most dramatic catalyst for the reconstruction of authority relationships is teacher power, especially as it is manifested in collective bargaining. Because teachers' working conditions are specified in great detail in the negotiated contract, authority relationships are becoming increasingly contractual, and expectations are made explicit. There is less paternalism and more collegiality in the interactions between the principal and his staff. In many situations, however, principals and the teaching staff are in an adversary relationship because the principal is perceived to represent management.

These developments have important implications for staff development. Some predictions about what will occur and some suggestions about what should be changed are related to these implications. First, changing authority relationships require readjustments of traditional expectations, roles, and decision-making structures. Hierarchical patterns of decision-making will be challenged and are likely to be replaced by collaborative patterns.

As roles and authority positions shift, there will be interpersonal and organizational strain. Participants within and outside of the school will have to find new ways of relating to each other and resolving conflicts in needs, interests, expectations, and goals.

The conflict between professional and bureaucratic modes of organization will increase. Changes that permit teachers greater opportunity for realization of professional potential will have to be found.

Teachers will have to resolve the discrepancy between their professional values, which emphasize service, and their power values, which emphasize control. New structures for decision-making and new norms will have to be established to enable teachers to exercise authority in professionally responsible ways.

Teachers will find that some of their previous autonomy is circumscribed by their negotiated contract and peer pressure to conform to teacher collectivity. Liberation from administrative arbitrariness probably will be paid for by pressure to "go along" with decisions made by teachers following majority rule, by union leadership, or by professional negotiators representing teachers at the bargaining table. Teachers will need to find ways to protect individual autonomy while enjoying the fruits of collective action. One way of ensuring that collective negotiations serve teachers, not rule them, is to establish guidelines for collective bargaining that promote flexibility, freedom to experiment, and openness to change between contract periods.

Conflicts between groups of teachers, administrators, and parents will have to be harnessed so that they lead to productive solutions. Dialogue, self-study, experimentation, research, information-seeking, and other means of cooperative exploration and problem-solving will have to be instituted.

NOTES

1. National Education Association, *Schools for the '70's and Beyond: A Call to Action,* staff report (Washington, D.C.: Center for the Study of Instruction, NEA, 1971), p. 104.

2. Roald F. Campbell, Luvern L. Cunningham, and Roderick F. McPhee, *The Organization and Control of American Schools* (Columbus, Ohio: Charles E. Merrill Books, 1965), p. 59.

3. William W. Wayson, "Power, Power, Who's Got the Power? Or, Where the Pressure's Coming From," *National Elementary Principal* 58 (March 1979): 18-19.

4. Robert J. Nash and Russell M. Agne, "The Ethos of Accountability—A Critique," *Teachers College Record* 73 (February 1972): 357-67.

5. National Education Association, *Schools for the '70's,* p. 30.

6. Tyll Van Geel, "Parental Preferences and the Politics of Spending Public Educational Funds," *Teachers College Record* 79 (February 1978): 356-62.

7. Albert L. Alford, "The Education Amendments of 1978," *American Education* 15 (March 1979): 6-14.

8. Don Davies, "Making Citizen Participation Work," *National Elementary Principal* 55 (March-April 1976): 20-29.

9. Dale Mann, "Political Representation and Urban School Advisory Councils," *Teachers College Record* 75 (February 1974): 287.

10. Ronald G. Corwin, *A Sociology of Education: Emerging Patterns of Class, Status, and Power in the Public Schools* (New York: Appleton-Century-Crofts, 1965), pp. 384-90.

11. Dan C. Lortie, "The Balance of Control and Autonomy in Elementary School Teaching," in *The Semi-Professions and Their Organization,* ed. Amatai Etzioni (New York: Free Press, 1969), p. 19.

12. Jack Culbertson, *Preparing Educational Leaders for the Seventies,* Final Report (Columbus, Ohio: University Council for Educational Administration, December, 1969), p. 254. ERIC Clearinghouse, ED 040 941.

13. Robert Bendiner, *The Politics of Schools—A Crisis in Self-Government* (New York: Harper & Row, 1969), p. 88.

14. State of Michigan, Labor Mediation Board, "North Dearborn Heights School District and Local 1439, North Dearborn Heights Federation of Teachers, Michigan Federation of Teachers," Case no. C 66-E-46 (June 28, 1966), p. 12.

15. Thomas Y. Hobart, Jr. "Pro-Education Team Wins, NYSUT Members Play Key Role in Carey-Cuomo, Abrams Victories," *New York Teacher,* 20 (Nov. 12, 1978), p. 4.

16. Ronald G. Corwin, "Teacher Militancy in the United States: Reflections on Its Sources and Prospects," *Theory Into Practice* 7 (April 1968): 97.

17. Sidney G. Tickton, *Teaching Salaries Then and Now, A Second Look* (New York: The Fund for the Advancement of Education, 1961), pp. 21-22.

18. Myron Lieberman and Michael H. Moskow, "Collective Negotiations for Teachers," in *School Policy and Issues in a Changing Society*, ed. Patricia Sexton (Boston: Allyn & Bacon, 1971), p. 286.

19. Ronald G. Corwin, *Militant Professionalism: A Study of Organizational Conflict in High Schools* (New York: Appleton-Century-Crofts, 1970), chap. 9.

20. Ben Brodinsky, "Teacher Power: Can You Trust It?" *National Elementary Principal* 58 (March 1979): 26.

21. Ibid.

22. Lieberman and Moskow, "Collective Negotiations for Teachers," pp. 284-87.

23. "A Model Teacher Standards and Licensure Act" (Washington, D.C.: National Commission on Teacher Education and Professional Standards in consultation with the National Commission on Professional Rights and Responsibilities and the NEA General Counsel, National Education Association, 1971).

24. Edward C. Pomeroy, "What's Going on in Teacher Education?" *Journal of Teacher Education* 26 (Fall 1975): 199.

25. Robert N. Bush and Peter Enemark, "Control and Responsibility in Teacher Education," in *Teacher Education*, Seventy-fourth Yearbook of the National Society for the Study of Education, pt. 2. (Chicago: University of Chicago Press, 1975), p. 284.

26. George W. Denemark and Joost Yff, *Obligation for Reform*, The Final Report of the Higher Education Task Force on Improvement and Reform in American Education (Washington, D.C.: American Association of Colleges for Teacher Education, 1974), pp. 2-3.

27. National Education Association, *In-Service Education*, Infopac. No. 7 (Washington, D.C.: Instruction and Professional Development, NEA, 1974), p. 2.

28. Maurice Leiter and Myrna Cooper, "How Teacher Unionists View In-Service Education," *Teachers College Record* 80 (September 1978): 107-25.

29. Allen A. Schmieder and Sam J. Yarger, "Teacher/Teaching Centering in America," *Journal of Teacher Education*, 25 (Spring 1974): 6.

30. National Education Association, "Teacher Centered Professional Development," mimeographed, (Washington, D.C.: Instruction and Professional Development, NEA, Fall 1974).

31. National Education Association, "What a Teacher Center Might Look Like," mimeographed, (Washington, D.C.: Instruction and Professional Development, NEA, Fall 1974), pp. 1-2.

32. Quoted in Bendiner, *The Politics of Schools*, p. 105.

33. Albert Shanker, cited in an article in *New York Teacher*, official publication of the New York State United Teachers, 19, 28 May 1978.

34. Reported in the *New York Times*, 25 March 1979.

35. Brodinsky, "Teacher Power," pp. 22-23.

36. Charles Cogan, "What Teachers Really Want from Boards," *American School Board Journal* 156 (February 1969), p. 10.

37. Cited in William L. Pharis, "The Principalship: Where are We?" *National Elementary Principal* 55 (November-December 1975): 4-9.

38. Editorial, "It's Late, but There's Still Time to Give Your Principals a Real Say in Management," *American School Board Journal* 163 (February 1976): 32-34.

39. Herbert C. Rudman, "The Dirty Dozen: The Principal and his Teachers," in *Professional Negotiation and the Principalship* (Washington, D.C.: Department of Elementary School Principals, NEA, 1969), p. 66.

40. Dale Mann, *The Politics of Administrative Representation* (New York: Lexington Books, 1976), p. 44.

41. See, for example, Lloyd E. McCleary, *An Essay on Role Attrition: Three Studies of the Job of the Principal* (April 1971), ED 077 135; and editorial "The Brewing—and Perhaps Still Preventable Revolt of School Principals," *American School Board Journal* 163 (January 1976): 25-28.

42. Rudman, "The Dirty Dozen," pp. 64-65.

43. Norman J. Boyan, "The Emergent Role of the Teacher and the Authority Structure of the School," in *Organization and Human Behavior: Focus on Schools,* eds. Fred D. Carver and Thomas J. Sergiovanni (New York: McGraw-Hill, 1969), p. 203.

44. Robert J. Braun, *Teachers and Power: The Story of the American Federation of Teachers* (New York: Simon and Schuster, 1972), pp. 252-60.

Teacher Autonomy and Authority

7

IN THE PRECEDING CHAPTERS, the three principles of authority—public trust, bureaucratic, and colleague—were traced. We saw that the meaning of these three principles changed over time, and that their relative importance shifted in different historical periods. The principle of public trust has been basic in American schooling, but the sources of public authority have varied, as has the extent to which local lay boards have controlled policy. For at least a century, administrators have run the schools, and the principle of bureaucratic authority has dominated. Until the contemporary era, teachers were not considered legitimate sources of policy-making authority, although for several decades they were consulted as experts in practice. The present era, although characterized by bureaucratic organizational arrangements, is marked by a press away from the bureaucratic principle and towards the principle of colleague authority. This is a result, in part, of a change in the way teachers view their role, and the political reality of teacher power, which buttresses their claims for professional authority with organizational strength.

The principle of colleague authority is the principle that much, if not all, authority should be in the hands of the school faculty. The school should be a self-governing community in which the faculty group has major control over policy, and the individual teacher has major control over what takes place in the classroom. Therefore, unless the colleague group exerts influence upon the individual teacher, he or she will exercise autonomous decision-making in the classroom.

Teachers' role conceptions and their position in the school's authority structure have changed since the advent of the common school. One of the factors influencing this change has been the evolution of motivational theory, which, in turn, has modified administrative theory and practice. Current thinking presumes a drive towards self-actualization in teachers and emphasizes the importance of teacher actualization for school renewal.[1]

Sociologists have pointed out that the bureaucratic organization restricts the possibility of experimentation, innovation, and the development of a unique personal style requisite to teacher self-actualization. Gary Griffin and Ann Lieberman, writing of the behavior of innovative school personnel say: "The rhetoric surrounding the word 'professional' includes constructs such as autonomy, self-governance, and self-renewal. These qualities are often in direct opposition with the leader/follower, management/labor, hierarchical organization of schools."[2]

According to some educators and teacher leaders, the strain between bureaucratic and professional modes of organization can only be resolved by recognizing that the teacher is a professional who must be accorded autonomy. This position is taken by Albert Shanker who states: "Teachers must possess the self-direction, independence, and decision-making power that is part of the definition of 'professional' and which distinguishes the professional from the employee on the assembly line."[3]

Another professional militant, David Selden, has stated that the hierarchical form of most school organizations inhibits teaching effectiveness, reduces teachers' self-concepts, and increases teacher frustration and feelings of powerlessness and statuslessness. He adds that if teachers are to be creative, imaginative, and effective, they must have the autonomy to be so.[4]

Underlying such statements are two assumptions: first, that teachers are full-fledged professionals who have the same relationship with clients as do doctors, lawyers, and other professionals granted high degrees of autonomy by the public; and second, that teacher actualization and teacher autonomy are concepts so closely related as to be almost synonymous, or at least that the former is a function of the latter. Both of these assumptions require analysis.

Teacher autonomy can be individual or collective. Individual autonomy means that teachers exercise their own judgments about curricula, program, and classroom management with little control exercised by parents and administrators. Collective autonomy means that control over policy is exercised mainly by the colleague group.

Autonomy has been defined as "absence from external constraints."[5] Advocates of teacher autonomy recognize professional and political limits to autonomy but desire large amounts of freedom from administrative and community interference with teachers' judgments. They also propose that the principle of colleague authority prevail in overall decision-making about the aims of the school and the means of achieving these aims. Are these proposals justified or desirable? These are questions we will consider.

Some researchers have noted that teachers have a great deal of individual autonomy, that some of it is necessary for achieving the general goals of the school organization, and that it is crucial in helping the organization adapt to its environment and achieve an optimal level of integration.[6] Others have noted that some kinds of teacher autonomy are dysfunctional for both teacher actualization and school renewal.[7] The "closed door" concept that isolates teachers from colleagues is inimical to teacher actualization in that it isolates the individual teacher from a major source of professional stimulation—the opportunity to share concerns and problems with those who are grappling with similar ones in the same local setting. Also, this isolation does not provide optimal conditions for discussions and problem-solving that might spur school renewal.

Collective teacher autonomy based on colleague authority also has its functional and dysfunctional aspects. More colleague authority than presently exists perhaps will lead to increased commitment and motivation for self-improvement if teachers are willing to assume the responsibility and control that go along with authority. But colleague authority that restricts individual teacher flexibility (by placing formal constraints on the amount of time a teacher may spend in curriculum development activities, for example) is dysfunctional. In addition, colleague authority that ignores the other sources of authority is not only dysfunctional, it is naive.

In this chapter, issues related to teacher autonomy will be explored. We conclude that the teacher's quasi-professional status and relationship to other sources of authority do not warrant the granting of the same kinds and amounts of "professional autonomy" accorded full-fledged professionals; that teacher actualization and teacher autonomy are not synonymous; and that the important issue for staff development is not "teacher autonomy or not teacher autonomy," but *how much* and *what kind* of teacher autonomy is optimal for meeting the dual and interrelated goals of teacher actualization and school renewal.

THE GROWTH OF ADMINISTRATIVE THEORY AND THE CONCEPT OF TEACHER ACTUALIZATION

The notion that the school should provide for teacher actualization paralleled a shift in thinking about the teacher's role away from "employee" toward "professional." New thinking about the teacher's occupational needs was influenced by the growth of motivational theory, which in turn influenced theories of school administration.

During the first quarter of the century, in the period of "efficiency orientation," Frederick W. Taylor's scientific management theories held sway. These theories were based on the view that human beings are motivated by rational-economic rewards: people work in organizations in order to make money, and economic rewards are controlled by management. The "line and staff" concept of the school hierarchy was considered essential for close supervision of work and for careful ordering and control of activities. The teacher was considered an employee who was to follow the rules and policies specified by administrators.

The research of industrial psychologist Elton Mayo and his colleagues led to a new understanding of work motivation: people work not only for money, but also for the satisfaction of being part of a social group. The concepts of morale—the importance of positive group identification—and leadership strategies based on group dynamics were developed in industry; they influenced theories of school administration. Although the formal hierarchical structure for decision-making remained, informally participative decision-making arrangements and more equal administrator-teacher relationships became common.

Psychologists like Chris Argyris, Douglas M. McGregor, and Abraham Maslow developed a third set of motivational assumptions related to the self-actualizing person. According to Maslow, human needs are arranged in a hierarchy. Needs at one level must be satisfied before the individual can seek satisfaction of needs at the next level. At the lowest level are safety and survival needs; then come social needs, needs for self-esteem, and needs for autonomy; at the highest level is the need for self-actualization. According to Maslow, this is the need to develop into "everything one can become." Maslow's theory of motivation provided the basis for principles of organizational leadership such as McGregor's Theory Y, which aimed towards the integration of individual higher-order needs and organizational goals. Maslow himself developed a Eupsychian management scheme that applied optimistic third force assumptions about human nature to strategies of organizational leadership.[8]

Applied to the school, Eupsychian management implies that the school organization should make it possible for an individual teacher to maximize his or her potential for achievement, competency, and creativity. This viewpoint led to an expansion of administrative theory from "human relations" to "human resources." This latter theory holds that the administrator's basic task is to create an environment that promotes teacher self-actualization, in addition to a pleasant climate and good morale.

Frederick Herzberg developed and tested a motivation-hygiene theory that sought to explain and predict what organizational factors are necessary to attract achievement-motivated individuals and to encourage people to seek higher-order satisfactions from their work. Herzberg postulated that the psychologically healthy adult has two drives: to seek satisfaction of his or her lower-order needs, which he called hygienic needs, and to seek satisfaction of higher-order needs, which he called motivation needs. Adequate presence of the hygienic factors—rewards such as a pleasant working environment, pay incentives, pension plans, and job security—are essential if organizational members are not to feel dissatisfied with their work. Herzberg proposed that job factors that relate to hygiene needs lead to dissatisfaction if not present, but not to job satisfaction if present. Other factors must be present for workers to gain deep satisfaction from their work. Among the things that bring satisfaction are achievement opportunities, recognition, rewards from the work itself, responsibility, and the opportunity for advancement. Herzberg discovered that people differ in the degree to which they are motivation-seekers. He found that some of those who are hygiene-seekers could become motivation-seekers if the environment provided increased opportunity for self-actualization.[9]

The work of Maslow, Herzberg, and others encouraged the idea that teacher self-actualization is a legitimate occupational and administrative goal. The "ideal teacher" began to be viewed not as a drudge who passes along the values of others, but as an active, thinking, creative, problem-solving person.

A goal of teacher education became teacher self-actualization. This is expressed by Arthur Combs's idea that teacher education is a "problem in becoming":

A self becomes. . . .Becoming is a problem in growth. It is an internal event
going on inside the learner and only in a limited degree open to external
manipulation. . . .Seeing the production of teachers as a problem of becoming,
however, calls for a different emphasis upon the development of beliefs, values,
purposes, and personal meanings, instead of behavior.[10]

A concern for developing opportunities for teacher "becoming" encouraged studies of teacher satisfaction and dissatisfaction, the teacher's position in the authority structure of the school, teacher alienation, and the conditions necessary for stimulating motivation-seeking behavior in teachers.

These studies and research on change processes suggested that teacher participation in decision-making is a critical factor in teacher satisfaction, staff commitment to school goals, and innovative behavior.

The combined effect of motivational theory, research on teacher actualization, studies of school change, teacher professionalism, and teacher power led to the insistence by some teacher leaders and educators that in order to become self-actualizing professionals, teachers should be granted "professional autonomy."

TEACHING AS AN OCCUPATION

Some claim that the teacher is a professional who should be accorded one of the basic privileges granted to those in the established professions: autonomy. On an individual basis, this would mean that the teacher would be independent of administrative, lay, and even colleague control in classroom decision-making, as long as she or he remained within the bounds of professional ethics and standards of competency. Collectively, it would mean that the principle of colleague authority would prevail. Teachers would control decisions about program, curricula, textbook and material selection, testing, child placement, grading, and professional matters such as teacher evaluation and tenure.

The demand for autonomy is based on claims that should be analyzed. Is the teacher a professional whose expert knowledge and skills justify having the authority to make autonomous decisions about program, curricula, and classroom management within his or her own sphere, the classroom? Can the school thrive under a laissez-faire approach to program and policy? What is the nature of educational decision-making, and what are the implications for the principle of colleague authority? What is the relationship between the professional and client communities? Should teachers make educational decisions without reference to the expectations and goals of the community they serve?

THE TEACHER AS A QUASI-PROFESSIONAL

Two aspects of the debate over the criteria to be used to judge whether or not an occupation is a profession are particularly relevant to the issue of teacher autonomy: (1) there are several generic criteria of professionalism, some of which have not yet been met by teachers; and (2) the mark of a profession is public acceptance of elite status claimed by practitioners, but teachers have not yet achieved such acceptance.

Howard Becker points out that not even the established professions such as medicine, law, and the ministry match point for point the ideal criteria that analysts say define the professions. He suggests that professional status is conferred to occupations that morally seem to deserve it.[11] Most students of the professions, however, believe that an occupation's professional status can be judged, in part, by the number of points of congruence between it and ideal criteria. Greenwood has distilled five elements that most analysts agree constitute the distinguishing attributes of a profession. Professions seem to possess: systematic theory, authority, community sanction, ethical codes, and a unique culture.[12]

Systematic Theory

Greenwood writes about the systematic theory of a profession.

The skills that characterize a profession flow from and are supported by a fund of knowledge that has been organized into an internally consistent system, called a *body of theory.* A profession's underlying body of theory is a system of abstract propositions that describe in general terms the classes of phenomena comprising the profession's focus of interest. Theory serves as a base in terms of which the professional rationalizes his operations in concrete situations.[13]

The knowledge that the professional has is technical, and acquired only through long, prescribed training. This knowledge is systematized and codified; it is neither too narrow (as a set of rules anyone can easily learn) or too broad or vague. To some extent, it is tacit and acquired through practical experience. This combination of esoteric technical and tacit knowledge creates an image of professional competency.

Professional Authority

In a professional-client relationship it is assumed that the client cannot, without help, diagnose his or own needs or find the best means of meeting those needs. The professional is invested with a monopoly of judgment in those areas within which he or she has been educated.

Community Sanctions

Harold Wilensky describes how community sanctions enter into professional status. "Any occupation wishing to exercise professional authority must find a technical base for it, assert an exclusive jurisdiction to standards of training, and convince the public that its services are uniquely trustworthy."[14]

Every profession strives to persuade the community to sanction its authority and give it certain powers and privileges. Its power includes control over its training centers and over accreditation of programs and licensing of practitioners. Among its privileges are legally protected confidentiality of professional-client communications, and relative immunity from community judgment on technical matters. In order to gain these privileges and powers the profession seeks to prove to the community that it will benefit by granting them.

Regulative Code of Ethics

A regulative code of ethics is needed because the monopoly of authority wielded by professionals can be abused, and because professionals often deal with matters of life and death. Ethical codes govern client-professional and client-colleague relationships. It is enforced by formal (for example, censure) and informal (for example, referral and consultation) regulation.

Professional Culture

Every profession operates through a network of formal and informal groups. Among the formal groups are: organizations through which professionals perform their services, such as the hospital and church; educational and research centers that replenish the profession's supply of talent, and through which its fund of knowledge is extended; and professional associations. Informal groups include cliques of colleagues based on specializations, affiliations with professional societies, residential and work propinquity, and personal attraction. The profession also has a special culture consisting of its values, norms, and symbols. The transformation of a neophyte into a member of a profession is essentially an acculturation process wherein an individual internalizes the values, norms, and symbols of the occupational group.

Professionals' autonomy in decision-making is granted by the community because it is believed that they possess highly esoteric technical knowledge and skills. A client consulting a professional generally believes that the professional is trustworthy and competent; the professional has had long years of training and socialization—the process of acquiring the knowledge, attitudes, and skills that make a person a member of a group—and belongs to a group that regulates it members' behavior. Since the professional's knowledge base is systemized, there are standards for his performance; the client may not be in a position to evaluate this performance, but the professional's colleagues are. The professional is judged by her or his ability to apply knowledge and her or his adherence to the values and norms of the professional culture.

The autonomy granted to professionals is considered necessary for competent work: the professional can perform effectively only if free to innovate, to experiment, and to take risks.

George Ritzer notes that although the teaching profession has invested time and energy to gain professional recognition it has failed to achieve community sanction of its claim to professional authority.[15] Among the reasons for this are: the nature of teaching as an occupation—teaching lacks many of the dimensions of professionalism previously discussed, the characteristics of the teaching cadre, and the occupation's visibility and lack of social distance from its clientele (parents).

THE NATURE OF TEACHING

Amitai Etzioni characterizes teaching as a semiprofession.[16] The goals of the school involve communicating, and to a lesser extent applying knowledge. The knowledge base of the occupation is weak, and is neither systematized nor codified. What technical knowledge is available is largely a potpourri of precepts derived from other disciplines.[17]

The teacher's period of professional training falls far below the five years that is average in the full-fledged professions. The process of learning to fit in the profession does not represent the shared-ordeal that characterizes professions such as medicine and the ministry, and thus it fails to create a strong professional culture, or solidarity and collegial feeling among practitioners. Teacher training does not involve an intensive acculturation process: there is no mediated entry (such as, slow induction with standards of accomplishment at each step); students are not subjected to sustained empirical and practice-oriented inquiry, and they have a relatively short apprenticeship.[18]

Teaching is characterized by intangible goals, an absence of concrete models for emulation, and multiple and controversial performance criteria.[19] Teachers work with immature students who attend school on a compulsory basis and do not necessarily desire the teacher's services; teachers also deal with students in groups. Getting students to learn is a complex task that involves motivating and eliciting attention, and interactions laden with emotion. Research studies indicate that teachers are unclear about objectives and the criteria for measuring successful performance.[20] (Spontaneous expressions of pupil interest and enthusiasm are among the most highly valued indicators of good teaching.) These characteristics of the teaching occupation make it difficult for teachers to insist upon professional autonomy. As sociologist T. Leggatt points out:

The difficulty that teachers have in eliciting respect for their learning and expertise when combined with this lack of clarity about the nature of success in teaching inevitably exposes them to criticism, and to the insecurity that can follow this, and undermines their claims to respect.[21]

CHARACTERISTICS OF TEACHERS

Ease of entry into the occupation, the high rate of turnover, and low commitment to career have led to a stereotype of the teaching cadre disadvantageous to teachers. Leggatt states that this is a consequence of certain primary characteristics of teachers as an occupational group, including the large size of the group, its high proportion of female members, and its lowly social class origin.[22]

The need for a large cadre of teachers has made it difficult to raise the qualifications for entry into the occupation, the standards of instruction, and the length and intensity of the experience of learning how to fit in the profession. Ease of entry into an occupation, and relatively low standards of accomplishment have not led to the sense of identity, career commitment, and shared values that are necessary for the establishment of a professional community; nor have they led to high prestige in the larger community.

The large proportion of female teachers perhaps will change as attitudes towards sex roles and responsibilities change. Until now, women have generally made their major commitment to family, and not to career. Teaching has been considered an occupation that offers a woman an ideal opportunity to earn money without relinquishing her "feminine self-image" and primary loyalty to family. It offers women practical and psychological benefits. For one thing, training to become a teacher is relatively easy compared with other professions. Teachers generally are certified to teach with only a bachelor's degree; their training is not rigorous; it does not consume time for years as it does in other professions. This means that women do not have to take "time out" of their personal lives to devote themselves to their professional training. Teaching also affords women the opportunity to use their college education in a way that does not make excessive demands upon the time that they and others may think should be spent caring for husbands and children. In addition, teaching involves nurturing children, an accepted feminine interest; it allows the opportunity to work alone in noncompetitive situations; and it offers the possibility of interrupting their careers at a point in their lives when the demands of family require that they do so. Teaching allows women to have an occupation without sacrificing their goals of marriage and children, and to combine work with family life. Relatively low commitment to career and professional self-improvement make for a loosely structured occupational group.

This is probably changing with the growth of the women's movement and feminine consciousness, but the high proportion of women probably has maintained the principle of bureaucratic authority, since women have traditionally accepted more submissive roles than men, and this probably has retarded the growth of professional militancy. The viewpoint that teaching is a feminized occupation also has contributed to public unwillingness to grant teachers autonomy.[23]

Teaching is underchosen by males in comparison with other occupations, and overchosen by both males and females from lower socioeconomic backgrounds, from small communities, and from minority group backgrounds.[24]

This "negative social selectivity" offers sharp contrasts with law and medicine, which tend to attract a disproportionate number of males and of individuals from high socioeconomic status and urban communities.[25] An occupational group that recruits so heavily from the lower social class and that provides social mobility has low-prestige standing. This is an impediment to high community regard, especially in middle- and upper-class communities where parents may be more highly educated and have more social status than teachers; parents thus are loathe to relinquish the principle of public trust in favor of the principle of colleague authority.

THE OCCUPATION'S VISIBILITY AND LACK OF SOCIAL DISTANCE FROM CLIENTS

Israel Gerver and Joseph Bensman point out that the process by which members of an occupation gain recognition as experts is related to social distance and visibility:

Experts do not arrive in society spontaneously but are the result of a complex process of institutional development, claims for recognition as experts, and the granting of social recognition is the *social visibility* of those claiming expertness and the *social distance* of the conferring groups from the alleged experts. The more distant groups, i.e., those least technically qualified, grant recognition which is based not upon a knowledge of expert procedures, methods and information, but instead upon the imputed consequences of expert action . . . The recognition of expertness, then, varies with the social distance of the conferring groups and their criteria of recognition.[26]

Teachers are highly visible to almost all the status-conferring community groups. Parents are in intimate contact with school life via their children, and keep the teacher's work under surveillance. Since most adults have gone through school, they have formed opinions about what constitutes good teaching, and have a strong sense of what the teaching task entails. Although parents may feel grateful to teachers for undertaking the job of educating their children, they are not necessarily impressed by the knowledge and skills required to do so. Most of us feel capable of judging a teacher's competency and are unwilling to abrogate our evaluative prerogatives. At the present time, teachers as an occupational group lack attributes that would make communities relinquish their own decision-making authority in favor of the principle of colleague authority. The school's visibility also makes it difficult for teachers to establish a professional mystique. The public stereotype of the teacher is not that of an expert who is a highly trained, high-prestige individual, as it is in the established professions.

Teachers may find, however, that some of the impediments to full professional status may recede as teachers progress towards higher levels of professionalization. Professionalization is "a dynamic *process* whereby many occupations can be observed to change certain crucial characteristics in the direction of a 'profession'."[27] Occupations are more or less professionalized, although a profession is a term applied to an ideal type of occupational group that does not actually exist.

What are some of the developments occurring in teaching that are likely to promote professionalization? First, new knowledge about the art of pedagogy may provide the theoretical base that can buttress teachers' claims to professional standing. Training in education may become sufficiently technical to create a gap between teachers and nonteachers. Technologies of teaching are being built that will improve teachers' skills in questioning, explaining, and in other areas. Robert Dreeben has suggested that although the teaching task is complex and composed of elements that are spontaneous, diffuse, and ill-defined, the field can and should develop technologies— that is, specific linkages between ends and means for the accomplishment of tasks. He predicts that technologies will be built in at least four areas: instructional processes, motivation, classroom control, and changing social arrangements within classrooms.[28] Joseph Schwab has suggested that an undistorted and viable educational theory can be built out of studies of classroom action and reaction.[29]

In recent years many researchers have gone into classrooms to study teaching in the belief that a technology and theory of teaching can indeed be built. *The Study of Teaching,* by Michael Dunkin and Bruce Biddle, describes hundreds of studies done since 1950 that shed light on classroom climate, management and control, the classroom as a social system, knowledge and intellect, logic and linguistics, and the sequential patterns of classroom behavior.[30]

Secondly, new designs in teacher education show promise of creating a more exacting experience of fitting people to be teachers, including a more intensive and longer apprenticeship, and the demonstration of competency at each stage of the program. Competency-Based Teacher Education (CBTE) already has initiated a dialogue among educators about the criteria for judging teacher effectiveness, and has encouraged research into teacher education, and new thinking about accreditation and certification processes.

Improvements in recruitment and selection, pre- and in-service education, maintaining standards in the occupation through licensure, accreditation, and work assignment, and advances in theory and research undoubtedly will overcome many of the shortcomings that have hampered teachers in their striving towards professional status. Finally, an increase in colleague authority could lead to changed roles and new responsibilities for teachers that will be more esoteric, more technical, and more prestigious.

THE VALUE-BASED NATURE
OF EDUCATIONAL DECISION-MAKING

The matter of teacher autonomy and the viability of the principle of colleague authority does not hinge entirely on the occupation's degree of professionalization. Educational authority is much more crucially related to the functions and aims of the school, and the nature of educational decision-making. The fundamental questions in education concern not *how,* but *what* and *why;* even if we had the knowledge related to teaching and learning that would prescribe an effective technology of teaching, the aims and functions of the school would still be controversial.

The philosophical issues outweigh in importance the technical issues. In education, ends and means are intimately related, and everyday decisions involve value judgments. Choices concerning curricula offerings, methodology, programs, classroom management, testing, and tracking are based on values concerning the function of the school in society, and assumptions about desirable outcomes of schooling. Controversy about the school's work, whether professional-professional or professional-public, is less often technical than philosophical. Decisions related to open versus traditional classrooms, heterogeneous versus homogenous grouping, emphasis on basic skills versus emphasis on the arts, whether or not to provide sex education, or special programs for the gifted, or whether to track students on the basis of IQ tests reflect diversity in value-orientations.

Teachers support values. "How best to achieve the school's goals?" can be informed by educational research and the disciplines of psychology and sociology, but educational goals themselves derive from conceptions about human beings and their relationship to society, about knowledge and its relationship to schooling, and from assumptions about the good life. Maxine Greene exhorts the teacher to "do philosophy."[31] Dwayne Huebner reminds us that educational decision-making is political, aesthetic, scientific, and ethical, as well as technical, and advises educators to broaden their purview by seeking insights from philosophy, theology, the arts, humanities, and social sciences, as well as from the behavioral sciences.[32] Greene and Huebner speak to the teacher in their plea that educational decision-making be based on a broad and deep understanding of diverse aspects of life and society—but are they not speaking also to everyone else who has an interest in the results of our educational system?

Parents and other laymen will not abrogate their rights to determine what kind of education children receive. Sol Elkin states:

The American public will not hand over to any professional group, no matter how high its standards, the power to determine the goals of education, the portion of our resources we choose to allot to schools, or our conception of the educated man . . . . . and this prerogative will not be, and should not be, surrendered to any single group within society.[33]

As has been discussed, it is unlikely that teachers will be able to convince the public that they should exercise a monopoly of judgment over policy-making, although they may be able to gain authority prerogatives in technical areas of decision-making.

TEACHER AUTONOMY AND THE AUTHORITY PRINCIPLE OF PUBLIC TRUST

If and when the teaching field establishes an esoteric knowledge base, and teachers are trained as philosophers and researchers as well as technical experts, teachers are likely to argue that they are better prepared than laymen to set school goals and to determine the means of achieving them—that is, to press for the principle of colleague authority. This view is not likely to be shared by the public in our pluralistic society, however. We also have considerable evidence that when professionally competent, highly educated teachers attempt to support their own values without reference to the values, aspirations, goals, and expectations of the community, neither teacher self-actualization nor organizational renewal takes place.

A Case Study

A case study documents how renewal can be thwarted when educators do not consider sufficiently the values of others.

In 1968, Roland Barth, then a well-known advocate of the open class-room, was hired as instructional principal of two public elementary schools in a lower-class, mostly black, inner-city school, as part of a plan that sought to enlist the resources of a foundation, a university, and a large public school system in order to develop an "important educational alternative." Barth hired six bright, highly educated and sophisticated teachers who were committed to open education; they proceeded to organize their classrooms according to British Primary School principles. Three months after the start of the year, their classrooms looked like conventional classrooms, and all of their innovative methods had been eliminated.[34]

What had happened? Barth and his six teachers assumed that it was their prerogative to create a classroom environment in accordance with their own cosmopolitan values. They also assumed that others in the school and its environment would embrace the innovation without reservation: children would respond according to the principles of learning upon which it is based; administrators would support the teachers' experimentation and provide resources; and parents would be impressed by the results. From the vantage point of the teachers and Barth, the efficacy of the open classroom had already been demonstrated in Britain and had worked in the upper middle-class communities where they had previously lived and worked. They did not consider that the needs felt by the children and parents and their values, goals, and expectations were antithetical to the open classroom, nor that administrators would not support the teachers' efforts for political reasons.

The teachers soon learned that the children had been conditioned to expect that school was either "firm and authoritarian" or "chaotic"; they interpreted the teachers' openness as lack of concern and weakness and as an invitation to bedlam.

Not only were the children resistant to the innovation, but the parents also were resistant. The tenets and practices of the open classroom were seen by parents as being in direct conflict with their aspirations for their children. The parents desired the rewards of white middle-class America for their children and insisted that they be trained in the mold of discipline, hard work, and striving that they believed led to high income and status in what they presumed was a society based on merit. The teachers' informal dress and manner and their easy relationships with the children were interpreted as lack of concern. And the activities selected were viewed as insulting to black children. As one parent saw it, "The young white teachers are condescending to our children; they don't think they are capable of writing, spelling, figuring, or thinking, so they let them play with blocks and animals."

The administrators, most of them black, became increasingly authoritarian as parents created pressure to establish a kind of "military academy," and insisted that administrators alter the open classroom teachers' behavior.

The teachers were unable to accomplish their goals in this situation. At first, they made concessions of form while keeping the substance of their efforts intact. They wrote, but did not use, formal lesson plans. They put desks in rows but changed them several times a day for activities. They dressed more conservatively. They changed the nomenclature used to describe activities so that these activities would not sound "open": playtime or freetime became "activity period," or "work period," although the function remained the same.

But altering appearances did not succeed, due to the high visibility of the program. Teachers then tried to convince administrators of the efficacy of the program by presenting logical arguments; the administrators applied whatever sanctions and pressures they could. For example, they carpeted the rooms and told the teachers that the custodian's union hereafter would forbid animals, crayons, paste or paint in the rooms. They demanded explicit lesson plans. They refused to supply funds out of petty cash for "creative materials."

The incongruency between teacher-community values made the project's goals of change unachievable; neither the teachers nor the parents modified their views. Thus, almost nothing new was allowed into the system, and the teachers' strivings for professional self-actualization were stymied. The teachers' response to the pressure from the community was withdrawal—at first emotional, then political, and finally physical—they quit. As one teacher put it: "I am what I am. I am incapable of doing what is expected of me; therefore, it is best for all concerned that I leave."[35]

The Barth case indicates that the importance attached to schooling by parents in terms of their aspirations for their children, their deeply held views about how their children ought to be prepared for society, and the high visibility of the school's program constrains teacher autonomy. Increasing professionalization of teaching may lead to increasing conflict between local communities and professional staffs unless teachers modify their own approaches to take into account the values and expectations of parents.

TEACHER AUTONOMY AND THE PRINCIPLE OF BUREAUCRATIC AUTHORITY

The principle of bureaucratic authority states that authority should be delegated to or assumed by bureaucratic officials. Underlying the principle is the assumption that bureaucratic arrangements are most efficient in meeting the goals of the organization, and that it is the bureaucratic official who is in the best position to ensure that goals are met.

Max Weber has described the ideal type of bureaucracy as including a formula of managerial precision and clearly delineated areas of competencies and work roles. According to Weber, bureaucracy is a rational organization of human effort. Its members are chosen on the basis of ability to perform specific tasks, and responsibility for accomplishing these tasks is incorporated into established positions, each of which is systematically related to other positions, usually in a hierarchical arrangement; responsibilities and duties are built into positions through a system of rules that specify the contribution of each position to the whole organization. The organization's mission underlies the entire system and provides the focus and justification for all the rules. Weber, while recognizing possible dysfunctions of bureaucracies for the human spirit, believed that bureaucratic organization is the most efficient and rational form of harnessing human energy that has been devised.[36] Robert Merton adds that if a bureaucracy is to operate successfully, it must attain a high degree of reliability of behavior and an unusual degree of conformity with prescribed patterns of action.[37]

The complex organization has a pattern of roles that comprises its formal structure. These roles are occupied by persons who behave in accordance with the established role prescriptions, and thus individuals are replaceable within the structure.

Many organizational theorists have noted that there is another structure that coexists with the formal structure just described—that is, the informal structure. The informal behavior of individuals and groups is patterned and socially organized, and these informal patterns are functionally related to the formal structure. For example, the informal chats among teachers about mutually known children may provide information and insight that help a teacher motivate a particular child to learn. Some theorists have considered the relationship between the formal and informal structures as highly functional: the formal structure focuses the organization on goals and the informal structure develops as the organization adapts to the specifics in the setting. An equilibrium develops between the formal and informal structures.

Other analysts have pointed out that there is autonomy among subsystem parts of the organization; rather than equilibrium, conflicts and strains exist. These tensions may be dysfunctional for the achievement of organizational goals.

Schools are, to some degree, bureaucratic organizations. Organizational charts usually present a picture of the school as a hierarchically arranged bureaucracy. This and the school's formal statements of goals suggest a formal structure where policy is made at superordinate levels and passed down the line and implemented by the teacher. Dan Lortie notes, however:

The bureaucratic model, in emphasizing the formal distribution of authority, does not prepare us for many of the events that actually occur in public schools . . . . The bureaucratic map of public schools, then, leaves out certain parts of the territory, notably those which point to power held by teachers (and of course, students) which are nowhere given formal sanction.[38]

PROFESSIONAL AND BUREAUCRATIC MODES OF ORGANIZATION

Charles Bidwell's analysis of the school as a formal organization indicated that school systems face two major functional problems: coordination of instructional activity of teachers and individual school units so that the sequence of activities is presented in a way that ensures a reasonable uniformity of outcomes; and the maintenance of sufficient latitude for the exercise of professional judgments about the kinds of specific educational outcomes that best serve the students and the constituency, and the procedures that are best adapted to these ends.[39]

The first problem points to a bureaucratic solution, and the second problem to a professional solution. Corwin's study indicated that administrators hold primarily bureaucratic expectations for behavior in schools, while teachers hold primarily professional expectations, and these differing expectations create a strain in relationships between the two groups.[40]

The bureaucratic mode of organization emphasizes rationalized activities: it stresses the uniformity of clients' problems, specific and universally applied rules and procedures, a task orientation, efficiency, loyalty to the organization and to superiors, and authority that stems from office (position). Rationalized activities are necessary for the functioning of the school system because the school system is responsible for a uniform product of a certain quality, and the process of preparing children and adolescents for adult roles is massive and complex. Schools deal with students over long periods of time and must provide educational services that comprise coherent sequences of increasingly differentiated and demanding tasks. To be coherent and sequential, these educational activities must be coordinated.[41]

The professional mode of organization emphasizes the individuality of clients' problems, diffuse rules stated as alternatives, a client orientation, and structural looseness.

The classroom teacher needs a great deal of autonomy in order to effectively deal with the diverse abilities of students, as well as the daily fluctuations in individual and group responses.

Some aspects of teaching require a professional mode of organization.

Informally, teachers have achieved a great deal of autonomy from the control of parents, administrators, and their colleagues. Some of this autonomy is necessary if teachers are to meet organizational goals and for professional development.

But certain kinds and amounts of teacher autonomy are dysfunctional for teacher actualization and organizational renewal. Lortie notes that the autonomy possessed by elementary teachers is not the collectively shared right of recognized professionals, and is not based upon the principle of colleague authority. It takes the form of "autonomy-equality" based on isolation from other sources of authority.[42]

The pattern of autonomy-equality grows out of teachers' needs that derive from the rewards and tasks of teaching, and is buttressed by the spatial work arrangements and the informal norms that are connected with those needs.

THE REWARDS OF TEACHING

Lortie's studies of the rewards of teaching shed some light on the issue of teacher autonomy. He discovered that the reward system of teaching gives teachers the opportunity to attain autonomy despite a hierarchical authority structure and a weak set of professional supports. Work rewards may be classified into three groups: (1) extrinsic rewards, such as money, prestige, and power; (2) ancillary rewards, which may be perceived as benefits, but since they are constant over time, become part of the job rather than income received for additional effort; examples are security, the work calendar, and the physical environment; and (3) intrinsic rewards that persons derive from their work; these rewards are subjective and vary to some extent from individual to individual. A person, having joined an occupation, concentrates her or his reward-seeking energies at those points where effort makes the largest difference in her or his total rewards. Intrinsic rewards are dominant for teachers; for a very large proportion of teachers the most important intrinsic reward revolves around "transitive" aspects of the role—that is, those rewards that arise when effective communication with students produces student responses the teacher defines as "learning."[43]

One of the consequences of this patterning of rewards is that it renders teachers more sensitive to students and less sensitive to administrative or collegial reactions. Since teachers' rewards depend primarily on what takes place in the classroom, they can be relatively independent of benefits controlled by administrators and colleagues.

SPATIAL WORK ARRANGEMENTS
AND COLLEGIAL INTERACTIONS

The rewards of teaching and certain aspects of teachers' work militate toward freedom from control. The spatial work arrangements for teaching —that is, the self-contained classroom—make it possible to achieve such freedom.

Teachers work separately from others during most of the day, and perform a wide variety of tasks for which they have almost sole responsibility. This lack of a division of labor means that teachers are not highly dependent upon other teachers in their daily work.

AUTONOMY-EQUALITY NORMS

Lortie points out that a set of norms exists to buttress the ecological separation of teachers, and the demand for autonomy that provides for maximization of classroom-related intrinsic rewards. The norms include: the teacher should be free from the interference of other adults while teaching, teachers should be considered and treated as equals (no merit pay or differentiated staffing), teachers should act in a nonintervening but friendly way toward one another. These three norms add up to the "autonomy-equality" pattern.[44]

This pattern has a number of consequences. It allows teachers to differ in their level of effort without having sanctions applied, favors variations in teaching style and content and allows teachers to express individual values and personality styles, weakens attempts to impose any single definition of "good teaching," encourages individualistic solutions, and, within limits, makes possible a laissez-faire, idiosyncratic approach to curriculum and classroom management.

TEACHER AUTONOMY AND THE
MISSION OF THE SCHOOL

Limits to the teacher's decision-making are set by national goals, the functions to be served by the school, knowledge in the academic fields, the professional culture, conditions in the teacher's immediate setting, and by decisions made in the local school system. Within the limits set by these conditions, though, the autonomy granted teachers could, theoretically, be extensive.

Some writers have concluded that teachers should be given large amounts of freedom from external constraints and freedom to express their own beliefs and values in the classroom.

In *The New School Executive,* Thomas Sergiovanni and Fred Carver state that the substantive goal of the school should be the self-actualization of students. Substantive and instrumental goals should be congruous. If the school holds as a goal the self-actualization of students, it should also hold this goal for teachers.[45]

They offer a prescription for school administration that will, supposedly, lead to the self-actualization of teachers. This will be accomplished through the creation of a social system "wide open" to suggestions from the teaching staff, not only as to the means of accomplishing school goals, but also in establishing and redirecting the goals themselves. The authors tell us that in order to fully bring out and utilize the human resources of the staff, the school leader must work towards "the liberalization and expansion of the zone of freedom so that the collective value system of the school is able to accommodate an assortment of individual belief systems."[46]

Let us examine this proposal. Suppose there existed a highly educated, professionally competent, motivation-seeking, self-actualizing staff of teachers who worked in a school where the community and administration delegated their own authority powers to the teaching staff, and gave them the mandate to meet the substantive goal of student self-actualization in individualistic ways.

What kind of experience would this provide for children? A child going through the grades might find himself or herself in classrooms using various approaches to learning, each with a different premise.

The first grade might follow the Montessori method. Its premise would be that children will self-actualize if their minds and senses are trained and disciplined in the early years. The teacher must carefully structure the environment to match the developmental needs and stages of children.

The second grade, with a Rousseauian, "free school" approach, would have the premise that children will self-actualize as they grow naturally with minimal adult intervention or structuring of the environment.

The third grade might follow the Skinnerian approach and premise that self-actualization can best be achieved if children's behavior is systematically "shaped." Adults should carefully structure the environment, norms, and rewards.

By fourth grade, there might be an open-education approach, with the premise that children will self-actualize most fully in an environment structured for play, discovery, creativity, and democratic problem-solving. The adult is a facilitator of learning who structures the environment and intervenes only when necessary.

In fifth grade, the child might find a realist approach. Its premise would be that self-actualization is best accomplished by mastering subject matter and the tools of thinking that will prepare children to function in the real world. It is not the child's interests that determine the curriculum, but the adult's perception of the child's needs. Therefore, the teacher must be highly directive.

Finally, in sixth grade, a classroom might follow the Rogerian approach, with the premise that self-actualization is best achieved by becoming in tune with one's inner world of personal meanings. The teacher is a nondirective leader.

Even without the "external constraints" placed upon the teacher by virtue of the public trust and bureaucratic principles of authority, the needs of children for continuity of experience make the Sergiovanni and Carver prescription one that is unlikely to lead to the substantive goal of student actualization, and consequently, not to the instrumental goal of teacher actualization. Teachers expressing highly individualistic values and using methods of instruction that do not coordinate with those of other teachers would find themselves having to redirect and retrain their new students each year. They would need to undo old patterns and habits before they could establish new ones. This would be a frustrating and probably ineffectual task.

When the common school was established a century ago, there was general agreement about its intended purposes. But, as the curriculum field progressed, curriculum workers had to grapple with the increasing complexity of Ralph Tyler's question, "What purposes should the school seek to obtain?" Today, that question is indeed complex. Will the school aim to foster conformity or creativity, to produce social activists or establishment people, intellectuals or practical people? Will it emphasize social skills or basic academic skills, flexibility or habits of discipline? Will it concentrate upon the arts or sciences, or balance the two?[47]

As Bruce Joyce remarks, the possible functions of education are so numerous that we need to impose a structure upon it.[48] This structure should enable us to articulate the central, unifying objectives of the school—that is, its mission. Furthermore, these objectives have to be linked with the means of achieving them. And as the technology of teaching becomes more elaborate and codified, and alternative means become as plentiful as ends, it will become even more essential that the school's staff achieve commitment to the school's mission and agree upon the way they will try to accomplish its goals.

SUMMARY AND IMPLICATIONS

In this chapter we have explored questions related to the issue of teacher autonomy. We noted that the notion that teachers must be given great latitude in the exercise of professional judgments is a contemporary one, and one that paralleled research on worker motivation, and the growth of teacher professionalization and teacher power. We noted that the demands made by some educators and leaders of teachers' unions that teachers be given "professional autonomy" is not warranted by teachers' professional status or their position in the authority structure of the school that mandates sharing control with other sources of authority.

Teacher autonomy also was analyzed in terms of its consequences for teacher professional self-actualization and organizational renewal. A certain amount of teacher autonomy not only is necessary for achieving the general goals of the school organization, but also is crucial in helping the organization adapt to its environment and to achieve an optimal level of integration.

Autonomy should not represent separation from a social context, however, nor activities that isolate a person from others. It should be "a force that binds people together."[49] This requires sharing of ideas and experiences by professional colleagues, and communication between and among teachers, administrators, and parents.

In the local situation, there are two kinds of teacher autonomy:collective—or colleague authority—and individual autonomy. In each category some kinds and amounts of autonomy are functional for teacher professional self-actualization and organizational renewal, and some dysfunctional.

There are various criteria for assessing how much and what kind of autonomy fills these dual and interrelated goals. Does the autonomy permit teachers to develop and express their own values and personal styles and be consistent with the values and needs of students, parents, and administrators? Does it lead to increased consensus among the three sources of authority and among the teaching staff about the school's mission and the means of achieving it? Does it enhance the development of shared meanings and goals? Does it bind people together? Does it increase the opportunity for collective problem-solving and conflict resolution among teachers, administrators, and other concerned individuals? Does it enhance the flexibility of individuals and the organization so that they can respond creatively to changed circumstances?

Using these criteria, it is possible to categorize certain kinds of autonomy as either functional or dysfunctional. On an individual basis, autonomy that takes the form of isolation from constructive supervision and colleague interactions is dysfunctional; autonomy that enables the teacher to experiment and innovate within the limits set by the overall mission of the school is functional.

In terms of collective teacher autonomy, or the principle of colleague authority, several generalizations might be made about dysfunctional and functional autonomy.

When dysfunctional autonomy exists among teachers, their authority ignores the values and expectations of the community, administrators' support or nonsupport, regularities in the school culture, or available resources. For example, teachers decide to transform the school overnight from a traditional to an open school, or to set up classes for gifted children without consulting the community, or to purchase a new set of textbooks when money is not available.

In another form of dysfunctional autonomy for teachers, authority restricts the flexibility of the individual teacher to innovate or participate in schoolwide events. Examples of this include restrictions placed upon the individual teacher by the negotiated contract as to how many faculty meetings a teacher may attend, or peer pressure to leave the building at three o'clock.

Or, authority may restrict the organization from adapting to changed circumstances. An illustration of this is a contract specification that mandates team-teaching in the first and second grades for the next three years.

Functional autonomy, in contrast, allows for authority that promotes the development of a professional community. Examples of this are the establishment of criteria by teachers for the selection of new staff members; peer evaluations; interclass peer observations and exchange of information based on these observations.

In functional autonomy, too, authority promotes improvements in program and curricula. This is illustrated by curriculum review councils including teachers, or strong teacher involvement in the design of the in-service program.

NOTES

1. See Jacob W. Getzels and Egon G. Guba, "Social Behavior and the Administrative Process," *School Review* 65 (Winter, 1957): 423-41.

2. Gary A. Griffin and Ann Lieberman, *Behavior of Innovative Personnel* (Washington, D.C.: ERIC Clearinghouse on Teacher Education, 1974), p. 6.

3. Albert Shanker, "Introduction," in Donald A. Myers, *A Bibliography on Professionalization and Collective Bargaining* (Washington, D.C.: American Federation of Teachers, 1974), p. 1.

4. David Selden, paraphrased in Robert A. Morgart, *Alienation in an Educational Context: The American Teacher in the Seventies?* paper presented at the Annual Meeting of the American Educational Research Association (Chicago: ERIC Clearinghouse, 1974), p. 67.

5. Fred E. Katz, *Autonomy and Organization: The Limits of Social Control* (New York: Random House, 1968), p. 4.

6. Ibid., p. 5.

7. Dan C. Lortie, "The Balance of Control and Autonomy in Elementary School

Teaching," in *The Semi-Professions and Their Organization* ed. Amatai Etzioni (New York: Free Press, 1969), p. 28; Robert Dreeben, *The Nature of Teaching: Schools and the Work of Teachers* (Glenview, Ill.: Scott, Foresman, & Co., 1970), pp. 85, 90; Sam D. Seiber, "Organizational Influences on Educational Innovation," in *Managing Change in Educational Organizations,* ed. J. Victor Baldridge and Terrence E. Deal (Berkeley, Calif.: McCutchan, 1975), pp. 85-86.

8. Abraham Maslow, *Eupsychian Management* (Homewood, Ill.: Irwin-Dorsey, 1965).

9. Frederick Herzberg, *Work and the Nature of Man* (New York: World, 1966).

10. Arthur W. Combs, *The Professional Education of Teachers: A Perceptual View of Teacher Preparation* (Boston: Allyn & Bacon, 1974), p. 38.

11. Howard S. Becker, "The Nature of a Profession," in *Education for the Professions,* Sixty-first Yearbook of the National Society for Study of Education, pt. 2 (Chicago: University of Chicago Press, 1962), pp. 27-40.

12. Ernest Greenwood, "Attributes of a Profession," in *Sociological Perspectives on Occupations,* ed. Ronald M. Pavalko (Itasca, Ill.: F.E. Peacock, 1972), pp. 3-16.

13. Ibid., p. 5.

14. Harold Wilensky, "The Professionalization of Everyone? *American Journal of Sociology* 70 (September 1964): 138.

15. George Ritzer, *Man and His Work: Conflict and Change* (New York: Appleton-Century-Croft, 1972), p. 61.

16. See Amatai Etzioni, *Modern Organizations* (Englewood Cliffs, N.J.: Prentice-Hall, 1964), p. 87. Seiber prefers the term "quasi-professional" and Leggatt "bureaucratic professional." See Seiber, "Organizational Influences on Educational Innovation," p. 75; and T. Leggatt, "Teaching as a Profession" in *Professions and Professionalization,* ed. J.A. Jackson (London: Cambridge University Press, 1970), p. 160.

17. Joseph Schwab, "The Practical: A Language for Curriculum," *School Review* 78 (November 1969): 8.

18. Dan C. Lortie, *Schoolteacher: A Sociological Study* (Chicago: University of Chicago Press, 1975), pp. 75-81.

19. Ibid., 136.

20. Ibid., Chap. 6; also see Philip Jackson, *Life in Classrooms* (New York: Holt, Rinehart, & Winston, 1968), chap. 4.

21. Leggatt, "Teaching as a Profession," p. 173.

22. Ibid., p. 161.

23. Richard L. Simpson and Ida Harper Simpson, "Women and Bureaucracy in the Semi-Professions," in *The Semi-Professions and Their Organization,* p. 247.

24. Ronald G. Corwin, "The New Teaching Profession," in *Teacher Education,* Seventy-fourth Yearbook of the National Society for the Study of Education, pt. 2 (Chicago: University of Chicago Press, 1975), p. 246.

25. Ibid.

26. Israel Gerver and Joseph Bensman, "Towards a Sociology of Expertness," *Social Forces* 32 (March 1954): 226-27.

27. Donald Myers, *Teacher Power: Professionalization and Collective Bargaining* (Lexington, Mass.: D.C. Heath, 1973), p. 19.

28. Robert Dreeben, *The Nature of Teaching: Schools and the Work of Teachers* (Glenview, Ill.: Scott, Foresman, 1970), chap. 4.

29. Schwab, "The Practical," p. 5.

30. Michael J. Dunkin and Bruce J. Biddle, *The Study of Teaching* (New York: Holt, Rinehart, & Winston, 1974).

31. Maxine Greene, *Teacher as Stranger: Educational Philosophy for the Modern Age* (Belmont, Calif.: Wadsworth, 1973).

32. Dwayne Huebner, "Curriculum Language and Classroom Meanings," in *Language and Learning*, ed. James B. MacDonald and Robert R. Leeper (Washington, D.C.: Association for Supervision and Curriculum Development, NEA, 1966), p. 14.

33. Sol M. Elkin, "Another Look at Collective Negotiations for Professionals," *School and Society* 98 (March 1970): 174.

34. Roland Barth, *Open Education and the American School* (New York: Agathon Press, 1973), chap. 3.

35. Ibid., p. 169.

36. Max Weber, *Economy and Society*, ed. G. Roth and C. Wittia (New York: Harper & Row, 1960).

37. Robert K. Merton, "Bureaucratic Structure and Personality," in *Reader in Bureaucracy*, ed. Robert K. Merton et al. (Glencoe, Ill.: Free Press, 1952), p. 365.

38. Dan C. Lortie, "The Teacher and Team Teaching: Suggestions for Long-Range Research." in *Managing Change in Educational Organizations*, p. 253.

39. Charles E. Bidwell, "The School as a Formal Organization," in *Handbook of Organizations*, ed. James G. March (Chicago: Rand McNally, 1965).

40. Corwin, "Professional Persons in Public Organizations," pp. 1-22.

41. Bidwell, "The School as a Formal Organization," p. 974.

42. Lortie, "The Teacher and Team Teaching," p. 257.

43. Lortie, "The Balance of Control and Autonomy," pp. 30-41.

44. Lortie, "The Teacher and Team Teaching," pp. 252-58.

45. Thomas J. Sergiovanni and Fred D. Carver, *The New School Executive: A Theory of Administration* (New York: Dodd, Mead, 1973), p. 36.

46. Ibid., p. 27.

47. Bruce Joyce, *Alternative Models of Elementary Education* (Lexington, Mass.: Blaisdell, 1969), pp. 53-54.

48. Ibid.

49. Katz, "Autonomy and Organization," p. 4.

Staff Development: Creating a Changed Future

8

AS WE HAVE SEEN, until the progressive era, the teacher frequently was considered a hired employee who, like a drone, would carry out policy determined by the public trust and the bureaucratic authority, or both. In-service education was based upon the premise that teachers had to overcome gross deficiencies in their attitudes, knowledge, and skills. Teachers attended institutes and workshops, took extension or summer school courses, and were given salary increments for college attendance. Where in-service courses were offered in the local setting, they focused upon organizational needs, such as implementing a new program, or using a new textbook brought in by an administration; or the courses attempted to overcome teachers' inadequacies, as perceived by superordinates.

In the progressive era, the purpose of in-service education shifted from upgrading the individual teacher's competency to that of promoting the professional growth of the entire school staff by engaging the staff in cooperative efforts to solve school problems. Teachers were encouraged to work on curriculum development, to serve on problem-solving committees, and to do action research; the theory was that such participation would increase the teachers' commitment to school goals and would facilitate school change.

Although concepts about in-service changed, old practices held tenaciously; even now, most in-service education focuses upon the individual teacher and aims to build knowledge and skills in anticipation of future use. Few in-service programs are related to an overall design for school renewal.

The lag between the awareness that in-service education ought to be directed toward school renewal and the change in in-service practices is due in large part to high teacher mobility and turnover until recent times. Since a principal could count on replacing as much as one-fifth of the staff each year,[1] it used to make more sense for a school district to hire people who would meet evolving organizational needs than to put resources into training people who were likely to leave shortly.

But now, and for the foreseeable future, mobility will be restricted due to a teacher surplus, the effects of teacher unionization, the need for multiple incomes per family—which results in an increased supply of available teachers, and the availability of maternity leaves.[2] Therefore, staff development has become a priority; school renewal can only be accomplished if existing staff members change sufficiently to be able to fulfill new organizational goals.

Staff development, then, is a concept that has been evolving during this century, but has come into its time only during the past few years. And like other new approaches, early attempts at making it work have not been markedly successful. These attempts, however, have given us insights about why they have failed, and about what is needed to make them succeed.

The contemporary period has been marked by attempts to make school change. The impetus has come from many sources—new national priorities, curriculum revision projects, federal programs, the courts and legislatures, community groups, university professors, and radical teachers. As we shall discuss in this chapter, studies indicate that attempts at change have run into many obstacles: federal programs have either not been implemented, or have been distorted by local districts; staff development projects have succeeded with teachers who felt the need for the training offered, but have failed with those who did not. Other programs have succeeded in motivating the staff to accept an innovation, but failed to get the innovation implemented or adopted in the school system. Still others succeeded in getting an innovation implemented only to have it later deteriorate because of parental opposition.

A multiplicity of factors caused these unfortunate outcomes; generally, failure to create change in any particular setting was a result of many interacting factors. Much of this failure, however, was due to the use of inadequate models of staff development.

Staff development plans usually are predicated upon the assumption that there is a chain of command in the school organization that makes it possible to move policy down the line in a linear, rational, and efficient manner. The presumed hierarchy of influence is represented by the formal organizational chart.

According to the model shown in figure 1, the community elects the school board and thereafter bows to its policy judgments, since the board is the duly elected representative body of authority. The board then hires a superintendent of schools to put its policies into effect. The superintendent and his staff delegate decision-making authority for each school to the prin-

Fig. 1: Formal Authority Relationships

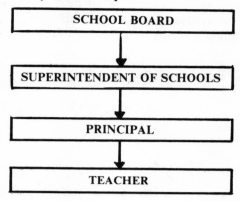

In the presumed hierarchy of influence in the schools, policy moves down in a linear way.

cipals, who develop their schools within the guidelines established by the central administration. Finally, the teacher, who had no say in policy-setting, implements the plans in the classroom.

In such a model, there is a separation between policy-making and implementation. The board has major responsibility for setting goals, presumably in line with the will of the people in the community. As authority moves down the line, there is less concern and responsibility for ends, and more responsibility for means.

This is not a bad ideal picture—everyone in the hierarchy has clearly delineated roles and responsibilities, and a spirit of rationality prevails. If this organizational chart represented reality, the major staff development task would be to educate and train the staff.

The assumption underlying staff development approaches based on this model is that if the teaching staff understands the school's goals, and can acquire the attitudes, knowledge, and skills required to implement them, the goals will be met. It is further assumed that teachers, being functionaries concerned only with means and not ends, will be able to adopt the necessary attitudes and values once they understand that they are necessary to meet school goals.

As we will see in this chapter, the literature on school change indicates that staff development approaches based upon these assumptions are not highly successful. We conclude that they fail, in part, because the model of the formal organizational chart does not match contemporary realities.

Today, although the formal (and legal) structure for decision-making is hierarchical and bureaucratic, the de facto state of affairs might be more accurately diagrammed as it is in figure 2.

Fig. 2: The Three Principles of Authority in the Contemporary Era

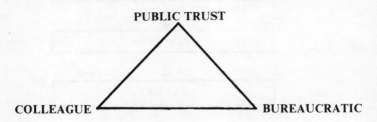

In today's actual structure for making decisions, each source of authority claims a right to frame policy.

The points of the triangle shown in figure 2 frequently represent points of conflict. Each source of authority is claiming a right to frame policy, and is struggling to establish—or retain—its own power prerogatives.

SHORTCOMINGS OF STAFF DEVELOPMENT MODELS

Staff development models often have one, or more, of various short-comings: (1) they are politically unrealistic; they are based on anachronistic assumptions about authority prerogatives; (2) they are overcommitted to rational strategies of change that focus upon organizational goals; thus they fail to take into account adequately the behavioral regularities in the school and its environment, and the need to make personal and normative changes; and (3) they are overcommitted to making personal change and thus do not make provision for organizational accommodation to these changes.

If the aim of staff development is to create a changed future condition, then the political question of who decides what this future condition shall be is crucial, especially in an era characterized by aggressive claims by diverse groups for a voice in policy-making. The issue is often ignored because old assumptions about authority are uncritically accepted, although they are no longer tenable, as we have seen.

Strategies based upon the bureaucratic model tend to accept "rational" assumptions about change; they optimistically assume that an innovation deemed good and beneficial by school board members, or the superintendent of schools will be embraced by teachers and implemented by them if they can acquire the necessary knowledge, attitudes, and skills. This may have been a reasonable assumption when the aims and functions of the school were relatively simple, and people generally agreed upon them; today, the plurality of goals means that there is disagreement about what is desirable. The proliferation of alternative methods of achieving goals means that there also is disagreement about how to accomplish what is desired.

Staff development models that are based upon rational strategies of change ignore the diversity and stability of individual values found in school staffs. They also insufficiently account for the diverse needs, aspirations, personality traits, self-interests, norms, habits, and existing behaviors of groups and individuals who are to make the change, or will be affected by the change. These factors are powerful variables that affect the acceptance or rejection of an innovation, and these factors are not easily manipulated.

As discussed in the previous chapter, the ends of teaching are value-based, and much less exclusively technical than other professions. The work is characterized by intangible goals and multiple and controversial assessment criteria. Thus, teachers are able to select goals and means, and evaluation criteria congruous with their own values and priorities. An innovation proven effective for certain objectives may be rejected by teachers because these objectives do not represent high-priority goals for them. Some of the evidence we will look at suggests that the assumption that there is a unitary set of values held by school people is incorrect, as is the assumption that teachers' values are extremely malleable.

In addition, rational approaches tend to ignore political realities. As we have seen, shifts in authority prerogatives and relationships mean that administrators have less sanctioning power, and teachers have more power to resist superordinate directives. More than ever, teachers have to be persuaded, not told, to implement innovations because of teachers' increased professional role conceptions, their demand for colleague authority or professional autonomy—or both, and teacher power that buttresses these demands and protects recalcitrant teachers.

Aside from the authority issue, rational strategies have other shortcomings. Goals and objectives are specified in advance, as is the sequence of steps toward their achievement. This approach incorrectly assumes a simplistic model of the school, in that it ignores the regularities—values, norms, habits, organizational structures, and rewards—in the school, which need to be changed before an innovation will be accepted, implemented, or incorporated. It also fails to account for the variables activated once the change process is set into motion; these variables alter the overall gestalt, making it impossible to predict in advance precisely what will happen.

The shortcomings of rational strategies of change have been noticed by many people who want to make changes and are aware of the necessity of personal and interpersonal change in order to foster school renewal. Some models of staff development thus focus upon changing the perceptions, attitudes, values, and problem-solving skills of individuals and groups. These have been referred to as "normative-reeducative strategies."[3] Examples of these strategies are: sensitivity training, Organizational Development, and T-groups. These approaches start with the premise that patterns of behavior are supported by sociocultural norms and by commitments on the part of individuals to these norms, as well as that school change requires that old normative orientations give way to new. In order for an innovation to be implemented, individuals have to modify their old attitudes and values, and to create norms that are in line with the innovation. Some normative-reeducative strategies have succeeded in making personal change. Individual and intergroup change, however, does not necessarily lead to organizational change.

Because the school is a social system composed of interdependent and interrelated parts, a change in one subsystem must be adjusted to by other subsystems if an innovation is to be successfully implemented and incorporated. Some of these subsystems are: goals, environment, technology, formal structure, and group and individual processes.[4] Therefore, any attempt at creating a changed future condition simultaneously has to deal with all relevant subsystems.

Students of change processes say that there are three distinct stages in successful change: initiation, implementation, and incorporation, or adoption. Successful initiation requires "unfreezing"[5] old perceptions and creating enough disequilibrium in those who are to implement the change to make them willing to accept it on some level. Sometimes this involves only providing new information, but often it requires a more extensive process aimed at overcoming resistance. The initiation stage has been given a great deal of consideration by organizational theorists, since some commitment to an innovation is clearly crucial to its successful implementation.

Recently, though, people have seen that "unfreezing," while essential, is insufficient to make successful change. Research indicates that the next step, implementation or changing, requires alterations in individual and group perceptions, attitudes and values, norms, and usual patterns of behavior. It also requires organizational adjustments: time, space, and materials need to be reorganized; rewards for new behavior must replace rewards for old;

administrators must support experimentation and new goals; resources must be provided; and rules and procedures must be realigned. Commitment to an innovation requiring that teachers plan together, such as team-teaching, will be insufficient to make it work if time is not provided for this during the school day; curriculum development projects based on teacher involvement will fail if the negotiated contract limits teachers' meetings to two per semester.

Although it is true that organizational change does not take place without appropriate changes in staff members' behavior, it is also true that the amount and kind of change that is possible for any individual is circumscribed by the amount and kind of organizational change that occurs. Jacob Getzels and Egon Guba have pointed out that individual behavior has two dimensions: the idiographic and monothetic. The former refers to the personal traits of the individual—personality and needs-disposition; monothetic refers to those behaviors shaped by the institution—role, expectation, and institutional goals. A change that takes place in the idiographic dimension as a result of new insights may not be expressed in behavior if changes in monothetic variables do not also occur.[6] For example, teachers who decide they would like to have more equal relationships with their pupils may find that institutional expectations about their role may force them to retain an authoritarian stance, as discussed previously in the Barth case.

In short, a staff development plan aimed at creating a changed future condition requires a process of mutual adjustment among persons, the organization, and the change desired. This adaptation will occur at each stage of the change process. In the initiation stage, acceptance of the innovation will depend upon its congruency with existing regularities: open classroom will mean something different to teachers in Scarsdale than it does to those in Ocean Hill-Brownsville. In order for both teacher groups to be committed to it, they will need to interpret it in the light of the particularities of their own situation. As people attempt to implement the innovation, it will have to be reinterpreted in line with unanticipated events: meanings will be revised, new norms created, and organizational adjustments made. In order for this to happen, the system has to be extremely flexible; procedures, rules, attitudes, ways of getting and dealing with feedback, and other aspects of the system must support this adaptive process.

It has been said that organizational renewal is best accomplished through self-actualizing individuals; but the degree to which an individual can self-actualize is, in part, a function of environmental conditions. Teacher actualization and organizational renewal are interrelated, not isolated, concepts. As many philosophers, psychologists, and sociologists have written, man's relationship with the environment is transactional—that is, one both shapes and is shaped by the environment. The teacher not only is a unique person, but a member of a school staff, and part of the community that comprises the school's environment. In order to fully realize professional potential, a teacher's work must be in tune with the needs, expectations, and values of others in the school and its environment, and must be supported by organizational elements such as rewards, resources, norms, and structures. On the other hand, the system must be open to influences stemming from the teacher's uniqueness.

If self-actualization is, as Maslow said, "becoming the best one can become" then the school that provides the opportunity for this is one allowing the teacher to contribute to shaping the environment, and to be shaped by it in a way that promotes professional growth.

If, as we shall see, adults' values are stable and not very malleable, and individual growth potential is greatest when the environment is compatible with an individual's values, then it follows that professional self-actualization is most likely to take place in an organization where superordinate goals are congruous with those of the people who are to implement them.

Organizational renewal is, in part, a function of the opportunity for professional self-actualization available to teachers. It is also a function of the organization's ability to change constructively at the same time it is evolving towards becoming a more integrated and more mature social system. School renewal requires that the school's mission become clarified, and that teachers and others become increasingly committed to it; in addition, it requires that the mission itself become transformed as people get new insights and perspectives and are influenced by changes occurring within and outside of the school. This dynamic process of change requires that organizational goals be compatible with the needs, values, expectations, and goals of the people in the school and its environment, and also that the process of change be gradual and incremental so that the organization and the people related to it can adjust at each step of the change.

This transactional, evolutionary, incremental approach is more conservative than many that have been tried. Some federal staff development projects aimed at making massive changes within a relatively short time, with the assumption that the people and organization rapidly would adjust to new demands stemming from the innovation. Other change efforts, like the one described by Louis Smith and Pat Keith, attempted to introduce an "alternative of grandeur" involving large-scale, simultaneous alterations in multiple components.[7] As we shall see, the evidence, unfortunately, suggests that the likelihood of affecting change in schools is low when such approaches are used. There are regularities in the school and its environment.

Teachers, administrators, and community members have values and expectations. These are reflected in patterns of behavior, conflicts among groups, and organizational arrangements. Any change has to be assimilated slowly so that the process of mutual adaption can take place. A staff development plan that provides for this process to occur must have three minimal foci: political, personal, and organizational.

Politically, the plan must be based on a realistic assessment of the values, needs, expectations, and existing regularities in the school and its environment. A salient aspect of the political condition is that of authority: who makes what decisions and how.

At the personal level, the plan must take into account the diversity and stability of values held by those who are to implement change, and to provide for readaptation of the staff.

Its organizational focus must provide changes in organizational subsystems—rewards, norms, technology, structures, procedures—in pari passu with evolutionary changes in the staff's goals; conversely, it must provide changes in organizational subsystems in order to effect changes in the staff's perceptions, attitudes, values, and goals.

So far in this book, we have explored one of the three shortcomings of staff development models: political. We noted that staff development models that are unrealistic about authority prerogatives are not likely to be effective.

In this chapter, we will examine the other two shortcomings. We will look at the models that focus almost exclusively on making personal change, and those that emphasize organizational goals and underplay the need to deal with personal change. In order to provide the background for this analysis, we will first review the historical development of the concept of staff development and current models of staff development. Then, we will look at the literature on personal and organizational change for insights about why staff development models that are overcommitted to either personal change or organizational goals are inadequate; finally, we will analyze case studies and other research related to various models of change.

HISTORICAL REVIEW OF IN-SERVICE EDUCATION

In-service education, from its inception in 1839, has been based upon the assumption that training before teaching begins cannot adequately prepare the teacher for the tasks of teaching. The concept of what those tasks entail, though, has changed radically; thus, the goals of in-service education have altered with changes in perceptions about the teacher's role.

From the middle of the seventeenth century to the last quarter of the nineteenth century, teachers' educational needs were considered obvious and easy to identify. As ideas changed about the aims and values of education, the nature of the learner and learning, and the functions of the school, and as advances were made in the fields of knowledge, questions relating to teachers' needs became more complex. Consequently, the goals of in-service education have become more controversial and problematical.

Until 1890, public schools were staffed by untrained, poorly educated, and often incompetent teachers. Many had no more than a common school education and a meager knowledge of subject matter. There were few or no requirements for certification, in part, because the demand for teachers exceeded the supply.

Before 1890, too, in-service education was directed towards correcting teachers' inadequate command of subject matter and their lack of professional skills. In the late nineteenth century, new demands were placed upon the schools; the goals of public education expanded beyond basic academic, vocational, and technical skills, and limited subject matter. In 1870, the influential William Tory Harris declared that education is the process "by which the individual is elevated into the species." The objective of the curriculum should be to make accumulated wisdom economically and systematically available to children. Harris's prescription for the curriculum reflected a change in the demands that were being placed upon schools, and thus upon teachers' competency.

From 1890 to the 1930s, the emphasis in in-service education was on upgrading teachers' cultural and professional skills and knowledge. The teacher institute, which was the primary means of in-service education in the previous period, continued to flourish, although it was coming under criticism by better educated teachers who rebelled against programs that duplicated pre-service training. Newer agencies for in-service emerged: summer normal schools, extension courses, and teachers' reading circles became prevalent.

The need of the schools to meet new demands, new developments in the curriculum field, and a new understanding of the learning process led to new thinking about teachers' educational needs. There was a rapid upgrading of teachers during this period. This was reflected in the rise of admission requirements of teacher-training institutes, an extension and enrichment of pre-service programs, and an adoption of higher standards for certification.

A change in administrative-supervisory approaches also took place. The shift went from inspection and criticism to helping teachers find new methods of instruction. During this period, supervision developed as a more important function of administration. Superintendents of schools increasingly delegated supervisory functions to head teachers freed from classroom duties, teaching specialists, and supervisors of special classes and functions. Teacher improvement was seen as the major task of supervision.

Although the earlier assumption that teachers could not, without help, analyze and correct their own weaknesses was becoming less tenable, direction from superordinates continued to be the guiding principle in most in-service programs. During this period of scientific-management, the supervisory staff was still the authority that determined the curriculum and teaching methods. Supervisors rated teachers on the basis of whether they successfully taught prescribed material by prescribed methods. Teachers became very much oriented to the authority of superordinates who defined the organization's goals. Teachers were considered specialists in classroom practice, as long as they stayed within the directives given by administrators.

From the 1930s to the mid-1950s, a new understanding of personality theory was reflected in the curriculum, in administrative theory, and in supervisory practices. Supervision focused upon the development of morale. The idea that direction by an expert was the best way of improving worker performance was modified. The approach changed to "human relations" or guidance. New programs of in-service education based on group activity led by a group member were implemented. Greater freedom for the teacher to experiment was reflected in the establishment of curriculum planning committees and policy-making boards, in which teachers participated.

In the mid-1950s, the workshop emerged as the panacea for in-service education. Except for college and university courses, the workshop had become the most widespread technique utilized for continuing education for teachers. The workshop normally consisted of a number of teachers acting in concert with resource persons and a director under conditions that were designed to provide for individual growth via group interaction. In theory there was no preplanned or arbitrary schedule of activities; participants worked on problems of their choice under the leadership of workshop members.

Action research—research done by teachers in order to improve their performance—also emerged during this period. This approach attests to the presence of an emerging concept that teachers did possess the intelligence and creativity to identify and research their own problems, as well as the motivation to do so.

There was a growing emphasis on assessing the needs of teachers, but this was done almost always by asking teachers and their supervisors what they thought teachers needed. To research in-service purposes, content, methods, and attitudes and needs of teachers, special techniques were devised and used: problem checksheets, attitude rating scales, inventories of instructional practices, opinion surveys, questionnaires, checklists, and other materials. The assumption underlying these procedures was that in-service education should grow out of the needs teachers felt.

The greater focus upon the needs of teachers, the concept of supervision as guidance, and an emerging emphasis upon democratic and participative planning did not occur until after teacher education and professionalization had advanced to the point where teachers became specialists in classroom practice. The concept of in-service could then evolve from that of training individual teachers to attempts by teachers, supervisors, administrators, and others to solve common problems.

Although thinking about the purpose of in-service education changed, actual practice did not change noticeably even up until the present time.

CURRENT MODELS OF IN-SERVICE STAFF DEVELOPMENT

The most common model of in-service education is individualistic. A common practice is to encourage teacher continuing education by offering released time or salary increments, or both, for a variety of professional growth activities, such as attendance at conferences and workshops, taking college and university courses, and travel. Underlying this approach is an assumption that "any professional development activity that a teacher undertakes singly or with other teachers after receiving her or his initial teaching certificate and after beginning professional practice" will add to a teacher's competency and should be rewarded.[8]

The individualistic approach has persisted for several reasons. It is congruous with historical models of in-service such as the teachers' institute, summer schools, extension courses, and workshops. It has been supported by the NEA, which has encouraged individual teachers to follow their own interests and needs in order to open up their own future and to increase their material benefits. Finally, the individualistic approach fits in with practical realities—it has been uneconomical for school districts to support staff development programs for a staff with a high rate of turnover.

Various factors have changed the thinking about the purpose of in-service education, as we have seen. These include lower teacher mobility and increased teacher commitment to career.

The shift has been from rewarding any professional growth activity to providing "continuous training that a teacher needs as a result of being assigned to certain teaching situations."[9]

Despite this shift, new models of staff development have not succeeded in harmonizing personal and organizational change in the pursuit of school renewal. Current models tend to fall into two categories: those having a personal change bias, and those having an organizational bias.

Personal Change Bias

Models with a personal change bias focus upon the improvement of individuals and groups in the school, on the assumption that better teachers will make a better school. Some of these models emphasize upgrading individual skills, knowledge, or attitudes assumed to be needed by teachers in the school. The needs selected for treatment may be those perceived by teachers' superordinates, a person exercising leadership for changes, or the teacher himself or herself. Examples of such models are: microteaching, which concentrates on a particular skill, such as questioning or explaining; advisory approaches, which provide help to the individual teacher according to needs felt by the teacher; and interaction analysis, which attempts to improve the individual teacher's classroom communication skills.

Another set of models with a personal change bias focuses upon changing the behavior of individuals and groups through clarification and reconstruction of their values and interpersonal behavior. These models often involve the intervention of a change agent who leads people through the change process. Examples of such models are: the National Training Laboratory (NTL) approach, which involves experimenters and subjects in the study of their own developing interpersonal and group behavior within a laboratory setting; T-groups, which focus upon the improvement of the problem-solving processes used by work groups; and Organizational Development, which focuses upon how people relate to one another in an organization, and aims at improving skills of problem-solving and communication, as well as at promoting openness to change and willingness to transform the organization.

Organizational Goals Bias

Models with an organizational goals bias emphasize developing the skills teachers need to carry out organizational goals determined by the school board or central office staff.

Examples of such models are: Needs-Assessment Competency-Based Teacher Education (CBTE) designs that entail identifying the competencies that teachers should have in order to carry out the school's program, and designing a program of teacher improvement based upon these competencies; specific program training, which helps teachers use a new textbook or program such as *Man, A Course of Study* (MACOS), or the

American Association for the Advancement of Science's *A Process Approach* (AAAS); and Federal change agent programs, which attempt to create local change in response to a national priority. These are usually based upon rational assumptions about change—that is, that a well-researched and developed innovation will be diffused throughout a school system if trainees can be given the appropriate attitudes, knowledge, and skills.

Both of these approaches to staff development have their strengths and weaknesses. Their weaknesses essentially are overcommitment to the assumptions that underlie the approach, and their neglect of assumptions underlying the other approach.

There are some models, however, that attempt to harmonize personal and organizational change. For example, the teacher center brings teachers together to work on curriculum development and other school-related problems and concerns, and provides in-service training in line with local needs and needs and interests felt by teachers. While overcoming some of the one-sidedness of the models described above, the teacher center often is unsuccessful for another reason: it does not always provide for political contingencies. For example, if the center does not provide a structure for decision-making about the goals of training, what often happens is that staff developers from the teacher center find themselves in conflict with district curriculum coordinators or administrators, or the teachers' union.

Organizational Bias: A Look at the Literature on Personal Change

Staff development programs that focus upon organizational goals often are based upon the assumption that the power of the innovation introduced will be the determining factor in its acceptance—that is, if it can be demonstrated that a particular change will promote student learning or creativity, or some other goal deemed important by a person working toward change, teachers will accept it and willingly strive to implement it. This rational assumption is not always warranted. Whether or not teachers are resistant or receptive to an innovation is a function not only of the merits of the innovation, but also of the teachers' own values, personality traits, and needs.

Research indicates how these latter factors influence acceptance or rejection of an innovation by an individual.

Personality characteristics make an individual generally resistant or accepting of change. Authoritarian personalities, for example, have been shown to be more resistant to change than democratic personalities.[10] A fear of failure, unwillingness to admit personal weaknesses, and a lack of self-esteem or feelings of competence also are associated with resistance to change.

In terms of specific innovations, those that require a modification of one of the important needs within an individual are likely to be rejected, while those that require only modifications of peripheral or less important needs are more likely to be accepted. Threats to one's self-image, status, or security also will negatively affect receptivity to an innovation.[11]

Values are a vital component of the behavioral change process. An innovation that is incongruous with a person's long-term, deeply held values and beliefs will be rejected, and one that appears to make a person's values more operational will be appealing.

As we have seen, values underlie all but the most trivial educational innovations. The Barth case, discussed previously, indicates what may happen if an innovation is not harmonious with community values. Mismatches of innovations with teachers' values also stymie change, since values are closely related to other components of the behavioral system and because they are stable and not very malleable.

Values: Some Definitions and Attributes

Milton Rokeach defines a value as: "An enduring belief that a specific mode of conduct or end-state of existence is personally or socially preferable to an opposite or converse mode of conduct or end-state of existence."[12] A value is a prescriptive or proscriptive belief—that is, a belief "wherein some means or end of action is judged to be desirable or undesirable."[13]

Values have cognitive, affective, and behavioral components. A value is a cognition about the desirable; it is affective in the sense that a person can feel emotional about it, be affectively for or against it, approve of those who exhibit positive instances of it, and disapprove of those who exhibit negative instances of it. A value has a behavioral component: it is an intervening variable in that it leads to action when energized. Values are related to attitudes, needs, interests and social norms. An individual's values are ordered into a value-system wherein each value is ordered in priority with respect to other values in terms of what is more desirable or what is desired. A value-orientation is a philosophical position within a specific dimension, such as, "human nature is good."[14]

Values and Innovations

What is valued as an end or a means of achieving agreed-upon ends by one teacher or administrator may not be valued by others. The differences in teachers' value orientations have been demonstrated by studies comparing alternative approaches to teaching.

Research on open classroom teachers indicates that there are indeed differences in the values of open and traditional teachers, and that these differences are reflected in personality traits, needs, and interests, as well as the kinds of social norms established by them in the classroom.

In a study of teachers' values, Anne Bussis and Edward Cittenden found that while there was considerable overlap and variability, distinct differences were found between open and traditional teacher groups. Teachers had different expectations for children, saw their role differently, and held different attitudes toward freedom, choice, equality, self-control, and the importance of self-expression and imagination. Open classroom teachers stressed individuality, self-actualization, and trust, and saw the world as changing progressively. Traditional teachers placed higher priority upon obedience and self-control, and emphasized academic achievement over self-expression.[15]

We turn now to another question: how malleable are adults' values? Or, can teachers be "given" a new set of attitudes and values as easily as they can be given new knowledge and skills?

The Stability of Values

Contrary to the rational assumptions underlying many approaches to making school change, a person's value system represents a fairly stable reference point in the normal course of events. Although attitudes and interests do change with experience and exposure to new ideas, values are highly stable and quite resistant to change.

Research on the values of college students indicates that even a powerful experience like college does not markedly alter a person's value orientation. Though Philip Jacob found that students' values do change to some extent during college, and for some students the change is substantial, most are surface changes that do not alter the essential standards by which students govern their lives. The values with which they arrive, which are integral elements of their personality, are still there when they leave. Students may have modified their opinions and learned how to get along with others, but most remain fundamentally the same persons, and they tend to make the same value judgments.[16]

Other researchers have found that where values do change, it is in the direction of strengthening original values; personal change is more likely to take place in a college situation that develops, extends, and makes workable a student's already established value orientation than in a situation that is in conflict with it.

In one study, incoming freshmen were given the Allport-Vernon-Lindsey *Study of Values* scale. The same men were given the scale again in May of their senior year, and they were then grouped according to their major field. The researcher found that there were characteristic differences in the patterns of value scores among different curriculum groups at the time of entrance to college, before they had selected a major field. In their senior year, differences in values were found. These differences, however, represented a strengthening of the values that characterized each curriculum group as freshmen. The scores did not tend to regress towards the mean.[17]

It is likely that value orientations are well established by the time a person enters college. Where the individual's educational or work environment is highly supportive of this value orientation, changes will occur in the direction of an accentuation of core values. Where the environment is in marked conflict with this value orientation, the individual will either leave it or comply with the demands of the environment without changing.[18]

Adult Socialization

An adult's values and commitments have been shaped by a process of socialization whereby the individual "is prepared, with varying degrees of success, to meet the requirements that society has set for his behavior in a variety of situations."[19] This behavior, developed as a result of cumulative experiences, is highly resistant to change; socialization is a much stronger force in the personal system than beliefs developed through gaining new knowledge. Therefore, it is likely that past history is the best predictor of future behavior, unless some fairly powerful interventions take place.

Orville Brim says that adult socialization frequently requires a replacement of old response patterns by new ones, or the creation of new combinations of old response elements.

A major aspect of adult socialization involves the taking on of new roles in marriage or in a career. Past experience and socialization can only partially prepare an individual for being a parent, or assuming a new work role.

Brim explains that there are three things persons require in order to perform satisfactorily in a role. They must *know* what is expected of them (in behavior and values); they must *be able* to meet the role requirements, and must *be motivated* to perform the role. He presents the following paradigm to describe aspects of changes in socialization:

	Behavior	Values
knowledge	A	B
ability	C	D
motivation	E	F

A&B: The individual knows what behavior is expected and what ends should be pursued.
E&F: The individual is motivated to behave in appropriate ways and to pursue designated values.
C&D: The individual is able to carry out the behavior and to hold appropriate values.[20]

Many programs of staff development focus upon Cell A. They deal primarily with overt behavior in the role and do not attempt to change basic values or motivation. This is unsatisfactory in that merely conforming behavior is unimaginative and limited, and is unlikely to persist.

In order for C & D to be accomplished, the individual must have knowledge, motivation, and the appropriate values. Therefore, any staff development plan that hopes to alter behavior must deal with attitudes, values, expectations, role changes, and even self-concepts, as well as knowledge and skills.

Many philosophers, psychologists, and sociologists have posited that the process of attitude and value change involves a dynamic interaction between old values and new requirements. Theories such as Dewey's "reconstruction of experience," Leon Festinger's "cognitive dissonance," Carl Rogers' "development of congruence," Theodore M. Newcomb's "strain for symmetry," Heider's "balance theory," Harry Helson's "adaptation level theory," and Nevitt Stanford's construct of "differentiation and integration" all hypothesize that development occurs as people encounter new conditions that create internal disharmony or dissonance, out of which a newer and more mature equilibrium is established.[21]

As we saw in the Barth case, however, an environment too incongruous with an individual's value orientation will lead to either conflict between the individual and the situation, unstable and superficial compliance, or to the person's leaving the situation. On the other hand, an environment congruous with the person's value-orientation may have the greatest potential to change behavior, as long as it creates sufficient disequilibrium within the individual to motivate him or her to clarify and reconstruct his or her values, and to try out new behaviors.

Implications: Participation and Power-Equalization

Staff development programs that focus exclusively on organizational goals and neglect the need to resocialize those who are to implement the desired change assume incorrectly that the critical variables in making change are convincing the staff of the efficacy of the innovation, and providing the requisite training.

This approach is naive in that it assumes that human motivations are "rational" and will not be influenced by idiosyncratic needs, self-interests, personality traits, and values.

Since educational innovations are value-based, values are important intervening variables in the acceptance or rejection of an innovation by staff members, as well as in their ability to carry it out. Since adults' values are stable and not particularly malleable, an innovation congruous with a person's value orientation is more likely to be accepted and to be properly implemented than one that is incongruous and requires massive value changes.

This is probably why participation in setting goals has been found to lead to more successful change than when goals are set unilaterally by superordinates. Since people are apt to make decisions in line with their existing value orientations, they are more likely to be more committed to these decisions, and to require less resocialization in order to implement them.

The principle of power-equalization holds: planned change is more likely to be successful when decision-making power is shared by all people at all levels of authority. Its underlying assumptions are: that people who are alienated from an organization will be reluctant to undertake the commitment necessary to change it (people blindly committed to an organization will have the same reluctance); that participation will minimize alienation and reduce the threat involved when innovations are unilaterally introduced by superordinates; and that consequently, subordinates will be more apt to cooperate in the agreed-upon changes.[22]

Another implication of the research on personal change is that it is probably easier to implement an innovation that is in line with existing values than to change values in line with an innovation. This suggests that goals of change ought to be conservative about the amount of change they hope to make in people, on the premise that a small amount of successful change is better than no change at all. This research also suggests that when radical behavioral change is required by an innovation, strategies of personal change and socialization are mandatory.

The Person Bias: A Look at the Literature on School Change

Perhaps the most prevailing strategy for change implicit in current reform programs is based upon the assumptions that institutions are the reflections of the people who operate them, and consequently, institutions can best be changed by changing people responsible for managing them.[23]

While it is true that organizational change is heavily dependent upon personal change, staff development strategies that focus primarily or exclusively upon personal change have several essential failings: they place too much faith in the malleability of persons; they incorrectly assume that changes in attitudes, knowledge, and skills invariably lead to behavioral change; they fail to realize that personal change is limited by the characteristics of the organization; and they ignore the necessity to change organizational variables in line with changes taking place in persons.

Paul Lawrence and Jay Lorsch diagram the relationship between the individual and the organization as shown in figure 3. How an individual is motivated to behave in a specific organizational position is a function of the developmental history of the individual as well as the nature of the organizational context.[24]

Fig. 3: The Individual Organizational Interface

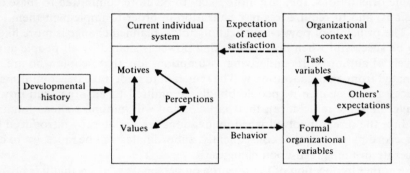

Paul R. Lawrence/Jay W. Lorsch, DEVELOPING ORGANIZATIONS: DIAGNOSIS AND ACTION, © 1969, Addison-Wesley, Reading, Massachusetts. Fig. 5, p 70. Reprinted with permission.

The behavior of people in organizations has different determinants from behavior outside of organizations; therefore, modifications in behavior within organizations require different strategies from those useful in private life. Insights can only lead to behavioral change if people's situations enable them to control the other variables that must be altered if change is to take place. Often, this is not the case in organizations. Daniel Katz and Robert Kahn note that change agents who focus on changing people in groups in organizations assume an incorrect chain of events. They assume that the individual will be provided with new insights and knowledge; these will produce some significant alteration in the individual's motivational pattern; these insights then will be retained when the person returns to the usual organizational role; the person will be able to adapt his new knowledge to the real-life situation; and the individual will be able to persuade co-workers to accept these changes and to change their behavior accordingly.[25]

As we shall see, studies on normative-reeducative strategies that make these assumptions indicate that because linkages between these events are not provided, the chain of events is not completed. Furthermore, even if those linkages are provided, and the individual moves from step one to step five, it does not necessarily mean that organizational change will take place.

Seymour Sarason has remarked that "the more things change the more they stay the same."[26] In schools, change limited to one subsystem can result in a preservation of the status quo. The school is a social system with subsystems so interrelated that a change in one subsystem affects other relevant subsystems. An innovation requires changes not only in one subsystem, but in an interlocking set of subsystems. Since the regularities that exist in the school are functional, there is pressure in the system to maintain the status quo, especially where the innovation will require alterations in highly valued or highly needed regularities. Therefore, where a change program focuses upon one subsystem to the neglect of important other subsystems—as illustrated by the Federal change agent projects to be discussed—the innovation becomes drastically modified to fit in with old patterns, and change does not take place.

As J. Victor Baldridge and Terrence Deal point out:

Educational change engages all the subsystems that together comprise complex educational organizations.
   These include the goals, the environment, the formal system or structure, and the technology of the organization, as well as individuals and groups in an informal system of relationships. These various organizational subsystems are related in systematic ways. Any subsystem can pressure another subsystem to change. A changing environment, for example, affects educational goals, technology, and the formal structure. A changing formal structure interacts with informal relationships.[27]

Just as one subsystem can pressure another to change, it can prevent another from changing as well. For example, two teachers may want to team-teach but lose their motivation when the required additional planning time can only be bought by giving up their lunch periods. Another teacher might try open classroom only to find that the teachers in her wing are outraged by the extra noise. A teacher who elects to take a leadership role in curriculum development may be contacted by the union representative with the message that such enthusiasm is making it "bad" for future negotiations.

In short, successful change requires simultaneous attention to all relevant subsystems. Change in people leads to organizational change only if organizational features—structures, norms, rewards, supports, and resources—also can change in conjunction with the changes taking place in persons.

Implementing Innovations

As we have previously noted, the first stage of the change process—initiation—requires that an innovation be accepted on some level by those who are to implement it; without a minimal commitment to the innovation, implementation does not take place. Because this is such a critical step, researchers and change agents have paid a great deal of attention to this stage and to strategies aimed at overcoming initial resistance. But, as indicated by a case study of an attempt to make school change, by Neal Gross, Joseph Giacquinta, and Marilyn Bernstein, failure to implement innovations cannot simply be explained by "initial resistance." Efforts to inform people about the innovation and to inspire them to be willing to try it is a necessary, but not sufficient, step.

These researchers documented the process of changing from a traditional to an individualized approach in an elementary school. Teachers were then expected to emphasize the process, more than the content of learning, to allow pupils maximum freedom in choosing their own activities, and to provide a rich environment stocked with a variety of self-instructional materials. Teachers would have new role prescriptions. They were to be facilitators of learning, rather than instructors in the conventional sense.

The individualized instruction innovation was introduced into a very favorable climate for change; parents, administrators, and teachers were eager for school improvement, and the staff was highly motivated to try this new approach. The initiation stage went very smoothly.

This case study shows that obstacles and frustrations arose during the period subsequent to initiation, during the period of implementation. Some of the barriers to change were factors characterizing persons, such as lack of motivation, knowledge, and skills, but other barriers were related to structural subsystems. The researchers identified organizational barriers encountered by teachers when they attempted to carry out the innovation: the unavailability of required instructional materials and equipment, and the incompatibility of organizational arrangements with the innovation. The latter included time schedules, assignment of pupils, grouping practices, and the type of report card used.

Because administrators incorrectly assumed that willingness to make the change on the part of the teachers would ensure successful implementation, the administrators did not sufficiently anticipate the problems that came up during the change process, nor did they create evaluation mechanisms to deal with these problems as they occurred.[28]

A case study by Harry Gracey provides further evidence of how the school structure can frustrate the attempts to change of even the most highly committed and motivated teachers. His study of a group of teachers who desired to teach in a nontraditional, humanistic, child-centered mode and were stymied by a host of pressures is additional testimony that structure plays an important role in organizational innovation.

Gracey looked at two kinds of teachers working in a prosperous suburban community supportive of the schools and of experimentation and innovation. Gracey calls teachers of one kind "craftsmen." These teachers believe that education should be tailored to the needs and capacities of individual children, and view teaching as a highly skilled profession involving constant creative work with individual children. The second kind of teacher does what Gracey calls "production teaching." This involves taking a class through the prescribed curriculum in the prescribed amount of time. Production teachers rely on textbooks, workbooks, tests, and instructional materials, and emphasize drill and repetition.

Gracey wanted to see how the bureaucratic structure supports or stymies these two kinds of teachers. He found that the characteristics of bureaucratic organizations support the practices of production teachers but seem to frustrate craftsmen teachers.

As in the Barth case, craftsmen teachers were blocked by parents' and administrators' expectations; other factors were students' desires for grades, the school's requirement that quiet and order prevail in classrooms, and the large number of students in each classroom.[29]

The implementation stage requires both a personal and organizational focus in the staff development program. The personal focus ought to help individuals and groups alter their perceptions, attitudes, and norms, to provide a socialization experience, and to adapt the innovation to the existing "person" regularities, as well as to adapt people to the innovation. The organizational focus should enable the system to readjust to the new requirements of the innovation as interpreted by the staff. Important subsystems such as time, space, materials, and resources have to be realigned, and rewards and supports provided for new behavior.

Incrementalism

Because it is impossible to specify in advance what will take place once the change process is begun, the principle of incrementalism, or gradualism, has been postulated by organizational theorists; this postulate has been supported by evidence from case studies on educational change.

A strong negative correlation has been found to exist between the level of ambition of change attempts and the degree of success.[30] Therefore, it is advisable to introduce change gradually and incrementally.

During the 1960s, "innovation" was the name of the game. In many places nothing short of a total reconstruction of philosophy, goals, and teaching practices was considered adequate to meet the demands of a society reaching towards a humane and civilized way of life. In some schools, the new mandate, issued from a source of authority desiring change, was stated in inspiring and grandiose terms.

In one school, studied by sociologists Louis Smith and Pat M. Keith the key words were: Individualize, Humanize, Dramatize, and Socialize. A five-year plan was mapped out to accomplish objectives that required vast alterations in all of the subsystems of the school—goals, rewards, norms, values, roles, climate, structures, technologies, and evaluation strategies. The project ran into tremendous difficulties. After two years, the school board, the superintendent, the curriculum director, and the principal all left or took leaves of absences. Most of the teachers quit or planned to leave. The innovation was not being implemented.[31]

Smith and Keith point to the lack of gradualism as the major source of the failure to implement the innovation. Commenting about the advantages of the incremental approach over the "alternative of grandeur" approach used in the school, they state that the incremental approach involves lower levels of uncertainty and fewer unintended outcomes, decreased time pressure, an increased interval for major change, and limited decisions related to the change. They add that concomitant with the decreased demand on resources will be an increased likelihood of success in initial goals. In turn, this adds opportunities to create a position of strength; this reinforces activities, increases individual esteem, and leads to further change.[32]

Successful change requires a process of mutual adaptation among people, the organization, and the innovation. This process must occur during each stage of the change process.

During the first stage, initiation, change goals must be interpreted by those who are to accomplish them; in order for people to become willing to try a new approach, or to become committed to it, they need to see how the innovation will fit in with existing regularities, and how it may be adjusted to the particularities of their own situation. It is necessary that information be provided and people be motivated, but also that people have the opportunity to discuss the innovation, to see it in operation, to work with the innovation in a small way, and to anticipate problems that might occur.

As we shall see, during the next stage, implementation, the need for mutual adaptation is even greater. Conflicts among people inevitably will arise; ways to legitimate, negotiate, and resolve these conflicts need to be devised. Some of this conflict will stem from the ambiguity and discomfort felt by people who are trying to implement the innovation without having sufficient clarity about its aims and methods. Discrepant interpretations about what should be done and how it should be done arise at this stage; provision ought to be made for activities and opportunities to develop shared meanings, expectations, and goals, and to develop new norms. Also at this stage, structural subsystems have to be adjusted as planning becomes more specific.

For successful change to occur, the process of mutual adaptation must continue until the innovation is diffused throughout the school and incorporated as a regular part of the system. It is hoped that at this point, new insights and perspectives gained throughout previous periods will provide enough disequilibrium so that the process renews itself.

STRATEGIES OF CHANGE: SOME CASE REPORTS

In recent years, researchers have been going into schools to document the process of change, with a view toward identifying the important factors that facilitate or impede the process. The case reports that have resulted from this research illustrate the complexity of the change process, and point out the multiplicity of the factors that are involved. It seems clear, however, that failure to accomplish change is due, in part, to the one-sidedness of the assumptions about the change process made by change agents, who plan, initiate, and guide the change.

We will now examine several case reports and analyze them in the light of the assumptions about change that were made in each situation. One set of faulty assumptions is the "organizational change bias," and the other is the "personal change bias."

Organizational Change Bias: Rational Strategies

The assumption underlying what Kenneth D. Benne and Robert Chin call "rational-empirical" strategies is that if a change is proposed by some group that knows of a situation that is desirable, effective, and in line with the self-interest of another person or group, the latter will adopt that proposed change if it can be shown by those who propose the change that the person or group will gain by the change.[33]

This was the assumption of a host of federal change projects in the sixties and seventies. Its acceptance derives from a positivist belief deeply entrenched in our culture that the inner person—one's motivations, aspirations, needs, and personal values—is less important in determining behavior than the rational assessment of an idea, or the impact of immediate environmental influences. Thus, it was assumed that if an idea had been researched and field-tested successfully, or if a solution to a national problem seemed to be available, it could be introduced into a local school district and successfully implemented there.

The notion that research and development was the crucial factor, and that diffusion in the local setting would take care of itself, underpinned many projects funded by the federal government and private foundations, including many change-agent staff development projects, including those connected with the 1965 Elementary and Secondary Education Act (ESEA). National priorities were determined, specific goals established, and research and development were initiated. The resulting products were put into the local school system, with a surprising naivete about the complexity of such systems. Such procedures were based on the assumption that the practitioner is passive, perhaps slightly resistant to the innovation, but easily brought around to accept it once it is explained; getting from the introduction stage to the incorporation stage simply is a matter of using sound training strategies that give the teachers the necessary knowledge, attitudes, and skills required to implement the innovation. Ernest House, who studied the impact of federal programs on local sites where they were introduced after having been researched and developed elsewhere, found that the "technocratic paradigm" underlying these research, development, and dissemination (R,D,& D) programs did not promote much innovation.[34]

As Sarason has reported, this approach ignores, among other things, the "culture of the school." He points out that regularities of time, space, and behavior exist in the school for functional reasons, and also that these regularities are interconnected, so that a change in one regularity affects the overall "ecology."[35] Therefore, an innovation that proved successful during the research and development phase in one setting may fail in another setting where the behavioral regularities conflict with the requirements of the innovation.

Some of the variables that determine whether change will take place are: the values and needs felt by the teachers; the goals and leadership style of the principal; the degree of consensus among teachers, administrators, and parents about goals and the means of achieving them; support of the central office for the innovation; and available resources.

THE RAND STUDY. The Rand Corporation was commissioned by the United States Office of Education in 1972 to examine 293 federally sponsored programs that were trying to promote educational change in the public schools by paying the costs of innovative projects for a trial period.[36] The researchers found that federal efforts to promote innovations have resulted in little consistent or stable improvement in student outcomes.[37] Rand analysts attribute this not to the inadequacies of the innovative ideas, but to the "difficult and uncertain process of implementing innovative efforts in an educational system that resists change."[38]

There were variations in the extent to which the different projects were successfully implemented, and also in the extent to which the local educa-tion authority (LEA) continued project activities after federal funds were withdrawn. A critical factor in the successful implementation and continua-tion of these projects was the extent to which the innovation fit with the regularities of the local site, including the attitudes and "felt needs" of the teachers who were to be trained. Unless opportunities for mutual adapta-tion between the project and LEA were provided, the projects were likely to be unsuccessful.

Two analyses by Rand researchers of federal change-agent staff develop-ment projects based upon the "technocratic paradigm" illustrate some of the problems of this approach. The first, by Dale Mann, indicates what happened when rational strategies were used to train groups that had dif-ferent "felt needs" for the training offered. The second analysis, by Milbrey Wallin McLaughlin, is of eight classroom organization projects. She con-cludes that successful implementation was more likely to occur when change agents took an organizational rather than a technological perspective, and focused primarily upon the user rather than upon the educational treatment of the innovation.

Mann's analysis of 29 change-agent projects points to the speciousness of the assumption that teachers necessarily will embrace and implement an innovation introduced by a change agent if they can be convinced of its value and provided with the appropriate training. He found that not much change took place; this lack of success could only be accounted for by a multiplicity of interacting factors. There were differences in success, he found. Mann related these differences to the needs felt by participants in the training program. The more successful projects had "volunteers" as partici-pants, the less successful projects "nonvolunteers." The former group stated that they were already dissatisfied with their performance or became per-suaded of its inadequacy, and most said they had already been doing a ver-sion of the innovation. The latter group did not feel the need for the training offered and therefore were resistant to it. Mann also found that when projects that started with volunteers, and were successful with them, shifted to nonvolunteers, project goals became less ambitious, the amount of behavior change expected from individuals lessened, and project trainers reduced their expectations about the proportion of people in any given site they would be able to reach.[39]

In short, rational assumptions about change were valid only under certain conditions. One important factor was whether or not there was a match between the innovation and the needs felt by those who were to be trained. Where there was not, plans deteriorated to the point where the innovation "contributed more to organizational maintenance than to organizational change."[40]

McLaughlin's analysis of five of the eighty-five classroom organization change projects sheds further light on why rational strategies are not always appropriate to most school situations.[41] She reports:

Where implementation was successful, and where significant change in participant attitudes, skills, and behavior occurred, implementation was characterized by a process of mutual adaptation in which project goals and methods were modified to suit the needs and interests of participants and in which participants changed to meet the requirements of the project.[42]

This was true even for highly technological projects. Unless adaptations were made in the original plans, significant changes in participants did not occur and implementation tended to be superficial or merely symbolic.

McLaughlin points out that receptivity of the principal actors—central administrators, principals, and teachers—was critical. But high levels of initial support and commitment formed a necessary but not sufficient condition for successful implementation. In addition, implementation strategies that allowed institutional support to continue and mutual adaptation to occur were necessary. Three critical strategies that interacted to produce successful results were: local materials development, ongoing and concrete staff training, and iterative, on-line planning, combined with regular and frequent staff meetings.

Local materials development provided the staff with a sense of involvement and a chance to "learn by doing," a sense of pride in accomplishment, and of "ownership" in the project. This local development also broke down the teacher's traditional isolation and provided a sense of professionalism and cooperation. But the most important result of local materials development was that it provided an opportunity for users to think through the concepts that were the basis for the innovation and to engage in experience-based learning.

The training sessions judged most useful were regular meetings of the project staff with local resource personnel in which ideas were shared, problems discussed, and support given; materials development often provided the focus for these sessions. Visits to other schools already implementing the innovation were felt by participants to be more useful than lectures from consultants. The staff training represented a kind of resocialization of teachers—that is, a learning and unlearning process that helped them develop new attitudes, behaviors, and skills required for a radically new role.

Adaptive or on-line planning is a continual process that establishes channels of communication and solicits involvement from participants. It also provides a forum for reassessing project goals and activities, monitoring activities, and modifying practices to conform to institutional and project demands. Plans that are laid out in advance and are very specific may not be too adaptive. Unpredictable problems and events inevitably arise during implementation. Therefore, planning activities that are ongoing, flexible, and congruous with the changing local setting are better able to respond to these factors.

McLaughlin concludes that adaptation of the original goals of a change project should be seen as an appropriate goal for practice and policy, and not an undesirable aberration. She states that although reinvention of the wheel may be an unpalatable prospect for program developers and policy makers, it is essential for individual development and thus for organizational renewal.

Personal Change Bias: Normative-Reeducative Strategies

Some philosophers, psychologists, and sociologists emphasize how much we are conditioned and stress the enormous influence of the environment upon behavior; others stress the active, seeking nature of people as they interact with the environment. Normative-reeducative strategies of change recognize both aspects of human existence, but emphasize the significance of the individual's values and needs in determining behavior, and therefore the importance of dealing with them in changing behavior.

According to Chin and Benne, normative-reeducative strategies differ from rational-empirical strategies in that they are built upon different assumptions about human motivation:

The rationality and intelligence of men [*sic*] are not denied. Patterns of actions and practice are supported by sociocultural norms and by commitments on the part of individuals to these norms. Sociocultural norms are supported by the attitude and value systems of individuals—normative outlooks which undergird their commitments.[43]

Change requires an alteration of normative orientations to old patterns and commitment to new. Chin and Benne describe these normative-re-educative approaches. These approaches bring change agents operating on a consciously worked out theory of change into contact with the client system. The client may be a person, a group, an organization, or a community.

The common elements in this set of change strategies are: all emphasize the client system and its involvement in working out programs of change and improvement; the way clients see themselves and their problems is brought into dialogic relationship with the way in which they and their problems are seen by the change agent; the problem confronting clients is not assumed a priori to be one that can be met by providing technical information, although this is not ruled out; the problem is assumed to lie in attitudes, values, norms, and the external and internal relationships of the client system, and to be one that may require alteration or reeducation; the change agent must learn to intervene mutually and collaboratively along with clients in efforts to define and solve the clients' problems; it is believed that nonconscious elements that impede problem solution must be brought into consciousness and publicly examined and reconstructed; the intervention is based on concepts and methods from the behavioral sciences—resources that the change agent and clients learn to use to deal with the problem and with similar problems in the future.

Two different sets of approaches are encompassed by normative-re-educative strategies: those oriented to the improvement of problem-solving processes utilized by a client system, and those focusing upon helping members of client systems to become aware of their attitudes, value orientations, and relationship difficulties through exploration of feelings.

Both sets have certain factors in common: they consider the clarification and reconstruction of values to be of pivotal importance in changing; they use the development of temporary systems as a medium of reeducation of persons and groups; they use a change agent (such as a trainer, researcher, consultant, therapist, or counselor) as an aid to growth; they do not accept the rationalistic biases of rational-empirical strategies; they emphasize experience-based learning as an ingredient of enduring changes in human systems; they emphasize norms of openness of communication, trust between persons, the lowering of status barriers between parts of the system and mutuality between parts as necessary conditions of the reeducative process; they believe that creative adaptations to changing conditions may arise within human systems and do not have to be imported from outside them; and they focus upon conflict-management.

Some of the approaches that fall into this group are human relations approaches like T-groups, sensitivity training, and Organizational Development.

THE BOWERS STUDY. Matthew B. Miles has sketched out the necessary components of the healthy organization. These are goal focus, communication adequacy, resource utilization, optimal power equalization, cohesiveness, morale, innovativeness, autonomy, adaptation, and problem-solving adequacy.[44] Several of the ten factors he considers essential are dealt with by normative-reeducative strategies: communication adequacy and power equalization, cohesiveness and morale, and problem-solving adequacy are all targets of these strategies. As a study by David Bowers indicates, however, these strategies deal with only one aspect of organizational change—person change—and do not necessarily result in lasting systemic changes.

Bowers collected data from more than 14,000 respondents in twenty-three organizations and analyzed them to see whether the normative-reeducative strategies used were effective. He found that treatments such as Interpersonal Process Consultation, Task Process Consultation, and Laboratory Training contributed to little or no organizational change and concluded that the data gives support to the argument that organizational change is a complex, systems-level problem in organizational adaptation, not merely an additive end result of participation in development activities.[45]

Sam Seiber, speaking about the evidence on the effectiveness of the socialization approach, adds that changes that occur tend to be temporary, with individuals reverting back to their usual attitudes once they have returned to the normal pressures of their jobs.[46]

The Nonmodel of Change

As has been discussed, rational-empirical strategies and normative reeducative strategies are based upon assumptions about human behavior and the change process that are both valid and one-sided. Neither approach is sufficient for creating organizational change.

In a study of eighteen elementary schools belonging to the League of Cooperating Schools I/D/E/A, Ann Lieberman and David Shiman found that school change, where it does occur, follows a pattern.

Step 1. First, people talk about the possibility of bringing about some kind of change within the school. Some of the talk comes from teachers who are hoping to have changes legitimized from superordinates. Some of the conversation emerges from the stimulation of the teachers and principals interacting with each other, and some comes from outside consultants. Expectations begin to rise. Big ideas are talked about. There is a great deal of uneasiness, and individual teachers begin to feel pressured to do something. There is disequilibrium. People want someone to tell them what to do to make change.

Step 2. Activity ensues. Some teachers begin to do something. One or two teachers may decide to work as a team. Others might try to individualize their reading program. It is rare that the whole school participates from the beginning. Usually a few people get excited about adopting a change, and with enough support, they try.

Step 3. Out of such activity, teachers begin to ask questions. The broader implications of the activity come to the fore. "Why am I doing this?" "Is this better than what I did before?" are questions asked. Discomfort is great at this time as the new activity has called upon people to try out new behaviors.

Step 4. The whole program begins to look "shabby" to those trying to implement it. Teachers who have attempted to individualize their reading programs, for example, now find it difficult to give the same spelling words to thirty children.

Step 5. The large philosophical questions get asked. Teachers begin to deal with goals for the first time. They ask, "How can we insure that our curriculum is relevant to our student population?" "How can I teach children to make decisions when I make all the decisions for them?"

These questions open up others and the process begins again. Teachers talk, they move into activities, they question their activities, they examine the whole school program, they raise philosophical questions, and they struggle to clarify their goals.[47]

The pattern just described—referred to as the "nonmodel" of change by Lieberman and Shiman—is quite different from patterns suggested by rational models of change:

Rational Model	Nonmodel
1. Both broad and specific goals are prespecified.	1. A broad goal is suggested, but specific goals arise out of action.
2. The individual teacher's needs, values, desires are not considered in the initiation stage.	2. The individual teacher's needs, values, and desires are the impetus for initiation.
3. The means of achieving the goals are laid out in advance.	3. The means of achieving the goals are determined through continual experimentation (problematic approach).

4. Environmental feedback causes modification, simplification, and telescoping of planned ends and means.
5. Diffusion throughout the school depends upon the training of resistant members.
6. The model is based upon a linear process.

4. Environmental feedback is essential input in determining ends and means.
5. Diffusion throughout the school depends upon a peer group (normative-reeducative) strategy.
6. The nonmodel is based upon a dialectical process.

The nonmodel is consistent with the research on behavioral change discussed in this chapter. Disequilibrium is created in some teachers who begin to see that alternatives exist that are more consistent with their values than are their present methods. Their initial experiments with such innovations raise further disequilibrium: they find that they cannot go very far with their new approach because it is in conflict with some old patterns of action, or because it is in conflict with existing regularities in the ecology of the school. They come together with peers to discuss emerging problems, and find that new issues arise out of these discussions. Ideals are viewed in the context of the realities that exist in the school and its environment. The innovation is reinterpreted and modified to fit these particularities. People realize that they are unclear about aspects of the innovation and unsure about how they can adapt it. They seek new information, new skills, new concepts. They think about what needs to be changed in the school—structures, norms, and other elements—and begin taking steps to make these changes. This process is dialectical and incremental. Original plans and specifications are abandoned and replaced by others as new meanings and needs are uncovered. New arrangements are tried: some work and others do not. The process of mutual adaptation among the innovation, the organization, and the people implementing it continues until the innovation is reformed so that it fits the realities inherent in the particular situation.

The pattern just described underlies an approach to school change called the "peer-group strategy." It proceeds this way: a specific innovation, such as individualized instruction is considered for adoption in the school; broad goals are set forth, but explicit specification of goals and objectives arise as people act—the specification is not laid out in advance; although the innovative idea may be introduced by the school board or the superintendent of schools, or another change agent, it is the colleague group that develops the innovation through collaborative effort.

This strategy generates opportunities for peer group members to serve as a source of information, inspiration, and aid to other teachers and interested outsiders, and to develop a peer group as a decision-making body capable of planning and implementing its own activities.

As researchers studying the results of this strategy conclude, it has the power to provide a process of mutual adaptation among persons and the organization as the change process proceeds dialectically and incrementally. They also note, however, that it can be successful only under certain conditions:

1. The district must be committed to the change
2. The principal must be open enough to become aware of teacher, community, and district needs during the change process, and the principal must support the teachers as they experiment (or fail)
3. The community must support the change
4. There must be some "early adopters" who will serve as an example and raise issues with the others
5. There must be a peer group climate that invites dialogue and problem-solving activities.[48]

SUMMARY AND IMPLICATIONS

In this chapter, we reviewed some of the literature relevant to making change in schools, and analyzed two one-sided approaches. The first approach has an "organizational goals bias"; it emphasizes organizational goals and rational strategies of change. The second approach has a "personal change bias," which assumes that personal change is the critical factor in school change, and thus tends to minimize other critical factors. This approach relies upon normative-reeducative change strategies.

Research on adult socialization suggests that adult values and commitments are malleable only under strong influences. Therefore, imparting new information and knowledge, or training new skills may not be sufficient to motivate people to change their behavior, or to be able to change it. Therefore, it is necessary to build into staff development plans socialization experiences aimed at changing people's motivation and attitudes, in addition to improving their knowledge and skills.

Making personal change is a basic aim of any staff development plan. Personal change will not necessarily result in school renewal, however; the latter requires that organizational adjustments be coordinated with changes taking place in people.

The assumptions underlying rational-empirical strategies and normative reeducative strategies are important and are valid under certain circumstances. But, they are inadequate as the basis for an encompassing staff development model.

Both of these approaches must be incorporated into a design for staff development at appropriate points. These points will be discussed in the next chapter. For now, it is important to note our thesis: a staff development model must be eclectic and use a variety of approaches; yet it must have three foci—political, personal, and organizational.

NOTES

1. Dale Mann, "The Politics of Training Teachers in Schools," *Teachers College Record* 77 (February 1976): 323.

2. Ibid.

3. Robert Chin and Kenneth D. Benne, "General Strategies for Effecting Changes in Human Systems, in *The Planning of Change*, 3rd ed., ed. Warren G. Bennis, Kenneth D. Benne, Robert Chin, and Kenneth E. Corey (New York: Holt, Rinehart & Winston, 1976), p. 31.

4. See Stanley Udy, "The Comparative Analysis of Organizations," in *Handbook of Organizations*, ed. James G. March (Chicago: Rand McNally, 1965), pp. 687-88.

5. This term was used by Kurt Lewin in describing the first stage in the process of change, and adopted by Edgar Schein. Edgar H. Schein, *Professional Education: Some New Directions* (New York: McGraw-Hill, 1972), chap. 8.

6. Jacob W. Getzels and Egon G. Guba, "Social Behavior and the Administrative Process," *School Review* 65 (Winter 1957): 429.

7. Louis M. Smith and Pat M. Keith, *Anatomy of Educational Innovation: An Organizational Analysis of an Elementary School* (New York: John Wiley, 1971), pp. 366-73.

8. Roy Edelfelt and Margo Johnson, eds., *Rethinking In-Service Education* (Washington, D.C.: National Education Association, 1975), p. 5.

9. Gilbert Shearron, "In-Service/Needs-Assessment/Competency-Based Education" (Paper presented at Research Conference on Competency Based Teacher Education, Houston, Tex., March 14, 1974), p. 2.

10. T. W. Adorno, et al., *The Authoritarian Personality* (New York: John Wiley, 1964), p. 597.

11. See Arthur W. Eve, "Variables of Institutional Change in Elementary and Secondary Schools," in *Literature Searches of Major Issues on Educational Reform*, comp. Alan Schmeider (Washington, D.C.: ERIC Clearinghouse on Educational Reform, February 1974), ED 090 144.

12. Milton Rokeach, *The Nature of Human Values* (New York: The Free Press, 1973), p. 5.

13. Ibid., p. 6.

14. These concepts and definitions were taken from Rokeach, *The Nature of Human Values*, pp. 7-22.

15. Anne M. Bussis and Edward A. Cittenden, "An Analysis of an Approach to Open Education," monograph (Princeton, N.J.: Educational Testing Service, August 1970).

16. Philip E. Jacob, *Changing Values in College* (New York: Harper, 1957), p. 6.

17. C.W. Huntley, "Change in Values During the Four Years of College," in *College and Student*, ed. Kenneth A. Feldman (New York: Pergamon, 1972), pp. 261-67.

18. John A. Bilorsky, "The Selection of Student-Initiated Courses: Student Autonomy and Curricular Innovation," in Kenneth Feldman, *College and Students* (N.Y.: McGraw-Hill, 1972), pp. 453-62.

19. Orville G. Brim and Stanton Wheeler, *Socialization after Childhood: Two Essays* (New York: John Wiley, 1967).

20. Ibid.

21. See John Dewey, *Democracy and Education* (New York: Macmillan, 1916), p. 92; Leon Festinger, "Cognitive Dissonance," *Scientific American* (October, 1962): 3-9; Carl Rogers, *On Becoming a Person* (Boston: Houghton-Mifflin, 1961), pp. 61-62; Theodore M. Newcomb, *The Acquaintance Process* (New York: Holt, Rinehart & Winston, 1961), p. 10; Harry Helson, "A General Theory of Perception," in *Theoretical Foundations of Psychology*, ed. Harry Helson with Howard Bartley (New York: Van Nostrand, 1951), pp. 379-85; Nevitt Sanford, "The Developmental Status of the Entering Freshman," *The American College*, ed. Nevitt Sanford (New York: Wiley, 1962), pp. 253-82.

22. Ronald Corwin, *Education in Crisis: A Sociological Analysis of Schools and Universities in Transition* (New York: John Wiley, 1974), p. 336.

23. Ibid., pp. 335-36.

24. Paul R. Lawrence and Jay W. Lorsch, *Developing Organizations: Diagnosis and Action* (Cambridge, Mass.: Addison-Wesley, 1969), p. 70.

25. Daniel Katz and Robert L. Kahn, *The Social Psychology of Organizations* (New York: John Wiley, 1966), p. 391.

26. Seymour B. Sarason, *The Culture of the School and the Problem of Change* (Boston: Allyn & Bacon, 1971), p. 2.

27. J. Victor Baldridge and Terrence E. Deal, *Managing Change in Educational Organizations: Sociological Perspectives, Strategies, and Case Studies* (Berkeley, Calif.: McCutchan, 1975), p. 10.

28. See Neal Gross, Joseph B. Giacquinta, and Marilyn Bernstein, *Implementing Organizational Innovations: A Sociological Analysis of Planned Educational Change* (New York: Basic Books, 1971).

29. Harry L. Gracey, *Curriculum or Craftsmanship: Elementary School Teachers in a Bureaucratic System* (Chicago: University of Chicago Press, 1970).

30. Amatai Etzioni, *Studies in Social Change* (New York: Free Press of Glencoe, 1961), p. 62.

31. Smith and Keith, *Anatomy of Educational Innovation*.

32. Ibid., p. 373.

33. Chin and Benne, "General Strategies," p. 23.

34. Ernest R. House, *The Politics of Educational Innovation* (Berkeley, Calif.: McCutchan, 1974), p. 213.

35. Sarason, *The Culture of the School*, chap. 1.

36. Paul Berman and Milbrey Wallin McLaughlin, *Federal Programs Supporting Education Change, Vol. IV: The Findings in Review*, prepared for the U.S. Office of Education, Department of Health, Education, and Welfare (Santa Monica, Calif.: Rand, 1975), p. 1.

37. Ibid., p. 5.

38. Ibid.

39. Dale Mann, "The Politics of Staff Development," (Paper presented at American Education Research Association [AERA], Washington, D.C.: March 1975), p. 25.

40. Ibid.

41. Material following this citation is taken from Milbrey Wallin McLaughlin, "Implementation as Mutual Adaptation: Change in Classroom Organization," *Teachers College Record* 77 (February 1976): 339-51.

42. Ibid., p. 341.

43. Benne and Chin, "General Strategies," p. 23.

44. Matthew B. Miles, "Planned Change and Organizational Health," in *Organization and Human Behavior*, ed. Fred D. Carver and Thomas J. Sergiovanni (New York: McGraw-Hill, 1969), pp. 375-92.

45. David G. Bowers, "OD Techniques and Their Results in 23 Organizations: The Michigan ICL Study," *Journal of Applied Behavioral Science* 9 (1973): 21-41.

46. Sam D. Seiber, "Images of the Practitioner and Strategies of Educational Change," *Sociology of Education* 45 (Fall 1972): 362-85.

47. Ann Lieberman and David A. Shiman, "The Stages of Change in Elementary School Settings," in *The Power to Change: Issues for the Innovative Educator*, ed. Carmen M. Culver and Gary J. Hoban (Glenview, Ill.: Scott, Foresman, 1971), pp. 52-63.

48. Ibid., pp. 62-63.

Summary and Model

9

As NOTED IN the preface, a great deal of energy, time, and resources has been devoted to making change in schools since the mid-fifties, but, in most cases with only modest results, if any at all. This poor track record has stimulated interest among educators and researchers in trying to assess the factors that contributed to both the failure and success of educational change efforts. Case studies of specific programs, analyses of political issues and national trends, and research into organizational and personal change have all provided insights. Our interest in this book has been to develop a framework for conceptualizing staff development that is informed by this literature.

In this chapter, we will summarize the argument presented in the preceding chapters, that staff development programs fail because they are based upon one-sided and shortsighted models, and also present a model that can lead to school renewal. The problem with most models of staff development is that they are: (1) biased toward fulfilling organizational goals through the use of rational change strategies; thus, they fail to adequately take into account the behavioral regularities and values that exist in the school and minimize the need to make attitudinal and normative changes or (2) they are biased toward making personal change and do not make sufficient provision for organizational accommodation to these changes; and/or (3) they are based on unrealistic assumptions about authority prerogatives; thus, they do not adequately deal with the political question of *who* makes *what* decisions and *how.*

One of the inadequacies of the organizational goals bias is that it is based on an assumption that the rational assessment of an idea is the critical factor in attitude and behavior change. Thus, if it can be demonstrated to teachers that an innovation is in line with school needs or that it is clearly superior to methods they are presently using, they will embrace it without reservation and assiduously set themselves to the task of acquiring the competencies needed to implement it. This "rational" assumption underestimates the degree to which persons' values, self-interests, previous experiences, expectations, aspirations, needs, and personality traits influence their acceptance or rejection of an idea, as well as their ability to use it.

As we documented in chapter 8, the efficacy of this rational assumption for school renewal is not borne out by the literature on school change. Time and again, case studies demonstrate that people influence the shape of an innovation more than the innovation shapes people's behavior. For this reason, socialization experiences aimed toward making personal change are essential in a staff development plan. Some of these experiences include opportunities for colleagues to discuss educational philosophy and goals, to rethink their assumptions about the teaching-learning process, to become more aware of the discrepancy between their "ideal" values as expressed in words and their "real" values as expressed in behavior; group process experiences that focus on changing interpersonal norms; and the opportunity to try out new behaviors on a small scale and to discuss resultant problems with others. It is also important that provision be made for what McLaughlin calls a "process of mutual adaptation," which enables staff members to modify aspects of an innovation so that they are more consonant with existing personal attitudes and behaviors, and what Sarason terms "existing regularities" in the school, that is, elements in the school's culture that are pervasive and difficult to change, such as social norms. These requirements put into relief another of the inaccurate assumptions of the organizational goals bias, namely that the more specifically plans for change are laid out in advance, the more likely it is that an innovation will be implemented. As we have demonstrated, the contrary is true. The more dynamic and open-ended the plan, the more likely that the process of mutual adaptation will occur, and that change will take place. The change will be gradual and incremental, but real.

The most predominant models of staff development are biased toward making personal change. Case studies, however, indicate that unless personal change is coordinated with organizational change, school renewal does not result. Teachers are not only individual practitioners; they are members of a school staff, and what they do individually interfaces with what is happening in the rest of the school. This means that although changing teachers' attitudes, knowledge, and skills is important, it is not sufficient for making school change. Organizational components also have to be adjusted to fit in with the changes taking place in people. For example, if the aim of a staff development effort is to change from a conventional to an open classroom approach, the following organizational subsystems would have to be altered: procedures for testing and reporting to parents; time schedules; the availability and use of materials, equipment, and other technologies; the assignment of pupils; grouping practices; and goals reflected in written documents such as curriculum guides. As we have indicated, if personal change in staff members takes place without accompanying organizational change, personal change tends to be temporary. Tension and frustration grow, and there is a tendency for people to revert to old behaviors, or to become dissatisfied, sometimes to the point of quitting.

In chapters 2 to 6, as we traced the three principles of authority from colonial to contemporary times, we indicated that until very recently, policy was made, not by teachers, but by school boards and administrators. Thus, there is historical precedent for the organizational goals bias. Legally and traditionally, teachers have been viewed, and have viewed, themselves as functionaries whose job it is to implement decisions made by others. As we saw in chapter 6, in the contemporary era things have taken a rapid turn. Teachers now consider themselves professionals having high levels of expertise and judgment and are pressing for a more determinative voice in school policy-making.

Authority relationships in school are now in flux. In addition to teacher power, we also have community power. Parents are insisting upon a more direct say in decisions that affect their children in school, and are challenging teachers' and administrators' practices, and school boards' policies. The chain of command suggested by the formal organizational chart wherein authority is passed down the line from school board to superintendent to principal to teacher, is no longer operative in most school systems. Therefore, the third shortcoming of staff development models that we have discussed has become salient. This is the political naivete underlying many models. School leaders often overlook the importance of realistically assessing political conditions, and they make serious errors related to authority prerogatives.

Today, it is no longer sensible to ask only, "Who has the right to make certain kinds of decisions?" The more fruitful questions refer to: "Who intends to make decisions?" and, "How can the various sources of authority be involved in making decisions?"

The argument made in this book is that an adequate conceptualization of staff development must have three foci: *political, personal,* and *organizational.*

The model presented here is intended to incorporate these three components.

The political question of educational authority is dealt with in the model in two ways. Parents, teachers, and administrators are all sources of authority who must be given a legitimate voice in policy-making. This should be done formally, by clarifying roles and responsibilities, determining decision-making prerogatives, and establishing structures for decision-making. In addition, the three sources of authority should be tapped in the process of determining what the school's mission will be, and in determining what alternatives to this mission should be provided for some parents, students, and teachers. For this reason, the first step in the model is a self-study. Its purpose is to assess the existing regularities in the school and its environment, and the goals held for the school's future by the three sources of authority.

Most staff development plans begin with long-range goals and objectives set out in advance. This approach is politically naive and inconsistent with the literature on personal and organizational change, as we have seen. Rational plans are important, but they should be made at the point where shared meanings and goals have evolved, and structures for decision-making have been established. The model, therefore, specifies that two stages ought to precede the rational planning stage: the self-study, and exploration.

In the exploration stage, normative-reeducative strategies of personal and interpersonal change should be dominant features. As staff members try out new behaviors related to the altered future condition, values will be discussed and clarified, points of conflict and points of agreement should become clearer and more manageable, and new ways of behaving will be tried out. During the exploration stage new meanings should emerge that make goals for the future better understood and consensual.

At this point, rational planning should take place. It is likely that rational plans will be on target because there already have been many discussions about what needs to be done, small-scale attempts to implement innovations related to the altered future condition, visits to other sites already involved with aspects of the future mission, and revisions of original goals because of these experiences.

Most rational plans are specific about goals, but vague (or restricted) about how these goals are to be achieved. The model presented here emphasizes the importance of being very specific about what subsystems need to be changed in order for the future mission to be fulfilled. These organizational subsystems include: technologies (materials, equipment, teaching methods); procedures, rules, routines, schedules; rewards; structures for decision-making; in-service education; and monitoring and evaluation of the change process. The major purposes of the planning stage are: to carefully think through all aspects or organizational change that will be required, to anticipate needs and problems likely to arise, and to make provision for these needs and problems so that chaos will be minimal. On the assumption that new goals will arise as the process unfolds, the plans should be flexible enough to allow for modifications.

The next stage of the model is implementation. Plans are put into effect on a large scale, and activity is highly goal-directed. Nonetheless, the implementation process should be gradual and incremental. For example, it might be wise to introduce change grade by grade, or only in one subject area across grades. Changes should be introduced gradually so that the process of mutual adaptation between the old and the new takes place. Inservice training and supervision must support implementation efforts.

The final step in the model is an evaluation of what has taken place and the formulation of new plans for school renewal. A new self-study might be undertaken after several years, or an ongoing self-study might be built into the staff development plan that documents the change process. The difference between the original self-study and the one initiated at this point is that there is much more information available in this later stage, and also that future plans will build on what has already taken place. The next round is likely to be less traumatic, although it might be more innovative.

The model appears to be linear. It is presented this way in order to suggest that there is a progression that is optimal. Aspects of each stage of the model take place at all times, however. Planning occurs right from the start—it is more tentative and its purview much more limited in the beginning stages, however, than in the planning stage. Aspects of the altered future condition will be implemented starting in the exploration stage. Exploration will be ongoing, as will evaluation and self-study.

STAFF DEVELOPMENT PRINCIPLES

Basic Principles

1. Staff development is a planned change process aimed toward creating a new future condition.
2. Staff development programs should be eclectic in their use of models of change and specific interventions; but
3. The programs should have three foci: political, personal, and organizational.
4. Staff development should provide for "a process of mutual adaptation" among persons, the organization, and the desired new future condition.
5. This process should lead to incremental change.
6. The process should be monitored so that feedback is provided throughout, and continuous evaluation takes place.

Political Principles

1. Superordinate goals reflecting the school's mission should be derived

Fig. 4: A Model for Designing In-Service Staff Development Programs

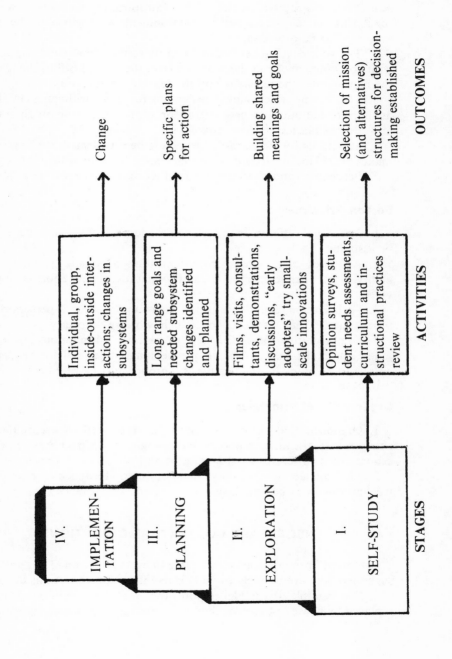

STAGES	ACTIVITIES	OUTCOMES
IV. IMPLEMEN-TATION	Individual, group, inside-outside inter-actions; changes in subsystems	Change
III. PLANNING	Long range goals and needed subsystem changes identified and planned	Specific plans for action
II. EXPLORATION	Films, visits, consul-tants, demonstrations, discussions, "early adopters" try small-scale innovations	Building shared meanings and goals
I. SELF-STUDY	Opinion surveys, stu-dent needs assessments, curriculum and in-structional practices review	Selection of mission (and alternatives) structures for decision-making established

from an assessment of the values, needs, goals, and expectations of parents, school board members, teachers, administrators, and students, and existing regularities in the school and its environment; alternatives to the mission may need to be provided.

2. The staff development model and its assumptions must be supported with commitments from the school board, the central office, the principal, the community, the teachers, and the teachers' association.

3. These commitments must be demonstrated in a willingness to alter old assumptions about, and new claims for, authority prerogatives; new roles and responsibilities must be carved out.

4. Structures for decision-making must be established; the issue of *who* makes *what* kind of decisions, and *how* must be dealt with.

5. Procedures and processes for conflict resolution must be established.

Person Principles

1. Individual differences in values, experience, skills, and felt needs must be assumed.

2. Activities that increase communication adequacy, problem-solving ability, trust, openness, empathy, and cooperative group effort must be provided.

3. Socialization experiences that focus upon values, perceptions, attitudes, and norms, as well as overt behavior are necessary.

4. Opportunities for individuals to exercise autonomous professional judgments and to develop a unique personal style, and for "expert" decisions to be made by the faculty as a group must be provided.

Organizational Principles

1. Organizational subsystems must be readjusted in accordance with changes in goals; time, materials, technologies, rewards, norms, rules, procedures, and structures must be altered and resources reallocated.

2. The change process must be monitored; feedback and evaluation mechanisms must be established.

NECESSARY CONTEXTUAL CONDITIONS

No "ideal" prescription is applicable to every situation. The applications suggested here are unlikely to be effective if certain conditions do not prevail. For example, the model requires that some old assumptions must be replaced by new ones, such as those related to authority prerogatives and to collective bargaining. If the staff development program based on this model is to succeed, it must be supported by attitudes and norms; roles, rewards, procedures, and structures; and leadership. Some fundamental conditions are suggested in this section:

Attitudes and Norms

1. Collaboration: The three sources of authority—the public (the school board and the community), administrators, and teachers (the rank-and-file teachers and the teachers' association) must agree to share decision-making and to establish new arrangements for doing so.

2. Flexibility: All groups must eschew behavior that prevents the system from adapting to unanticipated events as the change process unfolds. An example of critical importance is collective bargaining. The teachers' association must agree to negotiate only those policy items that describe procedures and processes, and avoid all items that specify curriculum content, required textbooks or testing programs, and other items that would limit flexibility.

3. Change and Experimentation: These are two norms that must be supported by the community, administrators, the school board, and teachers. A status quo orientation will undermine the program, since the change process is likely to be characterized, especially in the beginning stages, by ambiguity, goal vagueness, and conflict.

Roles, Rewards, Procedures, and Structures

1. Roles and Responsibilities: These must be reworked to be congruous with the collaborative approach underlying the model.

2. Rewards: Rewards must be changed in order to encourage teachers to expend effort on out-of-classroom staff development activities. Examples of rewards that could be provided are: released time; differential titles; temporary administrative, advisory, or other nonteaching roles; money; paraprofessional assistance; the opportunity to write and present papers, to teach in the staff development teacher center, and to do research. Money grants might be given to a teacher to do action research or to pilot-test and document an aspect of the program; bonuses might be given for contributions to curriculum development or instruction in the teacher center. Two teachers might share one class for a year so that they would have the time and energy to document the change process, to write and develop materials, and to lead discussion groups. Teachers who demonstrate leadership ability in the staff development program might be released from classroom duties for a year or two to work as advisors to other teachers or as master teachers

working with beginning or junior teachers.

3. Structures: New structures for decision-making must be established. Examples of structures that extend the range of sources of input are: in-service planning committees; parent advisory councils; cross-group committees of teachers, parents, administrators, students, and possibly representatives from higher education. Decisions must be made about who makes what kind of decisions. For example, it may be agreed that superordinate goals and broad policies are determined on a parity basis, but that expertise governs decisions about implementation. Structures and procedures for conflict resolution also must be established. Grievance committees, "beef sessions," confrontation meetings, arbitration, and other procedures will provide ways of handling conflicts in a constructive way, as well as give teachers and others a sense of power and control over events.

Leadership

1. Support: The central office staff, principals, and the school board must be committed to the open-ended quality of the model, and must have faith in the community's and staff's ability to cope with it. (An administrator intent upon "producing" tangible results in a short time can undermine the process.)

2. Climate: The principal must create a climate of trust and support teachers' attempts at innovation, experimentation, and willingness to take risks.

3. Management: Administrators must facilitate the change process by co-ordinating events, interpreting feedback data, monitoring the various components, and providing resources; administrators must also lead in changing appropriate subsystems.

4. Shared Leadership: Administrators must share leadership roles with teachers and the staff of the staff development center and give parent groups meaningful responsibilities and important roles.

STAGE I. THE SELF-STUDY

Assumptions

1. Successful change is most likely to be achieved when superordinate goals are congruous with the values, needs, aims, and expectations of those who will implement or be affected by the change, and with other regularities in the school and its environment.

2. The school's program should be responsive to the values, needs, aims, and expectations of all, or most, community members; therefore, it may be

necessary to establish alternatives to the basic mission in order to provide programs for those whose values and needs will not be reflected by this mission. These alternatives, however, must be compatible with the basic mission, so that the school does not become several schools within one school.

3. The staff development plan should start with *what is* and not with ideal goals; however laudable the ideal goals are, they may be untenable, given the existing regularities in the school and its environment.

4. All three sources of authority—public trust (the school board and the community), administrators, and teachers—should have input into the determination of superordinate goals and broad policy.

Objectives

1. To disclose information about existing values, instructional practices, curricula, children's needs, available resources, and goals for the future held by those in the school community.

2. To select a general mission and one or more alternatives from this data.

3. To establish initial short-range plans for exploring the mission and one or more alternatives.

4. To establish procedures for monitoring, evaluating, and providing feedback.

5. To establish an in-service staff development committee and other decision-making bodies.

6. To schedule time for in-service and other staff development activities.

7. To establish mechanisms for conflict resolution.

Sample Activities

1. Opinion surveys, open-ended questionnaires, Delphi forecasting procedures (a means of assessing people's goals and projecting a new future).

2. Assessments of student needs.

3. Curricula review.

4. Teachers' self-reports and peer observations about instructional practices.

5. Review of time schedules and other procedures.

STAGE II. EXPLORATION

Assumptions

1. Clarity about the desired new future condition probably does not exist

at this point; although the mission and one or more alternatives may be congruous with people's values and aims, there are diverse perceptions and interpretations, and uncertainty about how goals are to be achieved.

2. There probably will be a high degree of enthusiasm among staff people, which will stimulate seeking information, discussion, and some action in the classroom.

3. As aspects of the desired change are explored (as early adopters try out new behaviors, consultants meet with staff, and other actions take place), the discrepancy between ideals and the reality of the existing situation will create disequilibrium. Discussions will raise problems and issues; there will be discomfort resulting from ambiguity and conflict.

4. From continued exploration and dialogue, meanings will come to be shared and clarified, new norms will be created, and specific proposals for action sketched out.

Objectives

1. To develop shared meanings and consensual goals.
2. To establish norms of experimentation, risk-taking, openness, and cooperation.
3. To put staff in contact with outside sources.
4. To begin action—pilots, small-scale experimentation with new behaviors.

Sample Activities

1. Viewing films, interacting with consultants, visiting other sites already doing the innovation, demonstrations, workshops, seminars.
2. Discussions, short-range planning sessions, analysis.
3. Small-scale action, such as early adopters individualizing the reading program; documentation of the pilot projects.

STAGE III. PLANNING

Assumptions

1. Long-range, precise planning should be done only after various sources of authority, especially the professional staff, have explored and interpreted the innovation or innovations. Objectives should reflect shared meanings and be based on a realistic assessment of available resources.

2. Planning should involve not only goals statements, but specifications of in-service needs, required alterations in subsystems, and plans for action.

3. Planning should be done collaboratively; teachers and administrators should have major roles, but parents and students should have some input.

4. Plans should be flexible; although long-range plans are sketched out at this point, action should focus on short-range, easily revised plans.

5. Plans should entail political, personal change, and organizational change components.

6. Attention should be paid to roles and responsibilities, rewards, rules, and procedures.

7. Plans should encourage experimentation, unique approaches to problem solution and goal achievement, and heterogeneity of teaching styles.

8. Plans should recognize differences in the experience, skill, and needs felt by individual teachers; in-service offerings should be based on this recognition.

9. Plans should provide for individual in-service experiences, group interactions, intergroup interactions, and interactions inside and outside the school.

Objectives

1. To think through and analyze the sequence of steps that are likely to lead to goal achievement, and to make some flexible, long-range plans for setting the process in motion.

2. To set out objectives and action plans for the in-service program that relate to long-range goals.

Sample Activities

1. Work groups prepare long-range and short-range goals statements.

2. The staff development committee prepares flowcharts suggesting the sequence of in-service program development and the interconnections among components of the program, and with other aspects of school renewal.

3. First in-service course offerings are planned; behavioral and expressive objectives for these courses are developed; evaluation procedures are established.

4. Plans for alterations in organizational subsystems are set out in detail.

STAGE IV. IMPLEMENTATION

Assumptions

1. The in-service program should have, minimally, the following characteristics: (a) many opportunities for collegial, teacher-administrator, and

staff-parent interactions, (b) provisions for unique teacher needs arising from different levels of experience, skill, and grade level, and from differences in interests, concerns, and felt needs, (c) inputs from within and outside of the school, including consultants, professors, community members, and students; teachers and administrators should teach and learn in the staff development center.

2. The staff development effort should include a wide variety of teacher-training strategies and have socialization, skills development, analytic, inquiry, research, curricula, program, and materials development components.

3. An important focus of the staff development program should be behavioral change in line with the mandates of the mission and one or more alternatives.

4. Implementation efforts must be supported by training, supervision, and organizational changes in line with new goals.

Objectives

1. To gradually and incrementally fulfill the goals underlying the altered future condition.

2. To provide experiences and support that will facilitate the evolution of a new future condition.

Sample Activities

1. Putting plans into effect: expanding pilot projects, altering existing regularities incrementally, monitoring the change process.

2. Individual Activities: one-to-one clinical supervision for teachers, self-designed activities, independent study, action research, documentation of classroom change, interaction analysis, microteaching, programmed instruction, modules, different points of entry in group activities, child study, materials development, instructing in staff development center, school-community relations activities.

3. Group Activities: values clarification, sensitivity training, Organizational Development, problem-solving teams, planning committees, curriculum development workshops, team-teaching, cross-group teams (teachers, parents, students, administrators) for specific problem-solving, instructional sessions, workshops, brainstorming sessions, discussions, group investigation and research, task forces, peer observations of classroom behavior and follow-up conferences, senior-junior teacher partnerships, group seminars on the mission and one or more alternatives.

4. Inside-Outside Interactions: meetings with staff and staffs of other

schools and districts, parent-teacher-administrator brainstorming sessions or councils, consultants, speakers, visitations, conferences, workshops at colleges, college courses, travel.

REFERENCES

Perry, Ione L., and Bishop, Leslee J. *Staff Development: Sources and Resources.* Atlanta: Center for Curriculum Improvement and Staff Development, Department of Curriculum and Supervision, University of Georgia, 1974. This is a useful beginning bibliography that includes references on the change process, designing a plan, needs-assessment, educational improvement programs, teacher competencies, implementation, management, evaluation, accountability, and reflections on the future.

United States Office of Education. *Educational Programs That Work* 4, San Francisco, Calif.: Far West Laboratory for Educational Research and Development, 1977. This is a compilation of descriptions of various projects in use around the country. Some of the projects are alternative schools, bilingual and migrant education, early childhood, parent involvement, environmental education, training, administration, special education, subject areas, Title I programs, and special interest areas. This is an invaluable resource for anyone interested in promoting school renewal.

THE SELF-STUDY

Baker, Eva L. "Parents, Teachers, and Students as Data Sources for the Selection of Instructional Goals." *American Educational Research Journal* 9 (1972): 403-11.

Bureau of Elementary and Secondary Education, "The Administrator and Organizational Renewal." Washington, D.C., 1973. ERIC Clearinghouse, ED 088 214. These are reports on the involvement of students, parents, and the community in needs-assessment and educational decision-making, with specific suggestions for action.

Bureau of Planning and Evaluation, "Faculty Self-Study in the Elementary School." Working papers, rev. ed. Harrisburg: Pennsylvania State Department of Education, 1973. A guide for the study of a school district by its faculty members and administrators, along with parents; it begins with suggested procedures for initiating and conducting a self-study.

Hall, Clarence. "Parent Information Survey." *Thrust for Educational Leadership* 1 (May, 1972): 40-43. Presents the parent information survey developed and used in a California school district. The 38-item survey is composed of four sections relating to (1) point of view, (2) the instructional program, (3) student attitudes, and (4) home-school communications.

Pierce, Milo C. "Participation in Decision-Making: A Selected Bibliography." Exchange Bibliography No. 258. Monticello, Ill.: Council of Planning Librarians, February, 1972. A seventeen page bibliography.

Powell, James P., Jr. *Needs Assessment Studies for Education.* Gainesville, Fla.: Center for Community Needs Assessment, 1975. This is a review of the literature on needs-assessment studies on all educational levels.

Unruh, Glenys. "Staff Development in University City." *Theory into Practice* 11 (October, 1972): 239-44. A description of self-study strategies used in University City, Missouri.

Waynant, Louise F. "Teachers' Strengths: Basis for Successful In-Service Experiences." *Educational Leadership* 28 (April, 1971): 710-13. Describes strategies of identifying teachers' strengths, interests, and concerns, and a program based upon such an assessment.

Weaver, Timothy W. "The Delphi Method." Mimeographed, working draft. Syracuse: Educational Policy Research Center, June 1970. A description of a technology useful for gathering information and generating a process of forecasting and planning a new future condition.

Whitmore, Joanne M. *An Experimental In-Service Teacher Education Program for Distressed Elementary Schools.* Palo Alto, Calif.: Stanford University, Stanford Center for Research and Development in Teaching, 1974 ERIC Clearinghouse, ED087 777. This book contains a "Teacher Attitude Inventory," which identifies teachers' positions in relation to educational issues, and "Thinking about My School," an inventory that taps pupil's perceptions of the elementary school environment.

EXPLORATION

Bentzen, Mary M. *Changing Schools: The Magic Feather Principle.* New York: McGraw-Hill, 1974.

Culver, Carmen M., and Hoban, Gary J. *The Power to Change: Issues for the Innovative Educator.* McGraw-Hill, 1973.

Goodlad, John I. *The Dynamics of Educational Change: Toward Responsive Schools.* N.Y.: McGraw-Hill, 1975.

These three books describe the "League of Cooperating Schools" model utilizing the "peer group strategy." The importance of exploration as a step in making change is documented in these books.

PLANNING

Bare, I.L. et al., *The Ann Arbor Public Schools Participative Model In-Service Staff Development Project.* Ann Arbor: The Ann Arbor Public Schools, 1971. This document gives details about planning, resources, participants, and other information on this project.

Educational Service Bureau. *Inservice Education for Teachers.* Washington, D.C.: Administrative Leadership Service, 1968. Included are descriptions of specific district-sponsored workshops, teacher-initiated activities, innovative practices, and guidelines for planning in-service education programs.

Finch, Arnold. *Growth In-Service Education Programs That Work.* Prentice-Hall, 1969. Guidelines for planning school district in-service education programs and effective means of making them genuinely useful in instructional improvement.

Harris, Ben M.; Bessent, Wailand; and McIntryre, Kenneth. *In-Service Education: A Guide to Better Practice.* Englewood Cliffs, N.J.: Prentice-Hall, Inc., 1969. A practical guide to the planning of effective in-service education programs.

Houston, W. R. *Tooling up for PBE Staff Development: Designing and Planning for Change, Professional Assessment.* Houston, Tex.: University of Houston, 1974-1975.

National Education Association. *In-Service Education.* Infopac no. 7 Washington, D.C.: Instruction and Professional Development, NEA, 1974.

Rubin, Louis J. *Improving In-Service Education: Proposals and Procedures for Change.* Boston: Allyn & Bacon, 1971.

IMPLEMENTATION

Commissioner's Report on the Education Progessions 1975-76. *Teacher Centers.* Washington, D.C.: United States Department of Health, Education, and Welfare, 1977. Contains a comprehensive indexed bibliography and a directory of teacher centers.

Educational Leadership 31 (March 1974). Articles on various models of implementation of in-service, such as the "self-as-instrument" model, and problem-solving models.

Hoen, Lilburn P., ed. *Teaching Behavior Improvement Program.* Detroit: Michigan-Ohio Regional Education Laboratory, 1969. Includes lists of books and materials that can be purchased, and materials on interaction analysis, behavioral objectives, microteaching, teaching skills, and student feedback.

Hoover, Kenneth H. *A Handbook for High School Teachers.* Boston: Allyn & Bacon, 1970. A guide to assist the teacher in developing instructional skills.

Houston, W. Robert, et al., eds. *Resources for Performance-Based Education.* Albany: Division of Teacher Education and Certification, New York State Education Department, 1973. Resources and materials produced since 1967 for teacher education.

Joyce, Bruce R., and Weil, Marsha. *Models of Teaching.* Englewood Cliffs, N.J.: Prentice-Hall, 1972. Describes models that represent four "families" of approaches to teaching—social interaction, information processing, personal sources, and behavior modification—and advises the teacher how to use them.

Meierhenry, W. C., ed. *Mediated Teacher Education Resources: Supplemental Media Resources for Preservice and In-Service Teacher Education Programs.* Washington, D.C.: American Association of Colleges for Teacher Education, 1970. Audiotapes, games and simulations, films, multimedia packages, slides, filmstrips, and videotapes are identified and listed.

Walter, Kenneth A. *Authoring Individualized Learning Modules: A Teacher Training Manual.* Rockville, Md.: Montgomery County Public Schools, 1970. A how-to manual on constructing individualized teaching packages.

Bibliography

Adams, Don, with Reagan, Gerald M. *Schooling and Social Change in Modern America*. New York: David McKay, 1972.

Adorno, T. W.; Frenkel-Brunswik, Else.; Levinson, Daniel S.; and Nevitt-Sanford, R. *The Authoritarian Personality*. New York: John Wiley, 1964.

Alford, Albert L. "The Education Amendments of 1978." *American Education* 15 (March 1979): 6–14.

Allen, Dwight W., and Seifman, Eli. *The Teachers Handbook*. Glenview, Ill.: Scott, Foresman, 1971.

Almond, Gabriel A., and Powell, C. Bingham, Jr. *Comparative Politics: A Developmental Approach*. Boston: Little, Brown, 1966.

"And Now From Those Same Wonderful People Who Sit Across Your Bargaining Table," editorial. *American School Board Journal* 162 (September 1975): 32–37.

Antell, Henry. "What Constitutes an Effective In-Service Teacher Education Program." *NASSP Bulletin* 40 (April 1956): 147–48.

Argyris, Chris. "Individual Actualization in Complex Organizations." *Mental Hygiene* 44 (April 1960): 226–37.

Baer, H. K. "Providing Time, Money, and Resources for In-Service Programs." In *The Teaching Profession Grows In Service*. Washington, D.C.: National Commission on Teacher Education and Professional Standards, NEA, 1949.

Bagley, William C., and Keith, John A. H. *An Introduction to Teaching*. New York: Macmillan, 1942.

Bailyn, Bernard. *Education in the Forming of American Society: Needs and Opportunities for Study*. Chapel Hill: University of North Carolina Press, 1960.

Baldridge, J. Victor, and Deal, Terrence E. *Managing Change in Educational Organizations: Sociological Perspectives, Strategies, and Case Studies*. Berkeley, Calif.: McCutchan, 1975.

Barnard, Henry. *Normal Schools and Other Institutions, Agencies and Means Designed for the Professional Education of Teachers*. Hartford: Case, Tiffany, 1851.

Barr, A. A.; Burton, William H.; and Brueckner, Leo J. *Supervision: Principles and Practices in the Improvement of Instruction*. New York: Appleton-Century, 1938.

Barth, Roland. *Open Education and the American School*. New York: Agathon Press, 1973.

Bates, Samuel P. *Method of Teachers' Institutes and the Theory of Education*. New York: A. S. Barnes & Burr, 1864.

Beale, Howard K. *Are American Teachers Free?* New York: Charles Scribner's Sons, 1936.

Bendiner, Robert. *The Politics of Schools—A Crisis in Self-Government*. New York: Harper & Row, 1969.

Bennion, John W. "The Teacher and the Principal in Curriculum Development." In

Professional Negotiation and the Principalship. Washington, D.C.: Department of Elementary School Principals, NEA, 1969.

Benson, George L. "The School Principal and Negotiations: A Middle Management Dilemma." *Oregon School Study Council Bulletin* 13 (January 1970): 3.

Bentzen, Mary M. *Changing Schools: The Magic Feather Principle.* New York: McGraw-Hill, 1974.

Berge, Marvin L.; Russell, Harris E.; and Walden, Charles B. "In-Service Education Programs of Local School Systems." In *In-Service Education.* Fifty-sixth Yearbook of the National Society for the Study of Education. Chicago: University of Chicago Press, 1957.

Bidwell, Charles E. "The Administrative Role and Satisfaction in Teaching." *Journal of Educational Sociology* 29 (September 1955): 41–47.

———. "The School as a Formal Organization." In *Handbook of Organizations.* Edited by James G. March. Chicago: Rand McNally, 1965.

Bilorusky, John A. "The Selection of Student-Initiated Courses: Student Autonomy and Curricular Innovation." In *The Impact of College on Students.* Edited by Kenneth A. Feldman and Theodore M. Newcomb. San Francisco: Jossey-Bass, 1969.

Binder, Frederick M. *The Age of the Common School, 1830–1865.* New York: John Wiley, 1974.

Blau, Peter M. *Bureaucracy in Modern Society.* New York: Random House, 1956.

Bobbitt, Franklin. "Some General Principles of Management Applied to the Problems of City School Systems." In *The Supervision of City Schools.* Twelfth Yearbook of the National Society for the Study of Education, pt. 1. Chicago: University of Chicago Press, 1913.

Borrowman, Merle. *The Liberal and Technical in Teacher Education, A Historical Survey of American Thought.* New York: Bureau of Publications, Teachers College, Columbia University, 1965.

———. *Teacher Education in America: A Documentary History.* New York: Teachers College Press, Columbia University, 1965.

Bowers, David. "OD Techniques and Their Results in 23 Organizations: The Michigan ICL Study." *Journal of Applied Behavioral Science* 9 (1973): 24–41.

Boyan, Norman. "The Emergent Role of the Teacher and the Authority Structure of the School." In *Organization and Human Behavior: Focus on Schools.* Edited by Fred Carver and Thomas Sergiovanni. New York: McGraw-Hill, 1969.

Boyce, Arthur C., ed. *Methods for Measuring Teachers' Efficiency.* Fourteenth Yearbook of the National Society for the Study of Education. Chicago: University of Chicago Press, 1915.

Bradbury, Dorothy E. *Four Decades of Action for Children: A Short History of the Children's Bureau.* Children's Bureau Publication, no. 358. Washington, D.C.: Government Printing Office, 1956.

Braun, Robert J. *Teachers and Power: The Story of the American Federation of Teachers.* New York: Simon & Schuster, 1972.

Bredo, Anneke E., and Bredo, Eric R. "Effects of Environment and Structure on the Process of Innovation." In *Managing Change in Educational Organizations.* Edited by Victor J. Baldridge and Terrence E. Deal. Berkeley, Calif.: McCutchan, 1975.

Brenton, Myron. *What's Happened to Teacher?* New York: Coward-McCann, 1970.

"The Brewing—and Perhaps, Still Preventable Revolt of School Principals," editorial. *American School Board Journal* 163 (January 1976): 25–28.

Brim, Orville G., and Wheeler, Stanton. *Socialization after Childhood: Two Essays.* New York: John Wiley, 1967.

Brodinsky, Ben, "Teacher Power: Can You Trust It?" *National Elementary Principal* 58 (March 1979): 21–29.

Broudy, Harry S. *The Real World of the Public Schools.* New York: Harcourt, Brace, Jovanovich, 1972.

Brubacher, John W. "Principals' Political Behavior." *National Association of Secondary School Principals' Bulletin* 396 (January 1976): 23–29.

Bush, Robert N., and Enemark, Peter. "Control and Responsibility in Teacher Education." In *Teacher Education.* Seventy-fourth Yearbook of the National Society for the Study of Education, pt. 2. Chicago: University of Chicago Press, 1975.

Bussis, Anne M., and Chittenden, Edward A. "An Analysis of an Approach to Open Education." Monograph. Princeton, N.J.: Educational Testing Service, August, 1970.

Butts, Freeman R., and Cremin, Lawrence A. *A History of Education in American Culture.* New York: Henry Holt, 1953.

Callahan, Raymond E. *Education and the Cult of Efficiency.* Chicago: University of Chicago Press, 1962.

Campbell, Roald F.; Cunningham, Luvern L.; and McPhee, Roderick F. *The Organization and Control of American Schools.* Columbus, Ohio: Charles E. Merrill, 1965.

Campbell, Roald F., and Layton, Donald H. *Policy Making for American Education.* Chicago: Midwest Administration Center, University of Chicago, July 1969.

Carnegie Commission on Higher Education. *Continuity and Discontinuity: Higher Education and the Schools.* New York: McGraw-Hill, 1973.

Carrington, J. W. "Developing and Sharing the Power of Group Dynamics." In *The Teaching Profession Grows In Service.* Washington, D.C.: National Commission on Teacher Education and Professional Standards, NEA, 1949.

Caruso, Joseph James. "Parity in Designing, Conducting, and Evaluating Teacher Education Programs: A Conceptual Definition." Ed.D. dissertation, Teachers College, Columbia University, 1974.

Caswell, Hollis L., and Campbell, Doak S. *Curriculum Development.* New York: American Book, 1935.

Chase, Francis S. "Factors for Satisfaction in Teaching." *Phi Delta Kappan* 33 (November 1951): 127–32.

———. "Professional Leadership and Teacher Morale." *Administrator's Notebook* 1 (March 1953): 1–4.

Cheng, Charles W. "Community Representation in Teacher Collective Bargaining: Problems and Prospects." *Harvard Educational Review* 46 (May 1976): 153–74.

Chickering, Arthur. *Education and Identity.* San Francisco: Jossey-Bass, 1969.

Chin, Robert, and Benne, Kenneth D. "General Strategies for Effecting Changes in

Human Systems." In *The Planning of Change*. 2d ed. Edited by Warren G. Bennis, Kenneth D. Benne, and Robert Chin. New York: Holt, Rinehart, & Winston, 1961.

Clark, Burton R. *Educating the Expert Society*. San Francisco: Chandler, 1962.

Clark, David L., and Marker, Gerald. "The Institutionalization of Teacher Education." In *Teacher Education*. Seventy-fourth Yearbook of the National Society for the Study of Education, pt. 2. Chicago: University of Chicago Press, 1975.

Coffey, Hubert S., and Golden, William J., Jr. "Psychology of Change within an Institution." In *In-Service Education*. Fifty-sixth Yearbook of the National Society for the Study of Education, pt. 1. Chicago: University of Chicago Press, 1957.

Cogan, Charles. "What Teachers Really Want from Boards." *American School Board Journal* 156 (February 1969): 9–11.

Cole, Stephen. *The Unionization of Teachers: A Case Study of the UFT*. New York: Praeger, 1969.

Combs, Arthur. *The Professional Education of Teachers: A Perceptual View of Teacher Preparation*. Boston: Allyn & Bacon, 1974.

Conant, James B. *The Education of American Teachers*. New York: McGraw-Hill, 1963.

Corey, Stephen M. *Action Research to Improve School Practices*. New York: Bureau of Publications, Teachers College, Columbia University, 1953.

Corwin, Ronald G. "Professional Persons in Public Organizations." *Educational Administration Quarterly* 1 (1965): 1–22.

――――. *A Sociology of Education: Emerging Patterns of Class, Status, and Power in the Public Schools*. New York: Appleton-Century-Crofts, 1965.

――――. "Teacher Militancy in the United States: Reflections on Its Sources and Prospects." *Theory into Practice* 7 (April 1968): 96–103.

――――. *Militant Professionalism: A Study of Organizational Conflict in High Schools*. New York: Appleton-Century-Crofts, 1970.

――――. "The New Teaching Profession." In *Teacher Education*. Seventy-fourth Yearbook of the National Society for the Study of Education, pt. 2. Chicago: University of Chicago Press, 1975.

Cremin, Lawrence. *The American Common School: An Historic Conception*. New York: Bureau of Publications, Teachers College, Columbia University, 1951.

――――. "The Heritage of American Teacher Education." *Journal of Teacher Education*, pt. 1, 4 (June 1953): 163–70; pt. 2, 4 (June 1953): 246–50.

――――. *The Transformation of the School: Progressivism in American Education 1876 –1957*. New York: Vintage, 1964.

――――. *The Genius of American Education*. New York: Random House, 1965.

――――. "Curriculum Making in the United States." *Teachers College Record* 73 (December 1971): 207–20.

Cronin, Joseph. "Can Local Lay School Boards Survive Much Longer without Any Real Power?" *American School Board Journal* 161 (April 1974): 55–59.

Cubberley, Ellwood P. *Changing Conceptions of Education*. Boston: Houghton-Mifflin, 1909.

————. *Public School Administration.* Boston: Houghton-Mifflin, 1917.

Culbertson, Jack. *Preparing Educational Leaders for the Seventies.* Final report. Columbus, Ohio: University Council for Educational Administration, December, 1969. ERIC Clearinghouse, ED 040 941.

Culver, Carmen M.; Lieberman, Ann; and Shiman, David A. "Working Together: The Peer Group Strategy." In *The Power to Change: Issues for the Innovative Educator.* Edited by Carmen M. Culver and Gary J. Hoban. New York: McGraw-Hill, 1973.

Curtis, D. K. "Pre-service and In-service Education of Elementary and Secondary School Teachers." *Review of Educational Research* 28 (1958): 208–21.

Darland, David. "Preparation in the Governance of the Profession." In *Teachers for the Real World.* Edited by B. Othanel Smith. Washington, D.C.: The American Association of Colleges for Teacher Education, 1969.

Davies, Don. "Making Citizen Participation Work." *National Elementary Principal* 55 (March-April 1976): 20–32.

Davis, John C. "Legal Trends in Teacher Dismissal Procedures." *NASSP Bulletin* 359 (December 1971): 49–55.

Delon, Floyd G. *Substantive Legal Aspects of Teacher Discipline.* National Organization on Legal Problems of Education, Topeka, Kansas. Eugene, Oregon: Oregon University, ERIC/CEM State-of-the-Knowledge Series, no. 23, 1972, ED 069 017.

Denmark, George W., and Yff, Joost. *Obligation for Reform.* Final report of the Higher Education Task Force on Improvement and Reform in American Education. Washington, D.C.: American Association of Colleges for Teacher Education, 1974. Cited in Caruso, "Teacher Education Programs."

DeNovellis, R. L., and Lewis, A. J. *Schools Become Accountable: A Pact Approach.* Washington, D.C.: Association for Supervision and Curriculum Development, 1974.

Dewey, John. *Democracy and Education.* New York: Macmillan, 1916.

————. *The Public and Its Problems.* 3d ed. Denver: Allan Swallow, 1954.

Dobson, Russell, and Shelton, Judith. *Parental and Community Involvement in Education and Teacher Education.* Washington, D.C.: ERIC Clearinghouse on Teacher Education, February 1975, ED 100 833.

Dodd, William Harvel. "An Awareness Paradigm: Framework for In-Service Education." Ed.D. dissertation, University of Georgia, 1970.

Dorros, Sidney. *Teaching as a Profession.* Columbus, Ohio: Charles E. Merrill, 1968.

Dreeben, Robert. *The Nature of Teaching: Schools and the Work of Teachers.* Glenview, Ill.: Scott, Foresman, 1970.

Dunkin, Michael J., and Biddle, Bruce J. *The Study of Teaching.* New York: Holt, Rinehart, & Winston, 1974.

Edelfelt, Roy. *Teacher Designed Reform in Teacher Education through Association Negotiations.* Final report. U. S. Department of Health, Education, and Welfare, Office of Education, National Center for Educational Research and Development, August 1972.

————. "In-Service Education of Teachers: Priority for the Next Decade." *Journal of Teacher Education* 25 (February 1974): 250–52.

Edelfelt, Roy, and Johnson, Margo, eds. *Rethinking In-Service Education.* Washington, D.C.: National Education Association, 1975.

Edwards, Newton, and Richey, Herman G. *The School in the American Social Order.* Boston: Houghton-Mifflin, 1963.

Eggert, C. L., and Jones, F. "A Program of Inservice Training for School Administration." *NASSP Bulletin* 42 (March 1958): 35–38.

Eliot, Thomas H. "Toward an Understanding of Public School Politics." In *Governing Education: A Reader on Politics, Power, and Public School Policy.* Edited by Alan Rosenthal. New York: Anchor, 1969.

Elkin, Sol M. "Another Look at Collective Negotiations for Professionals." *School and Society* 98 (March 1970): 173–75.

Elsbree, Willard S. *The American Teacher, Evolution of a Profession in a Democracy.* New York: American Book, 1939.

Etzioni, Amatai. *Studies in Social Change.* New York: Free Press of Glencoe, 1961.

————. *Modern Organizations.* Englewood Cliffs, N.J.: Prentice-Hall, 1964.

————, ed. *The Semi-Professions and Their Organization.* New York: The Free Press, 1969.

Evenden, E. S. "Contributions of Research to the Education of Teachers." In *The Scientific Movement in Education.* Thirty-seventh Yearbook of the National Society for the Study of Education, pt. 2. Chicago: Public School Publishing Co., 1938.

Fayal, Henri. *General and Industrial Management.* Translated by Constance Starrs. London: Sir Isaac Pitman and Sons, 1949.

Federal Security Agency. *Schools at Work in Forty-eight States.* Office of Education Bulletin, no. 13. Washington, D.C.: Government Printing Office, 1952.

Feldman, Kenneth. *College and Students.* New York: McGraw-Hill, 1972.

Ferguson, Dorothy C. "The Teacher as a Member of a School Staff and Profession: A Synthesis of Current Thought." Ph.D. dissertation, Michigan State University, 1970.

Festinger, Leon. "Cognitive Dissonance." *Scientific American* (October 1962): 3–9.

Flexner, Abraham. "Is Social Work a Profession?" Proceedings of the National Conference of Charities and Correction. Chicago: Hildmann Printing, 1915. Reported in Becker, Howard. "The Nature of a Profession." In *Education for the Professions.* Sixty-first Yearbook of the National Society for the Study of Education, pt. 2. Chicago: University of Chicago Press, 1962.

Frazier, Benjamin W. "History of the Professional Education of Teachers in the United States." In *National Survey of the Education of Teachers in the United States.* Bulletin no. 10. Washington, D.C.: Government Printing Office, 1935.

Gage, N. L. *Handbook of Research on Teaching.* Chicago: Rand McNally, 1963.

Galbraith, John Kenneth. *The New Industrial State.* Boston: Houghton-Mifflin, 1967.

George, Thomas W. "Upheaval in School Law." *NASSP Bulletin* 57 (May 1973): 118– 26.

Gerver, Israel, and Bensman, Joseph. "Toward a Sociology of Expertness." *Social Forces* 32 (March 1954):226–35. Cited in Holger R. Stub, "The Professional

Prestige of Classroom Teachers: A Consequence of Organizational and Community Status." In *The Sociology of Education, A Sourcebook.* Edited by Robert R. Bell and Stub Holger. Homewood, Ill.: The Dorsey Press, 1968.

Getzels, Jacob, W., and Guba, Egon G. "Social Behavior and the Administrative Process." *School Review* 65 (Winter 1957): 423–41.

Getzels, Jacob W.; Lepham, James M.; and Campbell, Roald F. *Educational Administration as a Social Process: Theory, Research, Practice.* New York: Harper & Row, 1968.

Giacquinta, Joseph. "The Process of Organizational Change in Schools." In *Review of Research in Education.* Edited by Fred Kerlinger. Itasca, Ill.: Peacock, 1972.

Gilchrist, Robert S.; Fielstra, Clarence; and Davis, Anna L. "Organization of Programs of In-Service Education." In *In-Service Education.* Fifty-sixth Yearbook of the National Society for the Study of Education. Chicago: University of Chicago Press, 1957.

Gitell, Marilyn. "The Participants." In *Governing Education: A Reader on Politics, Power, and Public School Policy.* Edited by Alan Rosenthal. New York: Anchor, 1969.

Glime, Raymond G. "Bargaining with Teachers: The Things the Board Should Demand." *American School Board Journal* 158 (June 1971): 21–23.

Goble, Frank. *The Third Force.* New York: Grossman, 1970.

Goode, William. "Encroachment, Charlatanism, and the Emerging Professions: Psychology, Sociology, and Medicine." *American Sociological Review* 25 (December 1960): 902–14.

Goodlad, John I. "The Consultant and In-Service Education." In *In-Service Education.* Fifty-sixth Yearbook of the National Society for the Study of Education. Chicago: University of Chicago Press, 1957.

———. "The Curriculum." In *The Changing American School.* Sixty-fifth Yearbook of the National Society for the Study of Education, pt. 2. Chicago: University of Chicago Press, 1966.

———. "Educational Change: A Strategy for Study and Action." *National Elementary Principal* 48 (January 1969): 8–10.

———. "Lag on Making Ideas Work." In *Change and Innovation in Elementary and Secondary Organization.* 2d ed. Edited by Maurie Hillson and Ronald T. Hyman. New York: Holt, Rinehart & Winston, 1971.

———. *The Dynamics of Educational Change: Toward Responsive Schools.* New York: McGraw-Hill, 1975.

Goodwin, Harold J., and Thompson, Gerald W. "Teacher Militancy and Countervailing Power." In *The Collective Dilemma: Negotiations in Education.* Edited by S. Carlton and Harold Goodwin. Worthington, Ohio: Charles A. Jones, 1969.

Gracey, Harry L. *Curriculum or Craftsmanship: Elementary School Teachers in a Bureaucratic System.* Chicago: University of Chicago Press, 1970.

Greene, Maxine. *The Public School and the Private Vision: A Search for America in Education and Literature.* New York: Random House, 1965.

———. *Teacher as Stranger: Educational Philosophy for the Modern Age.* Belmont, Calif.: Wadsworth, 1973.

Greenwood, Ernest. "Attributes of a Profession." In *Sociological Perspectives on Occupations.* Edited by Ronald M. Pavalko. Itasca, Ill.: F. E. Peacock, 1972.

Griffin, Gary A., and Lieberman, Ann. *Behavior of Innovative Personnel.* Washington, D.C.: ERIC Clearinghouse on Teacher Education, August, 1974, ED 093 857.

Gross, Neal; Giacquinta, Joseph B.; and Bernstein, Marilyn. *Implementing Organizational Innovations: A Sociological Analysis of Planned Educational Change.* New York: Basic Books, 1971.

Gulick, Luther, and Urwick, L., eds. *Papers on the Science of Administration.* New York: Institute of Public Administration, Columbia University, 1937.

Gutek, Gerald Lee. *An Introduction to American Education.* New York: Thomas Y. Crowell, 1970.

Guzzetta, Dominic. "Growth Through Inservice Training." *Phi Delta Kappan* 36 (May 1955): 311–12.

Hall, Richard. "Professionalization and Bureaucratization." *American Sociological Review* 33 (February 1968): 92–104.

Harris, Ben M., and Bessent, Wailand. *In-Service Education: A Guide to Better Practice.* Englewood Cliffs, N.J.: Prentice-Hall, 1969.

Hazard, William R. "The Court: Policy Making for Education." *Journal of Educational Research* 68 (March 1974): Inside front cover.

Heider, Fritz. *The Psychology of Interpersonal Relations.* New York: Wiley, 1958.

Helson, Harry. *Theoretical Foundations of Psychology.* Edited by Harry Helson with S. Howard Bartley. New York: Van Nostrand, 1951.

Herrick, Virgil E. "Approaches to Helping Teachers Improve Their Instructional Practices." *Elementary School Journal* 62 (1954): 527–34.

————. "The Evaluation of Change in Programs of In-Service Education." In *In-Service Education.* Fifty-sixth Yearbook of the National Society for the Study of Education. Chicago: University of Chicago Press, 1957.

Herzberg, Frederick. *Work and the Nature of Man.* New York: World, 1966.

Hightower, F. W. "Inservice Education." *Educational Supervision and Administration* 38 (April 1952): 243–44.

Hofstadter, Richard. *The Age of Reform.* New York: Vintage Books, 1955.

House, Ernest R. *The Politics of Educational Innovation.* Berkeley, Calif.: McCutchan, 1974.

Houston, Robert W., and Howsam, Robert B., eds. *Competency-based Teacher Education: Progress, Problems, and Prospects.* Chicago: Science Research Associates, 1972.

Howsam, Robert B. *Educating a Profession.* Washington, D.C.: Report of the Bicentennial Commission on Education for the Profession of Teaching of the American Association of Colleges for Teacher Education, 1976.

Huebner, Dwayne. "Curriculum Language and Classroom Meanings." In *Language and Meaning.* Edited by James MacDonald. Washington, D.C.: Association for Supervision and Curriculum Development, NEA, 1966.

Huntley, C. W. "Changes in Values During the Four Years of College." In *The Impact of College on Students.* Edited by Kenneth A. Feldman and Theodore

M. Newcomb. San Francisco: Jossey-Bass, 1969.

Iannocone, Laurence. "Three Views of Change in Educational Politics." In *The Politics of Education*. Seventy-sixth Yearbook of the Society for the Study of Education. Chicago: University of Chicago Press, 1975.

Immegart, Glenn L., and Pilecki, Francis J. *An Introduction to Systems for the Educational Administrator*. Cambridge, Mass.: Addison-Wesley, 1973.

"It's Late, but There's Still Time to Give Your Principals a Real Say in Management," editorial. *American School Board Journal* 163 (February 1976): 32–34.

Jackson, Philip W. *Life in Classrooms*. New York: Holt, Rinehart & Winston, 1968.

Jacob, Philip E. *Changing Values in College*. New York: Harper, 1957.

Johnson, Clifton. *Old-Time Schools and School-Books*. New York: Henry Holt, 1925.

Jones, Philip C. "Should the Public Join You and Your Teachers at the Bargaining Table?" *American School Board Journal* 162 (September 1975): 27–31.

Joyce, Bruce. *Alternative Models of Elementary Education*. Lexington, Mass.: Blaisdell, 1969.

———. "Conceptions of Man and Their Implications for Teacher Education." In *Teacher Education*. Seventy-fourth Yearbook of the National Society for the Study of Education. Chicago: University of Chicago Press, 1975.

"A Juggernaut for a Federal Bargaining Law," editorial. *American School Board Journal* 162 (September 1975): 15.

Karier, Clarence; Violas, Paul; and Spring, Joel. *Roots of Crisis*. Chicago: Rand McNally, 1973.

Katz, Daniel, and Kahn, Robert L. *The Social Psychology of Organizations*. New York: John Wiley, 1966.

Katz, Fred E. *Autonomy and Organization: The Limits of Social Control*. New York: Random House, 1968.

Katz, Michael. *Class, Bureaucracy, and Schools*. New York: Praeger, 1971.

Kerr, Norman D. "The School Board as an Agency of Legitimation." In *Governing Education: A Reader on Politics, Power, and Public School Policy*. Edited by Alan Rosenthal. New York: Anchor, 1969.

Kessing, Felix M. "Acculturation." In *A Dictionary of the Social Sciences*. Edited by Julius Gold and William L. Kolb. New York: Free Press of Glencoe, 1964.

Kilgras, Donald C. *Administration as an Adversary Role: Bargaining—Collective Negotiations*. Eugene, Ore.: Oregon School Study Council, April 1973, ED 078 541.

Kimball, Solon T., and McClellan, James E., Jr. *Education and the New America*. New York: Vintage, 1966.

Kimbrough, Ralph B. *Administering Elementary Schools: Concepts and Practices*. New York: Macmillan, 1968.

King, James. "New Directions for Collective Negotiation." In *Professional Negotiation and the Principalship*. Department of Elementary School Principals, NEA, 1969, ED 135 075.

Kinnick, B. Jo. "The Teachers and the In-Service Education Program." In *In-Service Education*. Fifty-sixth Yearbook of the National Society for the Study of

Education, pt. 1. Chicago: University of Chicago Press, 1957.

Koerner, James D. *The Miseducation of American Teachers.* Boston: Houghton Mifflin, 1963.

Lawrence, Paul R., and Lorsch, Jay W. *Developing Organizations: Diagnosis and Action.* Cambridge, Mass.: Addison-Wesley, 1969.

Leggatt, T. "Teaching as a Profession." In *Professions and Professionalization.* Edited by J. A. Jackson. London: Cambridge University Press, 1970.

Leiter, Maurice, and Cooper, Myrna. "How Teacher Unionists View In-Service Education." *Teachers College Record* 80 (September 1978): 107–25.

Lewin, Kurt. "Group Decision and Social Change." In *Readings in Social Psychology.* Edited by Theodore Newcomb and E. Hartley. New York: Holt, Rinehart & Winston, 1947.

Lieberman, Ann, and Shiman, David A. "The Stages of Change in Elementary School Settings." In *The Power to Change: Issues for the Innovative Educator.* Edited by Carmen M. Culver and Gary J. Hoban. New York: McGraw-Hill, 1973.

Lieberman, Myron. "Teacher Militancy." In *The Teacher's Handbook.* Edited by Dwight W. Allen and Eli Seifman. Glenview, Ill.: Scott, Foresman, 1971.

———. "Local Control of Education." In *Conflict and Decision: Analyzing Educational Issues.* Edited by John Martin Rich. New York: Harper & Row, 1972.

Lieberman, Myron, and Moskow, Michael H. "Collective Negotiations for Teachers." In *School Policy and Issues in a Changing Society.* Edited by Patricia Sexton. Boston: Allyn & Bacon, 1971.

Lindsey, Margaret. "Decision-Making and the Teacher. In *Curriculum Crossroads.* Edited by A. Harry Passow. New York: Bureau of Publications, Teachers College, Columbia University, 1962.

———. "Performance-based Teacher Education: Examination of a Slogan." *Journal of Teacher Education* 24 (Fall 1973): 180–86.

———, ed. *New Horizons for the Teaching Profession.* Washington, D.C.: National Commission on Teacher Education and Professional Standards, NEA, 1961.

Lins, L. J. "Origin of Teacher Improvement Services in the United States." *Journal of Educational Research* 38 (1945): 697–707.

Lippitt, Ronald, and Fox, Robert. "Development and Maintenance of Effective Classroom Learning." In *In-Service Education: Proposals and Procedures for Change.* Edited by Louis J. Rubin. Boston: Allyn & Bacon, 1971.

Longstreet, Wilma S. "The School's Curriculum." In *The Elementary School in the United States.* Seventy-second Yearbook of the National Society for the Study of Education, pt. 2. Chicago: University of Chicago Press, 1973.

Lortie, Dan C. "The Balance of Control and Autonomy in Elementary School Teaching." In *The Semi-Professions and Their Organization.* Edited by Amatai Etzioni. New York: The Free Press, 1969.

———. *Schoolteacher: A Sociological Study.* Chicago: University of Chicago Press, 1975.

———. "The Teacher and Team Teaching: Suggestions for Long-Range Research." In *Managing Change in Educational Organizations.* Edited by Baldridge and Deal.

Lowry, Charles D., ed. *The Relation of Principals and Superintendents to the Training and Improvement of Their Teachers.* Seventh Yearbook of the National Society for the Study of Education, pt. 1. Chicago: University of Chicago Press, 1908.

Mackenzie, Gordon. "The Inservice Job." *Educational Leadership* 3 (October 1945): 2–6.

Mann, Dale. "Political Representation and Urban School Advisory Councils." *Teachers College Record* 75 (February 1974): 279–309.

————. "The Politics of Staff Development." Paper presented at the American Educational Research Association (AERA), Washington, D.C., 1975.

————. *The Politics of Administrative Representation.* New York: Lexington, 1976.

————. "The Politics of Training Teachers in Schools." *Teachers College Record* 77 (February 1976): 323–38.

Martin, Roscoe C. "School Government." In *Governing Education: A Reader on Politics, Power, and Public School Policy.* Edited by Alan Rosenthal. New York: Anchor, 1969.

Maslow, Abraham, H. *Motivation and Personality.* New York: Harper & Row, 1954.

————. *Eupsychian Management.* Homewood, Ill.: Irwin-Dorsey, 1965.

Mattingly, Paul H. *The Classless Profession: American Schoolmen in the Nineteenth Century.* New York: New York University Press, 1975.

Maucker, J. W., and Pendergraft, Daryl. "Implications of In-Service Education Programs for Teacher-Education Institutions." In *In-Service Education.* Fifty-sixth Yearbook of the National Society for the Study of Education. Chicago: University of Chicago Press, 1957.

McCleary, Lloyd E. *An Essay on Role Attrition: Three Studies of the Job of the Principal.* April, 1971, ERIC, ED 077 135.

McClure, Robert M. "The Reforms of the Fifties and Sixties: A Historical Look at the Near Past." In *The Curriculum: Retrospect and Prospect.* Seventieth Yearbook of the National Society for the Study of Education, pt. 1. Chicago: University of Chicago Press, 1971.

McGivney, Joseph H., and Moynihan, William. "School and Community." *Teachers College Record* 74 (December 1972): 209–24.

McLaughlin, Milbrey Wallin. "Implementation as Mutual Adaptation: Change in Classroom Organization." *Teachers College Record* 77 (February 1976): 339–51.

McMahon, Lois G. "Survey of a Study of In-Service Education Programs in Selected California Public School Systems." Ed.D. dissertation, Berkeley, Calif.: University of California, June 1954.

McNally, Harold J. "The Principalship: A Shared Responsibility." *National Elementary Principal* 55 (November-December 1975): 26.

Meade, Edward, Jr. "No Health in Us." In *Improving In-Service Education: Proposals and Procedures for Change.* Edited by Louis J. Rubin. Boston: Allyn & Bacon, 1971.

Meagley, R. L., and Evans, N. D. *Handbook for Effective Supervision of Instruction.* Englewood Cliffs, N.J.: Prentice-Hall, 1970.

Merton, Robert K. "Bureaucratic Structure and Personality." In *Reader on Bureaucracy.* Edited by Robert K. Merton, Aelsa P. Gray, Barbara Hockey, and Hanan C. Selvin. Glencoe, Ill.: Free Press, 1952.

Miel, Alice M. *Changing the Curriculum: A Social Process.* New York: Appleton-Century-Crofts, 1946.

Miles, Mathew B. "Planned Change and Organizational Health." In *Organization and Human Behavior.* Edited by Fred D. Carver and Thomas J. Sergiovanni. New York: McGraw-Hill, 1969.

Miles, Matthew B., and Passow, A. Harry. "Training in the Skills Needed for In-Service Education Programs." In *In-Service Education.* Fifty-sixth Yearbook of the National Society for the Study of Education. Chicago: University of Chicago Press, 1957.

Miles, Raymond E. "Human Relations or Human Resources?" *Harvard Business Review* 43 (July-August 1965). Cited in Sergiovanni and Carver, *The New School Executive.*

Milstein, Mike M., and Jennings, Robert E. "Principals Can Affect State Education Policy." *NASSP Bulletin* 60 (January 1976): 43–49.

Mitchell, James R. "The Workshop as an In-Service Education Procedure." A study conducted and reported by the Subcommittee on In-Service Education of Teachers. *North Central Association Quarterly* 28 (April 1954): 421–57.

"A Model Teachers Standards and Licensure Act." Washington, D.C.: National Commission on Teacher Education and Professional Standards in consultation with the National Commission on Professional Rights and Responsibilities and the National Education Association General Assembly, NEA, February, 1971.

Monks, Robert. "What About the Principal's Right to Due Process?" *The Clearing House* 49 (October 1975): 62–63.

Morgart, Robert A. *Alienation in an Educational Context: The American Teacher in the Seventies?* Paper presented at the Annual Meeting of the American Educational Research Association, Chicago, Ill., ERIC Clearinghouse, April 1974, ED 090 220.

Morris, J. R. "Why an Inservice Program?" *NASSP Bulletin* 44 (February 1960): 123–25.

Myers, Donald. "The Declining Power of the Principal." *The National Elementary Principal* 54 (September/October 1974): 18–26.

―――. *Teacher Power: Professionalization and Collective Bargaining.* Lexington, Mass.: D. C. Heath, 1973.

Nasaw, David. *Schooled to Order: A Social History of Public Schooling in the United States.* New York: Oxford University Press, 1979.

Nash, Robert J., and Agne, Russell M. "The Ethos of Accountability—A Critique." *Teachers College Record* 73 (February 1972): 357–70.

National Education Association. *The Development of the Career Teacher: Professional Responsibility for Continuing Education.* Washington, D.C.: National Commission on Teacher Education and Professional Standards, 1964.

―――. *Schools for the '70's and Beyond: A Call to Action.* A staff report. Washington, D.C.: Center for the Study of Instruction, NEA, 1971.

―――. *In-Service Education,* Infopac no. 7. Washington, D.C.: Instruction and Professional Development, NEA, Fall 1974.

―――. "A Negotiations Strategy for In-Service Education." From Organizational Aspects of In-Service Education, pt. 2, of Teacher-Centered In-Service Education. Mimeographed. Washington, D.C.: NEA, 1974.

———. "Teacher Centered Professional Development." Mimeographed. Washington, D.C.: Instruction and Professional Development, NEA, 1974.

———. "Teacher Power for In-Service Education." In *In-Service Education.* Mimeographed. Washington, D.C.: Instruction and Professional Development, NEA, 1974.

———. "What a Teacher Center Might Look Like." Mimeographed. Washington, D.C.: Instruction and Professional Development, NEA, 1974.

———, Research Division. "In-Service Education of Teachers." Mimeographed. Washington, D.C.: NEA, February 1954.

———. "Ten Criticisms of Public Education." *Research Bulletin* 35 (December 1957): 131–75.

NEA Task Force on Practicing Teacher Involvement in Teacher Education, Letter of Transmittal, "Guidelines for Guaranteeing the Involvement of Practicing Teachers in the Initial Preparation of Teachers." Presented to the Fifty-second Representative Assembly of the National Education Association, July 3-6, 1973, Portland, Oreg.

National Society for the Study of Education. In *In-Service Education for Teachers, Supervisors, and Administrators.* Fifty-sixth Yearbook of the National Society for the Study of Education, pt. 1. Chicago: University of Chicago Press, 1957.

Newcomb, Theodore M. *The Acquaintance Process.* New York: Holt, Rinehart & Winston, 1961.

Nissen, Myra H. "Table Talk with Albert Shanker." *National Elementary Principal* 53 (March/April 1974): 44–50.

Nolte, Chester. "Citizen Power over Schools: How Much Is Too Much?" *American School Board Journal* 163 (April 1976): 34–36.

Nuthall, Graham, and Snook, Irvan. "Contemporary Models of Teaching." In *Second Handbook of Research on Teaching: A Project of the American Research Association.* Edited by Robert Travers. Chicago: Rand McNally, 1967.

Olesen, Virginia, and Whittaker, Elvi I. *The Silent Dialogue: A Study in the Social Psychology of Professional Education.* San Francisco, Calif.: Jossey-Bass, 1968.

Openshaw, Karl. "Attitudes for Growth." *Educational Leadership* 20 (1962): 90–92.

Osborne, R. T. "The Preferential Training Needs Record." Ph.D. dissertation, University of Georgia, 1950.

Owens, Robert G. *Organizational Behavior in Schools.* Englewood Cliffs, N.J.: Prentice-Hall, 1970.

Pangburn, Jessie M. *The Evolution of the American Teachers College.* New York: Bureau of Publications, Teachers College, Columbia University, 1932.

Parker, Cecil J. "Guidelines for In-Service Education." In *In-Service Education.* Fifty-sixth Yearbook of the National Society for the Study of Education, pt. 1. Chicago: University of Chicago Press, 1957.

Parsons, Talcott. "Suggestions for a Sociological Approach to the Theory of Organizations." In *Complex Organizations: A Sociological Reader.* Edited by Amatai Etzioni. New York: Holt, Rinehart & Winston, 1961.

Perry, Charles R., and Wildman, Wesley. *The Impact of Negotiations in Public Education: The Evidence from Schools.* Worthington, Ohio: Charles A. Jones, 1970.

Pestalozzi, Johann H. *How Gertrude Teaches Her Children.* Translated by Lucy E. Holland and Francis Turner. London: Swan Sonnenschein, 1907.

Pharis, William L. "The Principalship: Where Are We?" *National Elementary Principal* 55 (November-December 1975) :4–9.

Philips, C. W. "What are the Characteristics of an Effective Inservice Program?" *NASSP Bulletin* 36 (March 1952): 357–61.

Piele, Philip, and Eidell, Terry L., with Stuart C. Smith. *Social and Technological Change: Implications for Education.* Eugene, Oreg.: The Center for Advanced Study of Educational Administration, 1970.

Polyani, Michael. "Tacit Knowing: Its Bearing on Some Problems of Philosophy." *Reviews of Modern Physics* 34 (October 1962). Cited in Wilensky, Harold. "The Professionalization of Everyone?" *American Journal of Sociology* 70 (September 1964): 149.

Pomeroy, Edward C. "What's Going on in Teacher Education?" *Journal of Teacher Education* 26 (Fall 1975): 196–201.

Prall, Charles E. *State Programs for the Improvement of Teacher Education.* Washington, D.C.: American Council on Education, 1946.

Prall, Charles E., and Cushman, Leslie C. *Teacher Education In Service.* Washington, D.C.: American Council on Education, 1944.

Prethus, Robert. *The Organizational Society.* New York: Alfred A. Knopf, 1962.

Rabinowitz, Frank, and Crawford, Kay E. "A Study of Teachers' Careers." *The School Review* 68 (Winter 1960): 377–400.

Redfern, George R. "Negotiation Changes Principal-Teacher Relationships." In *Professional Negotiation and the Principalship.* Washington, D.C.: Department of Elementary School Principals, NEA, 1969.

Rehage, Kenneth J., and Denemark, George W. "Area, State, Regional, and National In-Service Education Programs." In *In-Service Education.* Fifty-sixth Yearbook of the National Society for the Study of Education. Chicago: University of Chicago Press, 1957.

Reutter, Edmund E., Jr. "Teachers' Freedom of Expression." *IAR Research Bulletin* 13 (February 1973): 7–9.

Rich, John Martin. *Challenge and Response: Education in American Culture.* New York: John Wiley, 1974.

Richey, Herman G. "Growth of the Modern Conception of In-Service Education." In *In-Service Education.* Fifty-sixth Yearbook of the National Society for the Study of Education, pt. 1. Chicago: University of Chicago Press, 1957.

Rieder, Corinne. "The National Institute of Education: What It Is and What It Plans to Do." *NASSP Bulletin* 68 (May 1974): 37–45.

Ritzer, George. *Man and His Work: Conflict and Change.* New York: Appleton-Century-Crofts, 1972.

Rogers, Carl. *On Becoming a Person.* Boston: Houghton Mifflin, 1961.

Rogers, Everett M. *Diffusion of Innovations.* New York: The Free Press of Glencoe, 1962.

Rokeach, Milton. *The Nature of Human Values.* New York: The Free Press, 1973.

Rosner, Benjamin. *The Power of Competency-based Teacher Education: A Report.* Boston: Allyn & Bacon, 1972.

Rudman, Herbert C. "The Dirty Dozen: The Principal and His Teachers." In *Professional Negotiation and the Principalship.* Washington, D.C.: Department of Elementary School Principals, NEA, 1969.

Ruedinger, William Carl. *Agencies for the Improvement of Teacher In-Service.* Bulletin no. 3. Washington, D.C.: Government Printing Office, 1911.

Rugg, Harold, and Withers, William. *Social Foundations of Education.* New York: Prentice-Hall, 1955.

Sand, Ole. "Curriculum Change." In *The Curriculum: Retrospect and Prospect.* Seventieth Yearbook of the National Society for the Study of Education. Chicago: University of Chicago Press, 1971.

Sarason, Seymour B. *The Culture of the School and the Problem of Change.* Boston: Allyn & Bacon, 1971.

Schein, Edgar H. *Professional Education: Some New Directions.* New York: McGraw-Hill, 1972.

————. *Organizational Psychology.* Englewood Cliffs, N.J.: Prentice-Hall, 1965.

Schmeider, Allen A., and Yarger, Sam J. "Teacher/Teaching Centers in America." *Journal of Teacher Education* 25 (Spring 1974): 5–12.

Schwab, Joseph. "The Practical: A Language for Curriculum." *School Review* 78 (November 1969): 1–23.

Seguel, Mary Louise. *The Curriculum Field: Its Formative Years.* New York: Teachers College Press, 1966.

Seiber, Sam D. "Images of the Practitioner and Strategies of Educational Change." *Sociology of Education* 45 (Fall 1972): 362–85.

————. "Organizational Influences on Educational Innovation." In *Managing Change in Educational Organizations.* Edited by Baldridge and Deal.

Seitz, Reynolds C. "School Law: Trends and Trials. Teacher Negotiations: The Legal Issues." *Nation's Schools* 87 (February 1971): 49–51.

Sergiovanni, Thomas. "Factors which Affect Satisfaction and Dissatisfaction of Teachers." *Journal of Educational Administration* 5 (May 1967): 66–82.

Sergiovanni, Thomas J., and Carver, Fred D. *The New School Executive: A Theory of Administration.* New York: Dodd, Mead, 1973.

Sergiovanni, Thomas J., and Starratt, Robert J. *Emerging Patterns of Supervision: Human Perspectives.* New York: McGraw-Hill, 1971.

Sexton, Patricia. *School Policy and Issues in a Changing Society.* Boston: Allyn & Bacon, Inc., 1971.

Shalala, Donna E., and Kelly, James E. "Politics, the Courts, and Educational Policy." *Teachers College Record* 75 (December 1973): 223–37.

Shanker, Albert. Introduction to *A Bibliography on Professionalization and Collective Bargaining,* by Donald A. Myers. Washington, D.C.: American Federation of Teachers, September 1974.

————. "Why Teachers Are Angry." *American School Board Journal* 162 (January 1975): 23–26.

————. "And Now from Those Wonderful People Who Sit across Your Bargaining Table." *American School Board Journal* 62 (September 1975): 32–37.

Shearron, Gilbert. "In-Service/Needs-Assessment/Competency-Based Education." A paper presented at Research Conference on Competency-Based Teacher Education, Houston, Texas, March 14, 1974.

Silberman, Charles E. *Crisis in the Classroom: The Remaking of American Education.* New York: Random House, 1970.

Simon, Herbert A. *Administrative Behavior.* New York: Macmillan, 1945. Cited in Getzels, Jacob W. *Educational Administration as a Social Process: Theory, Research, Practice.* New York: Harper & Row, 1968.

Simpson, Richard L., and Simpson, Ida Harper. "Women and Bureaucracy in the Semi-Professions." In *The Semi-Professions and Their Organization.* Edited by Amatai Etzioni. New York: The Free Press, 1969.

Slager, F. G. "What are the Characteristics of an Effective Professional Growth Program?" *National Association of Secondary School Principals Bulletin* 38 (April 1954): 206–209.

Small, Walter H. *Early New England Schools.* New York: Arno Press and *New York Times,* 1969.

Smart, James H. *Teachers Institute.* Circulars of Information of the Bureau of Education, no. 2, 1885. Washington, D.C.: Government Printing Office, 1885.

Smith, Louis M., and Keith, Pat M. *Anatomy of Educational Innovation: An Organizational Analysis of an Elementary School.* New York: John Wiley, 1971.

Smith, Othanel B. "Science of Education." In *Encyclopedia of Educational Research.* Edited by Walter S. Monroe. New York: Macmillan, 1950.

Spring, Joel. *Education and the Rise of the Corporate State.* Boston: Beacon Press, 1972.

Stub, Holger R. "The Professional Prestige of Classroom Teachers: A Consequence of Organizational and Community Status." In *The Sociology of Education: A Sourcebook.* Edited by Robert R. Bell and Holger R. Stub. Homewood, Ill.: The Dorsey Press, 1968.

Sweet, Samuel N. *Teachers' Institutes or Temporary Normal Schools.* Utica, N.Y.: H. H. Hawley, 1848.

Tickton, Sidney G. *Teaching Salaries Then and Now, A Second Look.* New York: The Fund for the Advancement of Education, 1961.

Tyack, David B. *Turning Points in American Educational History.* Lexington, Mass.: Blaisdell, 1967.

Udy, Stanley. "The Comparative Analysis of Organizations. In *Handbook of Organizations.* Edited by James G. March. Chicago: Rand McNally, 1965.

"U. S. House Committee on Education and Labor." In *School Policy and Issues in a Changing Society.* Edited by Patricia Sexton. Boston: Allyn & Bacon, 1971.

Van Geel, Tyll. "Parental Preferences and the Politics of Spending Public Educational Funds." *Teachers College Record* 79 (February 1978): 356–62.

Watson, Goodwin. "The Surprising Discovery of Morale." *Progressive Education* 19 (1942): 33–41.

Wayson, William W. "Power, Power, Who's Got the Power? Or, Where the Pressure's Coming From." *National Elementary Principal* 58 (March 1979): 12–20.

Weber, Max. *Economy and Society.* Edited by G. Roth and C. Wittia. New York: Harper & Row, 1960.

Wertheim, Sally H. "The Myth of Local School Control." *Intellect* 102 (October 1973): 55–59.

White, Clyde R. "Social Workers in Society: Some Further Evidence." *Social Work Journal* 34 (October 1953): 161–64.

White, Ralph, and Lippitt, Ronald. *Autocracy and Democracy: An Experimental Inquiry.* New York: Harper & Row, 1960.

Wiebe, Robert H. *The Search for Order, 1877-1920.* New York: Hill & Wang, 1967.

Wilensky, Harold. "The Professionalization of Everyone?" *American Journal of Sociology* 70 (September 1964): 137–58.

Wiles, David K., and Houston, Conley. "School Boards: Their Policy-Making Relevance." *Teachers College Record* 75 (February 1974): 309–19.

Woodring, Paul. *New Directions in Teacher Education.* New York: The Fund for the Advancement of Education, 1957.

———. "A Century of Teacher Education." In *A Century of Higher Education.* Edited by William Brickman and Stanley Lehrer. New York: Society for the Advancement of Education, 1962. Cited in Gutek, Gerald Lee. *An Introduction to American Education.* New York: Thomas Y. Crowell, 1970.

———. "Development of Teacher Education." In *Teacher Education.* Seventy-fourth Yearbook of the National Society for the Study of Education, pt. 2. Chicago: University of Chicago Press, 1975.

Wormser, Rene A. *Foundations: Their Power and Influence.* New York: Devin Adair, 1958.

Wright, Arthur D., and Gardner, George E., eds. *Hall's Lectures on School-Keeping.* Hanover: Dartmouth Press, 1929.

Young, William F. "Curriculum Negotiation: How? To What Extent?" *Educational Leadership,* 30 (April 1972): 576–78.

Ziller, Robert Charles. *The Social Self.* New York: Pergamon Press, 1973.

Index